A VISION FOR THE CHURCH

J. P. M. Sweet

A VISION FOR THE CHURCH

*Studies in Early Christian Ecclesiology
in Honour of J. P. M. Sweet*

Edited by

MARKUS BOCKMUEHL and MICHAEL B. THOMPSON

T&T CLARK
EDINBURGH

T&T CLARK LTD
59 GEORGE STREET
EDINBURGH EH2 2LQ
SCOTLAND

First published 1997

ISBN 0 567 08573 2 HB
ISBN 0 567 08579 1 PB

British Library Cataloguing-in-Publication Data
A catalogue record for this book is available from the British Library

Typeset by Waverley Typesetters, Galashiels
Printed and bound in Great Britain by Bookcraft Ltd, Avon

Contents

v

Preface

When we first hatched the idea of honouring John Sweet with a *Festschrift* on his 70th birthday, it was heartening to see the enthusiastic responses from his friends and former students whom we approached as contributors. It quickly became clear that here was a man whose nearly four decades of teaching the New Testament at Cambridge have endeared him to his colleagues and students as a scholar, a Christian pastor, and (as one contributor puts it) a prince of teachers. He is someone whose selfless service, putting the needs of others before his own concerns, has won him the unreserved affection of all who know him.

This volume is itself designed to express and bear witness to three important foci of his work. It is a book intended in the first instance for students. Second, in keeping with John Sweet's life-long engagement for the Church, it surveys the earliest Christian writers' ideas of what the Church should be and become. And third, its title alludes to the vision which John of Patmos had of and for the Church, a vision creatively expounded by John Sweet in his commentary on *Revelation* (London: SCM, 1979; 2nd edn., 1990).

The remarkable variety of scholarly approaches represented in this volume is itself an indication of the wide range of John Sweet's contacts and friendships, and of the affectionate regard in which he is held in many parts of the Church and beyond it. Even on its own restricted terms, our *Festschrift* can offer only incomplete evidence of this. Several others would very much have liked to contribute, but were either prevented at the last minute by other obligations or else did not learn of this venture in time. Already beset by serious illness, Ernst Bammel repeatedly re-affirmed his desire to write even a few pages to honour his former colleague; sadly, his failing strength left him unable to do so before he passed away on 5 December 1996. Many others, in this country and abroad, have indicated their desire to join with the contributors in offering to John and Mary Sweet heartfelt congratulations and fond good wishes.

MARKUS BOCKMUEHL / MICHAEL B. THOMPSON
Cambridge, 7 June 1997

Foreword

C. F. D. MOULE

A 'profile' of Prebendary John Sweet appeared in *The Church Times* on 15 October 1993, charming in its contents but bearing the unfortunate heading, 'A theologian with faith still undamaged' – as though that was surprising. Of all people, it is John Sweet who shows how unsurprising and natural it is. Looking at evidence coolly and not, to use a phrase of his own, 'blinkered by inherited assumptions',[1] he finds that it endorses the convictions at the heart of the Christian faith. So far from damaging the faith, the evidence undergirds it. His critique of the late Professor S. G. F. Brandon's theory that Jesus was in sympathy with Jewish extremists who advocated the use of violence against the Romans is effective precisely because, with courtesy and moderation, he simply looks at the evidence and exposes the weaknesses in Brandon's thesis.[2]

It was at Oxford that he began his academic training. Born in India, where his parents were in the Forest Service, he went to Eton and then read Greats at New College. After national service he returned to Oxford to read theology, moved by Bishop Stephen Neill's addresses in an Oxford University Mission. Then came training at Westcott House, Cambridge, a year at Yale on a Harkness Fellowship, and a Curacy at St Mark's, Mansfield, Nottinghamshire, before he was appointed Chaplain at Selwyn College, Cambridge, and, soon afterwards, a Lecturer in the University. He was made a non-residentiary Prebendary of Chichester in 1962.

His commentary on the Revelation is a model of its sort – compact, lucid, perceptive, and quietly enthusiastic. His comments on the apparently vindictive attitudes displayed by the seer reflect his own patience and openness. He agrees that a reader who cannot think himself into the presuppositions behind those attitudes

> cannot deny his repugnance or meekly agree to call ugly beautiful. But he can be asked to be patient, and to be willing to open himself to an unfamiliar context and to new ways of seeing and hearing. He may not in

---

[1] *Revelation* (London: SCM Press, 1979) 1.
[2] 'The Zealots and Jesus', in E. Bammel and C. F. D. Moule (eds.), *Jesus and the Politics of his Day* (Cambridge: Cambridge University Press, 1984) 1–9.

the end be changed, but unless he is *willing* to be changed there is no possibility of real communication and enrichment. (p. 52)

For some years before my retirement, in days before bureaucracy had made such irregularities difficult, John Sweet, at my request, used generously to deliver, gratis, the closing lectures in my course at Cambridge on the theology and ethics of the New Testament. It was not just laziness on my part. It was because I felt particularly helpless when it came to dealing with the theology and ethics of the Apocalypse, and because I knew with what skill he would deputize for me out of the material that was to go into his commentary. It was, of course, a great success. I used myself to sit with the class, enjoying with them the pleasing change before us on the dais.

That elegantly written commentary, with apt allusions to modern literature and art, shows the sort of quality we might have had in quantity, but for his deep loyalty to his pastoral office. The same quality marks such other publications as he has found time for. The Cambridge studies on miracles which I edited contain a perceptive essay by Sweet on the theory of miracles in the Wisdom of Solomon.[3] It reflects not only great learning but an ability to grasp the wider questions, philosophical and religious, which are raised by the subject. His contribution to a *Festschrift* for Geoffrey Styler is a subtle piece of advocacy for the view that, in the Apocalypse, the final victory of truth over illusion lies not in over-whelming force but in the power of sacrifice.[4] In addition, there are articles in journals and dictionaries and, latterly, contributions to the work of the Liturgical Commission. But persons take precedence over books, and publication has never been so high on his agenda as pastoral ministry. It has been said that people – not least the unattractive and tiresome – would queue at his door for the counsel and help which he never failed to provide, at no matter how much cost of time and energy. Such was his charity that, to quote an observer, 'persons who are cantankerous and trying in the extreme come out of his description as delightfully eccentric characters'. The attitude of domestic staff is generally a faithful mirror of a pastor's worth. At Selwyn, on their own initiative, they gave John Sweet and Mary his wife a farewell party.

For such a one, the Lambeth Doctorate, conferred in 1994, was a specially fitting accolade, combining in one the recognition both of academic and of pastoral ministry, and, as was said at the time, lifting the large bushel under which he liked to hide his light.

[3] 'The Theory of Miracles in the Wisdom of Solomon', in C. F. D. Moule (ed.), *Miracles: Cambridge Studies in their Philosophy and History* (London: Mowbray, 1965) 113–26.
[4] 'Maintaining the Testimony of Jesus: The Suffering of Christians in the Revelation of John', in W. Horbury and B. McNeil (eds.), *Suffering and Martyrdom in the New Testament* (Cambridge: Cambridge University Press, 1981) 101–17.

In this collection of essays there is intended to be a note of vision, in the sense that they aim not only to look at each New Testament writer's understanding of the Church as it then was, but also to discern the direction in which their vision for the future might point. This is eminently appropriate to the occasion. Getting the priorities right and recognizing the paramount value of persons means seeing the transcendent in the immanent; and that is the substance of vision. The last words of John Sweet's commentary on the Apocalypse are: '*God* was at the centre at the end of John's vision (22⁵): at the end of the letter whose aim is to make that vision effective the centre is *Jesus*' (p. 320). Our own seer John, with his devoted wife Mary, shares this perspective. We hope that they will like this little present.

Abbreviations

❧❦❧

AB	Anchor Bible
ABD	*Anchor Bible Dictionary*
AF	Apostolic Fathers
ANE-OT	Ancient Near East-Old Testament
AUSS	*Andrews University Seminary Studies*
b.	Babylonian Talmud
BCE	Before Christian Era
BETL	Bibliotheca ephemeridum theologicarum lovaniensium
Bib	*Biblica*
BiKi	*Bibel und Kirche*
BTB	*Biblical Theology Bulletin*
CBQ	*Catholic Biblical Quarterly*
CRBS	*Currents in Research: Biblical Studies*
EdF	Erträge der Forschung
EKK	Evangelisch-Katholischer Kommentar
ET	English Translation
ETL	*Ephemerides theologicae lovanienses*
ExpT	*Expository Times*
FS	Festschrift
HTR	*Harvard Theological Review*
IBS	*Irish Biblical Studies*
JBL	*Journal of Biblical Literature*
JETS	*Journal of the Evangelical Theological Society*
JR	*Journal of Religion*
JSNT	*Journal for the Study of the New Testament*
JSNTSup	Journal for the Study of the New Testament Supplement Series
JSOT	*Journal for the Study of the Old Testament*
JSOTSup	Journal for the Study of the Old Testament Supplement Series
JTS	*Journal of Theological Studies*
KEKNT	Kritisch-Exegetischer Kommentar zum Neuen Testament

LXX	Septuagint
NICNT	New International Commentary on the New Testament
NovT	*Novum Testamentum*
NovTSup	Novum Testamentum Supplements
NRSV	New Revised Standard Version
n.s.	new series
NT	New Testament
NTAbh	Neutestamentliche Abhandlungen
NTS	*New Testament Studies*
OT	Old Testament
RB	*Revue Biblique*
SANT	Studien zum Alten und Neuen Testament
SBLDS	Society of Biblical Literature Dissertation Series
SBLMS	Society of Biblical Literature Monograph Series
SNTSMS	Society of New Testament Studies Monograph Series
SNTU	Studien zum Neuen Testament und seiner Umwelt
Str.-B.	Hermann L. Strack and Paul Billerbeck, *Kommentar zum Neuen Testament aus Talmud und Midrasch*, 7 vols. (Munich: Beck, 1922–1961)
THKNT	Theologischer Handkommentar zum Neuen Testament
TJT	*Toronto Journal of Theology*
TPINTC	Trinity Press International New Testament Commentary
TRE	*Theologische Realenzyklopädie*
TynB	*Tyndale Bulletin*
VT	*Vetus Testamentum*
WBC	Word Biblical Commentary
WMANT	Wissenschaftliche Monographien zum Alten und Neuen Testament
WTJ	*Westminster Theological Journal*
WUNT	Wissenschaftliche Untersuchungen zum Neuen Testament
y.	Jerusalem Talmud

Abbreviations for cited texts may be found in the Index of Ancient Sources.

I

Septuagintal and New Testament Conceptions of the Church

WILLIAM HORBURY

VISIONS *of* as well as for the Church were known at the time of Christian origins. The dreamers of dreams in Israel saw the people as a threatened flock, and Jerusalem as a mourning and rejoicing mother and bride (1 Enoch 89–91, 2 Esd 9–10); and the Christians followed them with visions of the Church and the holy city as a mother and bride, an aged yet joyful woman and a tower (Rev 12.1–6, 19.7–8, 21.2; *Hermas, Vis.* 1–3). These visions of sorrow and hope in turn contributed to patristic and later distinctions between a visible and an invisible Church, presenting a contrast which could be used to console or reform the empirical congregation.

The four apocalypses just cited were of disputed value in ancient times, and remained on the verges of the LXX and NT book-collections. Their visions of the Church were shaped, however, by the more generally accepted scriptures. 'No doubt a genuine vision lies behind, but the details evoke scriptural passages' (Sweet 1979:195). The visions concretize some of the similitudes applied to Israel and Jerusalem in the OT.

Against the background formed by these apocalypses it seems likely that, when the scriptures were read at the time of Jesus and Paul, even non-visionary hearers shared conceptions of the congregation which arose from association and development of the manifold biblical descriptions and images. The Christians were keenly aware of their separate loyalty (1 Cor 16.22), but this was owed to the messiah of Israel; they spoke and thought of themselves as essential Israel, and applied to themselves most of the relevant biblical vocabulary. So in the biblical manner, without special introduction, Paul could speak of betrothing the Corinthian church as a pure virgin to Christ (2 Cor 11.2). To a great extent, therefore, NT conceptions of the Church were ready-made before the apostles preached; and this is true not only of the imagery most readily applicable to the pre-existent or ideal Church, but also of descriptions of the empirical assembly.

To *what* extent, exactly, were such conceptions ready-made? One important contribution towards an answer is offered by the Greek translations constituting the LXX, individually and as a collection of books (briefly surveyed by Schürer and Goodman 1986:474–504). The LXX translations are mainly pre-Christian, and formatively influenced the Greek-speaking Christianity reflected in the Greek NT. The collection as a whole shared something of the enormous prestige accorded to the Greek Pentateuch in particular (the 'Septuagint', or work of the seventy translators, in the strict sense), and was abidingly revered by Christians, from the NT period onwards.

Here attention is concentrated on the two Songs and the Blessing of Moses (Exod 15 and Deut 32; Deut 33), and the Wisdom of Solomon. These texts form no more than a particle of the LXX material for conceptions of the congregation, but their significance is considerable. The Pentateuch is the oldest and most widely familiar part of the LXX; the two Songs and the Blessing took a high place, even within this sacrosanct corpus, as prophecies of Moses. This is plain from Philo and Josephus, and can be glimpsed from the NT (Rev 15.3–4).[1] The two Songs were also transmitted as the first two canticles in the LXX book of Odes. This book is a Christian collection in its present form, and it attests the importance of the two Songs in Christian thought and worship; at the same time it probably reflects Jewish usage in its treatment of the Songs of Moses and other OT canticles independently of their biblical context. The Song of Exod 15 enjoyed widespread veneration among Jews (Hengel 1995:n. 6) and had a specifically communal character, discussed below. Deut 32 is regularly called 'the Great Ode' in Philo (*Leg.* 3.105 and elsewhere), perhaps partly as 'the Greater' Song of Moses as opposed to the lesser Song in Exod 15 (*Plant.* 59, cited in n. 1, above); and in the context of Maccabaean martyrdom it was quoted as 'the Ode of Open Protest' (2 Macc 7.6, recalling Deut 31.21 LXX; see Harl in Dogniez and Harl 1992:319–20). In the NT, similarly, the two Songs were both influential, and the greater Song with its martyr-links was one of 'the early church's favourite texts' (Sweet 1979:240).

The book of Wisdom, by contrast, is relatively late, perhaps of the early first century BCE, but in thought it shows kinship with the Pauline writings. It is another document of martyr-theology, and it was probably known to first-century Christians (Horbury 1995). The LXX collection of books, in which Wisdom and other approved but non-canonical works are associated with the generally accepted scriptures, probably represents

[1] See Philo, *Plant.* 54–59, where the two Songs of Moses are considered together; *Virt.* 72–77, on the Deuteronomic Song and Blessing; and *Mos.* 2.288–89, on the Blessing; also Josephus, *Ant.* 2.346, 4.303, on the two Songs as composed by Moses in hexameters and preserved in the temple, and 4.320, on the prophetic Blessing. The joint influence on the NT of a pair of eschatological verses from the two Songs (Exod 15.17 and Deut 32.35) is considered against this background in Horbury 1996:210–11. In Rev 15.3–4 'the song of Moses, the servant of God' is that of Exod 15, but the song sung by the victorious martyrs echoes and parallels that of Deut 32.

a widespread Jewish reading practice which was continued by early Christians.[2]

All these texts are poetic compositions, presented in Greek in lines which echo the stressed metre of Hebrew verse. They differ markedly from Greek verse written in the quantitative classical metres, and probably reflect by their very form a pride in the ancestral biblical tradition.

The general context of this small-scale inquiry is that explored especially by Dahl 1941 – the relation of early Christian conceptions of the Church to conceptions of the nation and congregation current in ancient Judaism. Within the study of Septuagintal theology (briefly surveyed with examples by Le Déaut 1984:175–85, and Schaper 1995:1–2 and n. 449), this political or ecclesiological topic has gained sporadic attention (notably from Seeligmann 1948:110–21, on Isaiah). Examination of the Songs and Blessing of Moses in this connection is facilitated by the valuable Septuagintal commentaries of Le Boulluec and Sandevoir 1989 and Dogniez and Harl 1992. The use made of Deut 32 in ancient Jewish and early Christian literature is surveyed by Bell 1994:200–85.

Here the LXX is read with an eye not simply to the importance of the Greek Bible for Greek-speakers, but also to the likelihood that it often reflects interpretations current in the homeland as well as the diaspora, even among Jews whose main language was not Greek. The contacts between Septuagintal and rabbinic exegesis noted from time to time below point in this direction. LXX material, used with due caution, may then at times suggest something of conceptions current among Aramaic-speaking Christians, as well as the Greek-speakers whose outlook is more directly mirrored in many NT writings.

The passages particularly considered deal with Israel during the Exodus, the miraculous time of union between the people and their God (Exod 4.22, 19.4–6; Deut 32.10–14; Isa 63.11–14; Jer 2.2; Ezek 16.8) and the pattern of future redemption (Deut 30.3–5; Isa 11.11; Ezek 16.60; Mic 7.15). Conceptions of the congregation are studied first through five attributes which stand out in the two Songs and Wisdom, and are also prominent in the NT, and then through some community titles common to the Jewish and Christian material.

ATTRIBUTES OF THE CHURCH

To begin with the lesser Song of Moses, it is through and through congregational as well as prophetic. As presented in Exod 15 it is com-

[2] M. Hengel, by contrast, holds that the collection was essentially Christian, albeit influenced initially by Jewish practice in Rome (Hengel, 'Schriftensammlung', discussed by Horbury 1997b); but the consistent Christian wish to accord with Jewish biblical usage suggests that the collection was more representatively Jewish than he allows.

munal rather than individual, and forms a congregational hymn. This is clear in the Hebrew as well as the LXX. The hymn was sung not only by Moses, but also by the children of Israel. The singers are articulated into a men's section and a women's section, as befits a comprehensive assembly. In the LXX they still more clearly form a double choir of men and women; Miriam the prophetess was precentor of (ἐξῆρχεν) the women (Exod 15.20–21).[3] This method of performance recalls Greek and Roman employment of antiphonal male and female choirs, for instance in Horace's ode for Augustus's Secular Games of 17 BCE; it probably had reflections in Jewish practice at the time of Christian origins, as Philo suggests when, echoing Exod 15.21 LXX, he says that the choir of the Therapeutae models itself on that formed at the Red Sea 'when the prophet Moses was precentor of (ἐξάρχοντος) the men, and the prophetess Miriam precentor of the women' (Philo, *V. Contempl.* 85–89). Practice is similarly suggested by probably second-century rabbinic debate on the performance of the song, handed down in the names of R. Akiba, R. Nehemiah and others (Mishnah, *Sotah* 5.4; Tosefta, *Sotah* 6.2–3).

The Song of Exod 15 thus has a congregational atmosphere which is enhanced in the LXX. Its LXX presentation has a number of features which reappear in NT conceptions of the Church. Five at least anticipate attributes of the Church as encountered and envisaged by Paul in particular.

The first of these is a constitutional point: the congregation comprises both men and women. The assignation of parts to men and women in a single assembly which has just been noted is an arrangement in principle taken for granted in 1 Cor 11–14. Thus, as is often pointed out, it seems uncontroversial that women may pray or prophesy in the assembly (1 Cor 11.5); these activities are close to the prophetically-led women's hymnody of Exod 15 LXX. The details left room for debate, as 1 Corinthians amply shows, but the principle of an articulated assembly with parts for men and women is a Pentateuchal and prophetic one, made still plainer in the LXX interpretation at this point. This principle contrasts with and to some extent modifies the more frequently noticed teaching on the subordination of women in the Pentateuch and its ancient interpretation. The principle of women's participation is further reflected in ancient Jewish practice (discussed in Horbury 1997a), for example, in the provision of a women's court in Herod's Jerusalem temple; and elsewhere

---

[3] Ἔξαρχος, the noun corresponding to the verb used in LXX here, could denote the song-leader in Greek cults (E. R. Dodds [ed.], *Euripides: Bacchae* [2nd edn., Oxford: at the Clarendon Press, 1960], 87, on line 141, where the chorus say that Bacchus himself is the ἔξαρχος); the noun is applied by Philo to the male and female precentors of the Therapeutae, in a passage ending with a paraphrase of Exod 15 using the verb, quoted in the text below (Philo, *V. Contempl.* 83, 87).

in Paul, as when (perhaps using an existing testimony-collection) he quotes prophecy concerning sons (2 Sam 7.8) in the adapted form 'you shall be to me for sons and daughters' (2 Cor 6.18). The Church following this principle reflected the Pentateuchal ethos of a comprehensive national community, despite its relatively small local 'churches'.

Secondly, the hymn of the assembly in the LXX is a confession of faith. 'They believed (ἐπίστευσαν) in God, and in his servant Moses. Then Moses and the children of Israel sang this ode to God' (Exod 14.31–15.1 LXX). The assembly here is a congregation of those who believe in God and his appointed ruler. This point becomes central in NT conceptions of the Church, as when οἱ πιστεύοντες or πιστεύσαντες denote church members in famous phrases from Acts 2.44, 4.32 on 'believers'; compare the ecclesiastical aspect of 'all who believe' and 'those who believe' in Rom 3.22, Gal 3.22. These phrases, no doubt in conjunction with the continuing importance of the LXX for early Christians, worked on patristic tradition and helped to shape later definitions of the Church as 'a congregation of the faithful'.[4] This point is illustrated in the earliest patristic antecedents of such definitions. Thus, in Cyprian's influential treatise on church unity, the Church is 'the new people of those who believe' (*novus credentium populus*), and the phrase is followed by a quotation of Acts 4.32 (Cyprian, *De Unitate*, 5.19 (25)). Compare also, nearly a century earlier, Justin Martyr, *Dial.* 63.5: 'the word of God addresses as daughter [in Ps 45(44).11 LXX] those who believe in him [Christ], as being of one soul and one gathering together (συναγωγή) and one ἐκκλησία, the *ecclesia* which came into being from his name and shares his name – for we are all called Christians'. Here a reminiscence of Acts 4.32 on the believers as of one soul is not unlikely, for possible contacts with Acts 4.13, 25–27 occur in Justin's *First Apology* (39.3, 40.6, 11). However this may be, his *Dialogue* here exemplifies early continuation of the conception of the Church as an ἐκκλησία of believers, illustrated above from Acts and Paul, and strikingly presented in the introduction of the lesser song of Moses (Exod 14.31–15.1 LXX).

Moreover, two small correspondences between these verses in Exodus and expressions later used by Paul deserve notice. In 14.31, the people have faith not just in God, but in God and his servant Moses. This binary

---

[4] For 'congregation of the faithful' see bishop John Hooper's fourth article of 1552, close to 'congregation of faithful men' in the 1552 text which became the Nineteenth of the Thirty-Nine Articles (both are quoted, with a further comment by Hooper using the word 'multitude', as in Acts 4.32, by C. Hardwick, *A History of the Articles of Religion* [Cambridge: Deighton, 1851], 290); the similar 'blessed company of all faithful people' had been used in the thanksgiving after communion composed for the English Prayer-Book of 1549. All are probably influenced by Luther, whose view of the Church as a 'communion of saints' in the sense of a congregation of pious believers builds on patristic tradition shaped by Acts as well as Paul (see the text, below).

pattern (found also at Num 21.5, here of *dis*belief) is comparable with the Pauline expression of communal faith in one God, and one lord – who as messianic leader takes Moses's place (1 Cor 8.6). Secondly, these two consecutive verses in Exodus, 14.31 and 15.1, when read together present praise as the fruit of faith. The two verses were indeed thus read together in rabbinic exegesis (so the Mekhilta, quoted below, with homiletic emphasis on the importance of faith); but this already occurred in the Persian period, as appears from the Exodus narrative in Ps 106 (LXX 105).12 'And they believed in [God's] words, and sang his praise'. The progression from faith to praise which the consecutive reading embodies later reappears in Paul: 'with the heart it is believed ..., with the mouth it is confessed' (Rom 10.10). Here Paul for a moment reverses the sequence 'mouth ... heart' derived from his earlier quotation of Deut 30.14 (Rom 10.8). As 'confession' (ἐξομολόγησις) in the Greek biblical tradition regularly has the sense of hymnic 'praise', in the Psalter and elsewhere (e.g. Tobit 14.1; Sir 39.13–15 LXX), it is not unlikely that Paul has in mind the classical instance of congregational faith and praise at the Red Sea. Ps 106 was quoted in Rom 1; and the mouth, important in Paul here, is picked out in Wisdom precisely in connection with the Song at the sea: 'Wisdom opened the mouth of the dumb' (Wisd 10.21).

It is very possible, therefore, that the sequence Exod 14.31–15.1 lies behind Rom 10.10. In any case, however, the pattern of communal faith leading to communal confession which is given here in Exodus will have facilitated Christian views of the Church as the community of faith and confession. The believing assembly of men and women in the lesser Song of Moses can be contrasted with God's 'sons and daughters' who provoked him, according to the greater Song, as 'children in whom is no faith (πίστις)' (Deut 32.19–20 LXX). The two Songs together, in their LXX form, therefore enforce the conception of the Church as a community of faith and confession. They belong to the biblical material which qualified the view that the congregation is perpetuated chiefly by physical descent.

A third and related conception of the Church, as the assembly whose confession is divinely inspired, appears in the interpretation of the lesser Song as attested in the Wisdom of Solomon. The prophetically-led congregational hymn of praise was taken to have been inspired, perhaps even ecstatic. In this hymn God opened the mouth of the dumb, and made the tongues of babes to speak clearly (Wisd 10.20–21, compare Isa 35.6); they roamed like horses and skipped like lambs as they praised the Lord who delivered them (Wisd 19.9, compare Isa 63.13 and Ps 114.6). In Philo, similarly, they are 'in ecstasy', ἐνθουσιῶντες, men and women alike (Philo, *V. Contempl.* 87).

The interpretation shared by Wisdom and Philo appears also in rabbinic tradition, for example in the Mekhilta: 'As a reward for the faith

6

with which Israel believed in the Lord, the holy spirit rested upon them and they uttered the Song, as it is written, And they believed in the Lord ... Then Moses and the children of Israel sang ... (Exod 14.31–15.1)' (Mekhilta, *Beshallah*, 6[7], on Exod 14.31). The formula 'the holy spirit rested upon Israel and they uttered the Song' is also found in versions of the rabbinic debate on the performance of the Song which has already been mentioned (Mekhilta, *Shirata*, 1, on Exod 15.1; Tosefta, *Sotah* 6.2, cited above).

The ecstatic aspect of this inspired utterance also reappears in rabbinic tradition, in general agreement with Wisdom and Philo. Thus, sucklings and unborn babes in the womb joined in the Song, together with the ministering angels – as 'God is my strength and my song' (Exod 15.2) suggests when set beside 'Out of the mouths of babes and sucklings hast thou established strength' (Ps 8.2–3). This probably second-century exegesis is found among other places at Mekhilta, *Shirata*, 1, on Exod 15.1. Comparably, the beginning of the Song of Songs, 'Let him kiss me with the kisses of his mouth', was uttered by Israel at the Red Sea, in an exegesis ascribed to the late third-century Caesarean teacher Hanina bar Papa; the verse so interpreted is paraphrased in the midrash with a variation on the formula of inspiration noted above, 'let him make the holy spirit rest upon us, and we will utter before him many songs' (*Cant. R.* i 2, 1) – probably taken to include the Song of Songs, with its exalted hints of mystical union, as well as the Song of Moses.

The LXX as understood in Wisdom and Philo therefore represents widespread interpretative tradition. Paul's assumption that the congregational cry of Abba is uttered by the Spirit (Rom 8.15; Gal 4.6) is closer in expression to the rabbinic version of this tradition, where 'holy spirit' regularly occurs; but it seems nonetheless to be continuous with the Septuagintal view of the redeemed congregation as uttering a hymn by divine inspiration.

A fourth attribute of the community of the Exodus is a relation between the congregation and the angels, both bad and good. This emerges with special reference to the hostile angels in the greater Song.

> 'When the Highest divided the nations, when he dispersed the children of Adam,
> he set the bounds of the nations according to the number of the angels of God;
> and the Lord's portion was his people, Jacob, the lot of his inheritance, Israel.' (Deut 32.8–9 LXX)

As is often noted, the translation 'the angels of God' here in verse 8 presupposes a Hebrew text such as is known from Qumran Cave 4, to be rendered with 'El' rather than, as in most English versions, 'Israel'; and the 'sons of El' are understood as angels, as happened with the 'sons of God' in Job. Some Greek copies have the rendering 'sons' (followed with discussion by Harl in Dogniez and Harl 1992:325–26); but it was no doubt considered to refer to angels, as in the majority Greek text. For the present purpose the translation process reconstructed here is less important than the understanding which governs it, also attested at Sir 17.17 and Jub 15.30–32, in line with Deut 4.19–20: each nation is allotted to an angel (from among the sun, moon and stars, all the heavenly host, the gods whom the heathen worship, according to Deut 4.19); but the Lord himself takes his own people. The people of God is therefore eyed jealously by the angel-deities of the nations, but protected by God (and his angels).

This understanding in turn leaves well-known traces in NT teaching. Sometimes its ecclesiological aspect remains largely implicit, for example when Paul states that we are redeemed by Christ from the power of the 'elements of the world' and 'not-gods' (Gal 4.3–5, 8–10), most plausibly understood as the cosmic host of the angel-deities of the nations; here it is membership of the redeemed people belonging to the true God which brings protection from the hostile powers to whom the nations are allotted, but the Church is unmentioned. The importance of the Church in this connection emerges more clearly in Eph 3.8–12, where the manifold wisdom of God will be made known to the principalities and powers in the heavens through the Church (Eph 3.10, διὰ τῆς ἐκκλησίας) – God's own people, now consisting, as it is presumed that the heavenly powers who eye his portion can see, both of Jews and Gentiles. The Church is viewed here, like God's own people in Deut 32.8, as an object of interest to the angels of the nations.

Lastly, the congregation of Israel is united around a ruler, Moses in the Exodus and another to come. This has already emerged through the binary faith of the congregation in God and in Moses, noticed above in connection with the introduction of the lesser Song (Exod 14.31–15.1 LXX). The importance of congregational faith in Moses is enhanced elsewhere in the LXX Exodus, in its version of the narrative of the signs given to Moses (Exod 4.1–9 LXX, where by comparison with MT 'in you' is added after 'believe' in vv. 5, 8 and 9). The significance of Moses as a ruler and the pattern of a messiah is evident in Philonic and rabbinic passages on Moses as king; see, for example, Philo, *Mos.* 1.148, 158 (he was named god and king of the whole nation); *Midrash Tehillim* 1.2, on Ps 1.1 (like David, he was king of Israel and Judah, as shown by Deut 33.5 – a passage from the Blessing of Moses discussed below). This point gains NT confirmation not only from Acts 7.35–38, on the legation of Moses as ruler and redeemer, but also from Paul's striking statement that all the fathers 'were baptized into Moses' (1 Cor 10.2), as the Christians were 'baptized into Christ' (Rom 6.3).

To return to the Pentateuch, in his final Blessing Moses foretells, according to the LXX, that 'there shall be a ruler in the Beloved, when the rulers of the nations are gathered together at one time with the tribes of Israel' (Deut 33.5 LXX). The future 'there shall be', contrasting with the past tense represented in the Massoretic pointing and in the rabbinic interpretation quoted above, makes this verse in the LXX a messianic oracle comparable with those of Jacob and Balaam (Gen 49.9–12; Num 24.7, 17 LXX). Deut 33.5 LXX, however, differs from these passages in envisaging the coming ruler as a monarch 'in the Beloved' – the elect people of God – reigning in an imperial council and forming the focus of the unity of Israel and, beyond, of the tributary nations of the world. Here the Blessing in its LXX form is not far from the Stoically-influenced Philonic and Pauline conception of the nation as one body, headed by the high priest or Christ, respectively (Philo, *Spec. Leg.* 3.319; Rom 12.5; Dahl 1941:226–27; Moule 1977:83–85). Hence, although the messianic links of the congregation in these LXX texts are less prominent than NT links between the Church and Christ, the LXX presents in the lesser Song and the Blessing of Moses the picture of a Church led by Moses as ruler, or by the greater messianic ruler still to come.

Thus far, then, the material studied from the LXX has disclosed five attributes of the congregation which are also prominent marks of the NT Church. Constitutionally and liturgically, it is a body in which men and women each take part, and it is governed by a divinely-appointed ruler. To turn to theological attributes, it can be described as a community of faith, the congregation of the redeemed who believe and confess. Correspondingly, in this corporate confession it is a community of the divinely inspired, and its confession is led by prophecy. As God's own peculiar people and portion, it is watched by the angel-deities to whom the heathen nations are allotted. Its faith is faith not only in God, but also in the appointed ruler, and a great ruler to come will be the focus of its unity. The shape and ethos of the Pauline churches are anticipated here; and although the theological attributes are not made normative in these texts, the fact that they are exhibited by the congregation of the Exodus as described in the Pentateuch accords them authority and influence.

These attributes give some substance to the view of the Church outlined in the LXX passages considered here. The sketch which begins to emerge constitutes a far-reaching anticipation of NT conceptions. Now this outline can receive further definition from the overlap between some LXX titles used for the congregation, and NT titles for the Church.

TITLES OF THE CHURCH

Within the two Songs, the Blessing and Wisdom the principal title of the Exodus congregation is 'people' (λαός). The Pentateuchal texts also have the correlative 'Jacob', 'Israel', and (for the national name Jeshurun) 'Beloved'. There is also occasional reference to 'ecclesia' and 'saints'. Here the evidently national title 'people' will be treated first, followed by the still national but less plainly ethnocentric 'Beloved', 'ecclesia', and 'saints'. All these terms reappear in the NT vocabulary referring to the Church, but their fresh application is not always straightforward.

The self-definition of the assembly as the people (λαός) of God just encountered in the 'Great Ode' is central in the LXX material considered here. In the lesser Song of Exod 15 the congregation, articulated into men and women, identify themselves emphatically as the elect people of God, 'this people whom you redeemed', 'this people whom you possessed' (Exod 15.13, 16). The greater Song, correspondingly, remembering the allotment of God's own people to himself in the presence of the angels of the nations (Deut 32.8 LXX, discussed above), expects the day when 'the Lord will judge his people', when the angels shall worship him and the nations shall rejoice 'with his people', and 'he shall purify his people's land' (Deut 32.36, 43 LXX). In the Blessing, similarly, he has had pity on his people, and there is none like Israel, 'a people saved by the Lord' (Deut 33.3, 29). Finally, in the later chapters of Wisdom the term λαός is even more clearly a focus of expressions of divine election; thus, in passages on the Exodus, Wisdom delivered a holy people, God did good to his people and fed them with angels' food (10.15, 16.2, 20); the Egyptians, on the destruction of their first-born, confessed 'the people' to be God's son (18.13); his people journeyed miraculously on when the Egyptians found a strange death, and in all things God magnified his people (19.5, 22). The theory of divinely-ordered yet rational miracle elaborated in Wisdom itself serves especially, as these verses show, to exalt God's 'people' (Sweet 1965:123–24).

The word λαός used here in the LXX, and emerging in Wisdom as *tout court* a current name for Israel, is rarely applied directly to the Christians in Paul. Like the name Israel, it occurs with primary reference to the Jewish people rather than as a straightforward title of the Church (Dahl 1941:210). This is probably the case when Deut 32.43 LXX 'rejoice, you nations, with his people' is quoted at Rom 15.10. Earlier in Romans, however, those Gentiles whom God has called are held now to share, correspondingly, in the title of his people and his children, as prophesied in Hosea: 'I will call the not-people (as) my people; and her that was not beloved (as) beloved' (Hos 2.25, freely quoted and followed by Hos 2.1 LXX, at Rom 9.24–25). Here Paul probably uses an existing testimony-chain, the compilation of which attests his own conviction that the Gentile Christians share the election of the Israelite λαός. Thus for Christians it was their 'fathers', with spiritual privileges like their own (1 Cor 10.1–4), who sinned when 'the people sat down to eat and drink' (1 Cor 10.7, quoting Exod 32.6). Correspondingly, another Pentateuchal verse on the 'people' is used in exhortation to Christians at 2 Cor 6.16, in a passage perhaps drawn from a source, as mentioned above. Here the series of texts on the congregation as the temple of God begins with Lev 26.11–12, quoted in a form near to Ezek 37.27, 'I will dwell among them . . . and they shall be my people'. The use of this text as the first of the series supports the view that a Pentateuchal understanding of the assembly as made up of men and women contributed to the specification of 'daughters' at the end of the series, as noted above.

The Christians thus belong to the λαός, but the title is not restricted to the Church. This is implied also in Acts, where λαός can be applied to the Jewish people, as noted below, but 'God made a visitation to take from the gentiles a people for his name' (Acts 15.14; cf. Deut 32.8; Rom 9.24). The same interpretation seems likely also to apply to famous texts on Christians as (belonging to) the people of God in Hebrews (4.9; 10.30, from Deut 32.40; see M. Bockmuehl, below); 1 Pet (2.9–10, from Exod 19.5–6, 23.22; Hos 2.25; see R. Bauckham, below); and Revelation (18.4 'come out of her, my people', from Jer 51.45). These books offer no anti-Jewish definition of λαός, by contrast with the frequent employment, from the *Epistle of Barnabas* onwards, of phrases such as 'the new people' (*Barn.* 5.7; see also Cyprian, *De Unitate* 5.19 [25], quoted above). The other side of this coin is NT continuation and awareness of the Jewish use of λαός as a Jewish national title. This was illustrated above from Rom 15.10 on 'his people'; but is also reflected in Acts (as at 7.17; 26.17, 23; 28.17, all in speeches by Christian Jews to non-Christian Jews) and Jude (v. 5; see R. Bauckham, below). Phrases like 'the new people' imply a doctrine of supersession, but they also recognize and continue the centrality in biblical and contemporary Judaism of self-definition as 'people of God' – the point brought home by the prominence of λαός in the LXX texts considered here. Λαός can therefore be reckoned only with qualification among NT titles for the Church, but the LXX references to an elect λαός are central in NT *conceptions* of the Church.

The election of the Jewish nation was also strikingly asserted in the LXX rendering of Jeshurun, the name for Israel occurring in the greater Song and the Blessing of Moses, by ὁ ἠγαπημένος, 'the beloved' (Deut 32.15, 33.5, 26, followed in the LXX translations of Isaiah (44.3) and the Psalms (29[28].6; see below). This interpretation fits the immediate context of Deut 32.15, a description of God's particular care for Israel from the time of his original choice (Deut 32.8–14), as well as the larger biblical context of the divine love shown in the Exodus (compare 'your sons whom you loved', Wisd 16.26). 'Beloved' appears as a messianic title in the NT (Eph 1.6) and in continuing Christian usage (e.g. *Barn.* 3.6); in both these instances ἠγαπημένος is used, but the similar ἀγαπητός also occurs in this sense, as in the Greek text of the *Ascension of Isaiah* (3.17).

'Beloved', which could in principle be represented by either Greek word, was probably already applied by pre-Christian Jews not only to Israel, but also to the messiah; thus in the Psalms the former sense seems to appear at Ps 29(28).6 LXX (ὁ ἠγαπημένος), the latter in the inscription of Ps 45(44) LXX 'for the beloved' (ὑπὲρ τοῦ ἀγαπητοῦ; Schaper 1995:78–79, taking Ps 29[28].6 LXX also as messianic, by contrast with the above).

The thematically related term 'son' has a similar dual application to Israel and the messiah (Exod 4.22; Ps 2.7). The stress on election in LXX application of the title 'beloved' to the congregation may be compared with the stress on Israel's sonship in Hebrew prayer known from Qumran: 'thou hast made us sons to thee before the eyes of all nations, for thou didst call Israel "My son, my first-born"' (4Q 504 iii.1–2, lines 3–5, quoting Exod 4.22).

In the NT the singular 'beloved' as a title is restricted to the messiah (Eph 1.6, already cited, but not in the epistles generally acknowledged as Pauline; for the title compare Mark 1.11, 9.7, and parallels, for the sense Col 1.13 'son of his love'). The plural 'beloved of God', however, is a title of the Christians collectively, as at Rom 1.7 (ἀγαπητοί); 1 Thess 1.4; 2 Thess 2.13; Col 3.12 (ἠγαπημένοι); cf. Rom 11.28 (ἀγαπητοί), of Israel. The link between the applications to Christ and to the Church appears in the immediate context of Eph 1.6, a blessing on God who 'picked us out through him [Christ] ... to be holy and blameless before him in love having foreordained us ...' (Eph 1.4–5). Against the LXX and NT background just noted, 'in love' (ἐν ἀγάπῃ) here probably refers to God's love for his people in election (so Origen), not theirs for one another. This passage could then rank with Eph 5.1 '[God's] beloved children' (τέκνα ἀγαπητά; cf. Wisd 16.26) as attesting the sense of the church title 'beloved' in slightly different language.

This usage directly continues, and applies to the Church in each place, the assertion of communal election made by the rendering 'beloved' in the greater Song and Blessing of Moses. Its continuity with the LXX is emphasized by the importance of 'beloved of God' (Rom 1.7; 1 Thess 1.4; cf. Eph 1.4–5, 5.1), despite the concurrence of the integrally related concept that the Church was loved by Christ; the two are fused at Rom 8.39.

The most famous and influential of all church titles, ἐκκλησία, occurs in the introduction of the 'Great Ode': 'Moses spoke to the end the words of this ode in the ears of all the ecclesia of Israel' (Deut 32.1 LXX). This title was quickly adopted by Christians (1 Thess 1.1, etc.), by contrast with their qualified use of λαός. Paul often uses it in the form 'ἐκκλησία of God' (1 Cor 1.2, etc.), thereby underlining the Christian share in the special relationship to God bestowed on the λαός. Although ἐκκλησία recalled the Israelite 'ecclesia in the wilderness' (Acts 7.38), for which it was regularly used in LXX Deuteronomy, it was not restricted to this sense. Factors which freed it from the strongly national associations of λαός will have included its absence from LXX Genesis to Numbers, where συναγωγή is used for the Israelite congregation. Another such factor will have been the broad usage of both ἐκκλησία and συναγωγή, and the Hebrew *qahal* and *'edah* and Aramaic *qᵉhala* and *kᵉnisha*, to which they often respectively correspond, for other assemblies as well as that of all Israel. Thus an application of Aramaic *qᵉhala* to a pious group is found at Babylonian Talmud, *Ber.* 9b, on the prayer practice of 'the holy congregation' in Jerusalem. (The use of this Aramaic phrase here and elsewhere is discussed in connection with NT vocabulary by Jeremias 1969:247–49.) Hence ἐκκλησία could be used for the separate Christian 'churches of the saints' (1 Cor 14.33; cf. Ps 89[88].6 LXX 'the ecclesia of the saints'); but it also presented the churches as continuous with the congregation of Israel described in the LXX Pentateuch.

Finally, 'the saints' appear as Israel corporately in the lesser Song and the Blessing of Moses. God is 'glorified among the saints (ἅγιοι)' (Exod 15.11 LXX), and 'all the sanctified (ἡγιασμένοι) are under his hands' (Deut 33.3 LXX). The first of these passages could have been taken as a reference to angels, but was perhaps more readily applicable to the congregation, the saints who are glorifying God by the hymn of Exod 15 which they are singing. The second passage is applied to the martyrs in 4 Macc 17.19. In the book of Wisdom, comparably, the martyr 'was numbered among the sons of God, and his lot is among the saints' (5.5); the theme of Israel's sonship (Exod 4.22) with which 'the saints' of Israel are here connected was noted above in Qumran prayer and elsewhere in Wisdom (16.26; cf. 18.13). Again in Wisdom, at the first Passover the Israelites covenanted 'that the saints (ἅγιοι) should share alike in good things and in dangers' (Wisd 18.9).

This Jewish designation of Israel as 'saints' is reflected in Acts when Gentile Christians receive 'a lot among the sanctified' (Acts 26.18; cf. 20.32, and the use of λαός for the Jewish people noted above in Acts). Phrases speaking of the 'inheritance' or 'lot' of the saints recur, with the same emphasis on sharing the privileges of Israel, at Eph 1.18; Col 1.11 (cf. the stress on the Church as beloved, noted above in Eph 1.4–5, 5.1; Col 3.12). This group of phrases on the saints' inheritance from Acts, Ephesians and Colossians correspondingly recalls the 'Great Ode' not only on 'the sanctified', but also on the election of Israel as falling to God's own 'inheritance' (Deut 32.8 LXX, discussed above).

The Christians, sharing this inheritance, are in the same way collectively entitled 'sanctified' (1 Cor 1.2) or, more usually, 'saints' (e.g. in 1 Cor 14.33, quoted above, and in epistolary addresses such as Rom 1.7; Phil 1.1). This title can readily accompany the title 'beloved', as at Rom 1.7, Col 3.12, both cited above. In the case of 'saints' a Pentateuchally-rooted title has been taken up, once again, in the Jewish community, as the LXX Pentateuch and Wisdom attest; and the Christians continue its application to Israel, but also apply it specially to their own churches.

The four titles now considered present the congregation of the Exodus as the redeemed people of God, God's beloved, and as the *ecclesia* of Israel made up of the 'sanctified' or 'saints'. When these titles are viewed together with the attributes noted above, the congregation as presented in this LXX material is more fully characterized. Constitutionally, it is both national and ecclesiastical, a national assembly for divine service, in which men and women take an appointed part. Theologically, it is not only a people descended from the Hebrew ancestors, but also a congregation of the saints who have faith in God and his servant Moses, and confess their divine Lord. Their corporate hymn of faith is divinely inspired, and collectively they are God's own Beloved, led and unified by God's appointed ruler, a people on whom the hostile gaze of the angel-deities is bent in vain.

To return to the opening question, just how far does this picture anticipate Christian conceptions of the Church? The view of the congregation of the Exodus offered in this LXX material would not be wholly inadequate as a sketch of the Church in the NT. Thus the Corinthian emphasis on spiritual gifts, and Paul's call in reply for decency and order, could both invoke the example of the Pentateuchal congregation as presented here in the LXX. The constitutive nature of faith for the Church, as met in Acts and Paul, is as much a feature of the Septuagintal portrait as is the importance of Jewish descent. The congregation appears in the LXX under designations characteristically used by Christians, 'the Church' and 'the saints', and the Pauline phrase 'ecclesia of God' (as at 1 Cor 1.2) recalls the Septuagintal view of the people as the Lord's own portion.

On the other hand, it has become clear that the transition from this portrayal to Christian conceptions and doctrines of the Church was not wholly straightforward. The conviction that Israel corporately were God's chosen and beloved, as LXX interpretation so strongly emphasizes, did not disappear. In this point the Paul of Romans was at one with the Paul of Acts (Rom 11.28, 15.10; Acts 26.23, 28.17, cited above). Hence, despite expectation that Israel in the end would be saved through Christ (Rom 11.25–27), and despite thorough Christian participation in the concept of the people of God, 'people' was not readily adopted as a church title until Christian claims to be the new elect people took root.

A second point in which the Christian development seems distinctive without being discontinuous is the link regularly made in NT sources between the congregation and the messiah. So in Paul the Church is 'the ecclesia of God', but it belongs primarily to God's messiah, and then, thereby, to God: 'you are Christ's, and Christ is God's' (1 Cor 3.23). This is a messianic expansion of the affirmation that the congregation belongs to

God noted above at Deut 32.8. Similarly, Paul betroths the Corinthian Church like a virgin to Christ (2 Cor 11.2), not directly to God; the Church is beloved by Christ as well as God, as noted already; and the Christians form one body in (here probably in the sense 'because of') Christ (Rom 12.5), or the body of (belonging to) Christ (1 Cor 12.27) (for these interpretations of the phrases, see Moule 1977:71–72). The communal faith is 'the faith of Jesus Christ' (Rom 3.22; Gal 3.22); although for many exegetes this faith is the faith exhibited by Christ, in the present writer's view the phrase more probably implies both faith that Jesus is the Christ of God, the bringer of God's redemption, and also faith in Christ like Israel's faith in Moses (the ecclesiastical aspect of 'believing' in these two Pauline passages was noted above).

Here, however, as this comparison recalls, the LXX has presented an antecedent noticed above, the binary faith of Israel in God and Moses (Exod 14.31; cf. Num 21.5). Similarly, the conception of the Church as the congregation belonging to and unified by the messiah (Rom 12.5; 1 Cor 12.27) is anticipated in the lesser Song and the Blessing of Moses (Deut 33.5). Here the NT development can be called not an adaptation, as in the case of λαός, but an intensification, occasioned by the ardent realized messianism of the Christians.

It can then be said, in conclusion, that the messianic element in Christian faith, and the concurrent Christian modification of the concept of the people of God, are foci of what can be called new in NT conceptions of the Church. Far more, however, is inherited from Judaism as represented by the LXX tradition, including what might be thought characteristically Christian associations of the Church with faith, confession, inspiration and the messiah.[5]

Postscript

John Sweet has cogently assessed the theory of miracles in Wisdom as exemplary for its hold on the doctrine of creation, but as undermined by the author's instinct for propaganda (Sweet 1965:125–26). Can the poems from the same LXX tradition studied here, imbued as they are with instinctive exaltation of Israel, then offer any vision for the Church to salute the honorand on his birthday? Perhaps at least two features of the poems might be picked out as exemplary. First, as it comes before us in these poems, from the Greek Pentateuch to Wisdom, the congregation of the Exodus is graced by a seemingly effortless conjunction of order and παρρησία ('free speech'). It has all the dignity of the solemn assembly of Israel, but in its antiphons it tastes the glorious liberty of the children of God. Secondly, the poems themselves in their Greek dress faithfully recall

---

[5] I am most grateful to Dr M. Bockmuehl for comments and suggestions.

by their stressed verse the strange and archaic scriptural sources, but in
their wording they are full of colour and vitality. These conjunctions of
order and liberty, fidelity and vitality, perhaps still have some exemplary
force for the Church in its services and its biblical interpretation. This
Septuagintal moralizing must abide John Sweet's verdict; but meanwhile
it can introduce a warm birthday greeting – offered with admiration for
his creative biblical work, and gratitude for his unfailing kindness and
encouragement.

Bibliography

Bell, R. H. 1994. *Provoked to Jealousy: The Origin and Purpose of the Jealousy Motif in Romans 9–11.* WUNT 2.63. Tübingen: Mohr (Siebeck).

Dahl, N. A. 1941. *Das Volk Gottes.* Oslo: Dybwad.

Dogniez, C. and M. Harl. 1992. *La Bible d'Alexandrie, 5, Le Deutéronome.* Paris: Les Éditions du Cerf.

Hengel, M. with R. Deines. 1994. 'Die Septuaginta als "christliche Schriftensammlung", ihre Vorgeschichte und das Problem ihres Kanons'. In M. Hengel and A. Schwemer (eds.), *Die Septuaginta zwischen Judentum und Christentum.* Tübingen: Mohr (Siebeck). 182–284.

Hengel, M. 1995. 'The Song about Christ in Earliest Worship' (revised English translation). In M. Hengel, *Studies in Early Christology.* Edinburgh: T. & T. Clark. 227–91.

Horbury, W. 1995. 'The Christian Use and the Jewish Origins of the Wisdom of Solomon'. In J. Day, R. P. Gordon and H. G. M. Williamson (eds.), *Wisdom in Ancient Israel.* Cambridge: Cambridge University Press. 182–96.

Horbury, W. 1996. 'Land, Sanctuary and Worship'. In J. P. M. Sweet and J. M. G. Barclay (eds.), *Early Christian Thought in its Jewish Setting.* Cambridge: Cambridge University Press. 207–24.

Horbury, W. 1997a. 'Women in the Synagogue'. In W. D. Davies, L. Finkelstein and J. V. M. Sturdy (eds.), *The Cambridge History of Judaism*, Vol. 3. Cambridge: Cambridge University Press.

Horbury, W. 1997b. *Jews and Christians in Contact and Controversy.* Edinburgh: T. & T. Clark.

Jeremias, J. 1969. *Jerusalem in the Time of Jesus.* Tr. by F. H. and C. H. Cave, with the author's revisions. London: SCM Press.

Le Boulluec, A., and P. Sandevoir. 1989. *La Bible d'Alexandrie, 2, L'Exode.* Paris: Les Éditions du Cerf.

Le Déaut, R. 1984. 'La Septante, un Targum?' In R. Kuntzmann and J. Schlosser (eds.), *Études sur le judaïsme hellénistique.* Paris: Les Éditions du Cerf. 147–95.

Moule, C. F. D. 1977. *The Origin of Christology.* Cambridge: Cambridge University Press.

Schaper, J. L. W. 1995. *Eschatology in the Greek Psalter.* WUNT 2.76. Tübingen: Mohr (Siebeck).

Schürer, E. and M. Goodman. 1986. E. Schürer, *Geschichte des jüdischen Volkes im Zeitalter Jesu Christi.* 3rd–4th edn., Leipzig, 1901–9. ET *The History of the Jewish People in the Age of Jesus Christ,* revised by G. Vermes, F. Millar, M. Black, M. Goodman and P. Vermes (i, ii, iii.1, iii.2). Edinburgh: T. & T. Clark. iii.1:470–704.

Seeligmann, L. 1948. *The Septuagint Version of Isaiah.* Leiden: Brill.

Sweet, J. P. M. 1965. 'The Theory of Miracles in the Wisdom of Solomon'. In C. F. D. Moule (ed.), *Miracles.* London: Mowbray. 115–26.

Sweet, J. P. M. 1979. *Revelation.* London: SCM Press.

2

Matthew's Vision for the Church

MICHAEL GOULDER

In one sense Matthew had a short-term vision for the Church. He was, we may suppose, writing in the later 70s (with Mark a familiar text), and he thought Jesus' generation would not have passed away before the Son of Man came (24.34; 16.28), that is, we may say, before 90. But there are those today who expect to see the Lord's return, but are not lacking in controversial policies for the Church; and Matthew was like that too. What makes his vision so attractive, and so effective, is his combination of spiritual idealism with practical moderation, rather a rare coupling in Church history.[1]

LOYALTY AND OPENNESS

The 70s were a critical time for the Church. In the 40s it had had a proper central organization at Jerusalem. The old triumvirate, Peter and the two sons of Zebedee, had been broken up by Herod's execution of James (Acts 12.1f); but it had been strengthened in fact in the advancement of his namesake, James, Jesus' brother, a man of principle and force of character, who rapidly became chairman of the Jerusalem three (Gal 2.9, 12; Acts 12.17, 15.13–21, 21.18). Paul felt that he had to square his preaching with the Jerusalem leadership (Gal 2.1–10), and James saw to it that their rulings were enforced (Gal 2.11–14), with the constant despatch of emissaries to Antioch, Galatia and later Corinth. Paul accepted this structure of authority, while maintaining his own position as apostle, and his 'gospel' as the true doctrine; but after his death, his followers resisted the imposition of Jerusalem rulings, and with the siege of the city and its destruction in 68–70, such resistance became increasingly practicable. We may see the pressures on the two sides by observing details in Mark, a radical Pauline, and Matthew, a middle-of-the-road conservative.

Jesus' family had been leading the Jerusalem church for thirty years, first in the person of James his brother, and then of his cousin Simeon

---

[1] It is an honour to have been asked to contribute to John Sweet's *Festschrift*. I have enjoyed an unclouded friendship with him since we were thirteen; and he represents the Matthaean ideal in modern form – wise conservatism, pastoral realism and unbounded aspiration.

(Hegesippus, the second-century historian, quoted in Eusebius, *Hist. Eccl.* 3.22); so naturally the primary issue was loyalty, or otherwise, to them. Mark is noticeably unfriendly to them: 'And when his relations (οἱ παρ' αὐτοῦ) heard [of Jesus' success] they went out to lay hands on him, for they said, He is out of his mind' (Mark 3.21). Matthew leaves out very few verses in Mark, but he leaves this one out. Mark goes on: 'And his mother and his brothers came, and standing outside they sent to him, summoning him.' The message is brought that they are outside, but Jesus looks about on those seated around and says, 'Whoever does the will of God, he is my brother and sister and mother' (Mark 3.31–35). What matters is to be in that circle, listening to Jesus and doing God's will: such people are Jesus' real family – his family according to the flesh were outside. Matthew includes the story, but he takes the sting out of it (Matt 12.46–50). Jesus' family came, and they waited politely outside because they 'wanted to speak to him'; they never thought of 'laying hands on him', or doubting his sanity; Jesus' spiritual family includes all his disciples as well as his physical family. It is the same with Jesus' unhappy preaching at Nazareth. Mark has him say, 'A prophet is not without honour save in his home-country, and among his relations, and in his house' (Mark 6.4): Matthew has, '. . . save in his home-country, and in his house' (13.57). Matthew does not want to speak ill of his relations: they are running the Church.

It is the same with the old triumvirate. Mark has some traditional stories to the credit of Peter, James and John – their call, their presence at the raising of Jairus' daughter, or the Transfiguration, or Gethsemane, but he also has a lot of hostile material. He calls James and John the Sons of Thunder, presumably an indication of their impetuous and angry temperament (Luke 9.54f); and Matthew leaves this out (10.2). Mark tells how Jesus told John off for trying to stop exorcisms in his name (Mark 9.37–40); and Matthew leaves this out too. Mark describes the brothers' humiliation when they ask Jesus for the seats at his side in heaven (Mark 10.35–45); this time Matthew tells the story, but cleverly shifts the odium on to their ambitious mother (20.20–28).

Mark has similarly quite a lot of unsympathetic matter about Peter. It is Peter who declares that Jesus is the Christ, but he gets no credit for it in Mark (8.29), whereas in Matthew he receives the highest praise – 'Blessed are you, Simon bar-Jonah! For flesh and blood has not revealed this to you, but my Father . . .' (16.17–19). In Mark, Peter takes Jesus aside and has the effrontery to rebuke him (Mark 8.32); in Matthew this is softened by adding 'God forbid it, Lord! This shall never happen to you', quite a mild 'rebuke' (16.22). In Mark Jesus then speaks the terrible words to Peter, 'Get behind me, Satan!' (8.33), again softened by Matthew's addition, 'You are [not just a rock but] a stumbling block to me' (16.23). There are many instances of Mark's rough treatment of Peter in the Last

Supper, Gethsemane and Denial stories in Mark 14; Matthew leaves most of these untouched, because Peter wins our sympathy in his weakness, but he makes things a bit easier – for example, Mark 14.72, '[Peter] began to weep', Matt 26.75, '[Peter] wept bitterly'.[2]

It would be possible to extend such comparisons much more widely by including the two evangelists' treatment of the disciples as a whole; but this much must suffice. There is evidence of a steady tendency in both writers. Mark gives a picture of the disciples generally, as of the Three in particular, as insensitive, ambitious, cowardly, self-regarding and generally unworthy: and this is best explained if he was a companion of Paul (Col 4.10, Phlm 24), who is resisting Jerusalem missionaries who claimed the authority of Peter for their doctrines ('of Cephas', 1 Cor 1.12). Matthew will not allow this. He is loyal to the Jerusalem leadership, Jesus' family (who are still there), the disciples, and especially Peter, who is so often their spokesman in his Gospel.

A CHURCH WITH A STRUCTURE AND A DISCIPLINE

With his Jewish background, Matthew saw the Church organized as a part of Judaism. Judaism had local courts with three judges to settle ordinary matters, and there was the Sanhedrin with seventy-one judges for capital and other serious cases (Mishnah, *Sanh.* 1). So Matthew writes as a Jew, 'I say to you, that anyone who is angry with his brother shall be liable to judgement [in his local church]; and whoever says to his brother, Raka [You idiot!], shall be liable to the Sanhedrin [the Jewish supreme court, still sitting in the neighbourhood of Jerusalem]; and whoever says, Moreh [You godless rebel!], shall be liable to hell-fire' (5.22). Christians have to be careful how they speak to one another. Anger itself will land them in front of the local court; for insult they will face the highest court on earth; and for serious insult it will be God's judgement, and condemnation to hell.

This is perhaps a rhetorical flourish, but Matthew is serious about discipline in the Church. In 18.10–17 'the disciples' are to be pastors of

---

[2] Peter was a problem for the Paulines. Some Christians at Corinth said they were 'of Cephas', so seeing him as leader of the opposition to the Pauline movement; but then historically he had been Jesus' senior apostle, and no Christian could be against him. Hence Mark's ambivalence towards him – some friendly traditions, some hostility – whereas Mark has no good word for Jesus' family. The tension is even worse in John. But in time, when Peter had been a good while dead, he was co-opted into the Pauline movement. 1 Peter, written perhaps around 90, is a thoroughly Pauline document, and can send greetings from 'Mark my son' in 'Babylon' (i.e. Rome); and so to Papias, and the tale of Mark's transcribing Peter's sermons. The first and most effective co-opter was Matthew.

'these little ones', their church members, on pain of being reported to God by the latter's guardian angels; if one of them 'is lost', that is commits a serious sin, they are to go after him, and if they 'find' him, there will be joy in heaven that he does not 'perish'. The evangelist explains what this means: if your brother [fellow-Christian] sins, you [singular, the local church pastor] are to speak to him privately; if he will not listen, you are to take one or two witnesses, as provided in Deut 19.15; if he is obdurate, you are to bring him before the local church; and the last resort will be to treat him as the Gentile and the publican – that is, excommunicate him. It is the same procedure which we find in Paul, who promises to invoke the witnesses of Deut 19.15 in 2 Cor 13.1, and requires 'separation from the unclean' in 2 Cor 6.14–7.1, and the handing over of sinners to Satan for the destruction of the flesh in 1 Cor 5.3–5. These shepherds of the flock mean business.

Matthew also takes over the Jewish idea of a continuous chain of authoritative interpreters: 'The scribes and Pharisees sit on Moses's seat: so whatever they tell you, observe and do' (23.2f). In the Mishnah the idea is that God's rulings were given to Moses, some of which he proclaimed in the Torah and some not; and through the succession of interpreters, through Ezra and the Great Synagogue, the right of legislation has passed to the present Sanhedrin, who 'sit on Moses's seat' (Mishnah, *Aboth* 1.1) – their rulings are valid for Christians too, who are still (in intention) a part of Judaism. But it should also be said that the true successors of Moses are seen not as 'their scribes' (7.29), but as Christian scribes (8.19), those who have been made disciples to the kingdom (13.52); in fact Jesus sent out not only scribes (like Matthew himself), but Christian prophets and sages (23.34, the highest echelons of Jewish religion, the predecessors of the rabbis).

There was however a second and greater source of divine law since Jesus came, and he had not only laid down many prescriptions for the Church himself, but had also set up a kind of Christian Sanhedrin, the Apostolic College, to interpret his rulings. Jesus had called Simon Cephas, the Rock; and Matthew took this to mean that he was like a foundation stone to the Church as a building, to which, in another metaphor, he held the keys. Matthew is a marvellous teacher, who first uses brilliant images like these, and then explains them. This meant that 'Whatever you bind on earth shall be bound in heaven, and whatever you loose on earth shall be loosed in heaven' (16.19). Binding and loosing were regular Jewish terms for the authority of Sages to enforce rules or make exceptions (Mishnah, *Ter.* 5.4, Mishnah, *Pes.* 4.5; Josephus, *Bell. Jud.* 11.5.2), and Peter is being given this same authority in the Church. Any enforcements or exceptions he makes, Jesus will ratify. Exactly the same words are used in the plural to the Twelve at 18.18, so Matthew sees the Apostolic College as a Christian equivalent to the Sanhedrin. Caiaphas was the chairman at

Jesus' trial in Matt 26, and Peter is similarly thought of as chairman of the Apostles. We may think the Church of England close to its origins here: the Jewish parallel makes Peter more a *primus inter pares* than a Pope, though his first-century successors behaved with more resolution than most Archbishops of Canterbury.

It is just at this point that Matthew is in two minds as to where he sees the Church going. As a conservative, he wants the Church to be part of Judaism, under the ultimate authority of the Sanhedrin, paying the temple tax lest the Jews be made to stumble (17.27), keeping the rulings of those on Moses's seat. But at the same time he loathed what he saw as Pharisaic ambition and show – being called Rabbi and Teacher (23.5–10), public piety (6.1–18), and the trivializing of religion (23.16–28) – and he could see that the mission to the Jews had failed (23.37–39). Against his instincts he senses that the future is with a different, apostolic structure.

KEEPING THE LAW AND INCLUDING THE GENTILES

The tension between Mark and Matthew had its origins in the success of Paul's mission to the Gentiles. The Jerusalem leaders had put their foot down about keeping Jewish food-laws in Paul's church at Antioch (Gal 2.11–14), and Paul (and Mark) knew that if this was insisted on all the way, that would be the end of the Gentile mission.[3] Hence Mark's critical attitude to these 'pillars': Jesus took Paul's side, he says (Mark 7.1–23, 2.23–28), and was often critical of them. But Matthew is loyal to Jerusalem, while often sympathizing with the Pauline position; and it is this which makes him such an interesting and winning person.

It has sometimes been doubted whether Matthew had much feeling for the Gentile mission, for in his Mission Discourse (ch. 10) Jesus says, 'Go nowhere among the Gentiles, and enter no town of the Samaritans, but go rather to the lost sheep of the house of Israel' (10.5f); and again,

[3] It is possible to read Gal 2 in other ways. Perhaps the Jerusalem leaders allowed that Gentiles could be saved without circumcision, provided they kept basic ('Noachide') laws, as in Acts 15; but they might object to Jewish Christians eating with Gentiles at Antioch, which would look as if keeping the full Torah did not matter: cf. M. Bockmuehl, 'The Noachide Commandments and New Testament Ethics', *Revue Biblique* 102 (1995) 72–101. Such an understanding would involve seeing the Galatian 'trouble-makers' as unauthorized by the Jerusalem leadership, and Gal 2.15–21 as unconnected with 2.11–14. But a more serious problem is Mark's (and John's) hostility to Jesus' family: why should these two evangelists attack such moderate Jewish Christians, doing their best for the Gentile converts? Note especially John 7.5, 'For not even his brothers believed in him' – and faith, believing, is the condition for salvation in John.

'you will not have gone through the towns of Israel before the Son of Man comes' (10.23). But it is important to notice that these words are spoken to the Twelve, and this is said three times (10.1, 5; 11.1). The Twelve understood their mission to be to 'the circumcision' (Gal 2.7f), and they agreed that Paul should have responsibility for the Gentile mission (Gal 2.9). So Matthew sees the Twelve as running the Palestine churches, and as being the final authority for any 'binding and loosing'; but the mission to Samaria, and to the Gentile world at large, was to be in other hands.[4] There is not the least doubt that Matthew accepted the Gentile mission with enthusiasm. He has Gentile astrologers at Jesus' cradle (2.1–12), and Jesus' final commission (to the Eleven and 'others') is 'Go therefore and make disciples of all nations' (28.17–19). The highest praise is reserved for the Gentile Centurion, 'I have not found such faith, no, not in Israel' (8.10), and in 24.14 'this gospel of the kingdom will be proclaimed throughout the world'. It is true that the evangelist can speak depreciatingly of 'Gentiles and tax-collectors' (18.17; cf. 5.47, 6.7); but then even Paul, the apostle to the Gentiles, can speak of 'sinners of the Gentiles' (Gal 2.15). In those days facing facts seemed more important than political correctness.

Matthew's vision of the Church is made (marginally) clearer in his Tares parable, with its interpretation (13.24–30, 36–43). We are told in the latter that the field is the world, and the good seed is 'the sons of the kingdom', that is, Christians in good standing; so we have the impression that Matthew sees the kingdom as the world. In one sense, of course, this is so: God is king of the whole universe, and the reaping stands for the judgement of all mankind. But then often in Matthew the kingdom is the Church: it has been subject to violence since the days of the Baptist (11.12), for example, and Peter has its keys (16.19). So too, here at the completion of the age the angels 'will gather out of his kingdom all scandals and those who do lawlessness', and it looks as if the Kingdom and the Church are now the same – as at the Marriage Feast, or with the Bridesmaids, where the unworthy are excluded. Matthew has a clearer head than most NT authors, but he can be inconsistent like the rest of us: the sons of the Kingdom are the Jews at 8.12, the good Christians at 13.38; the Pharisees' teaching is leaven to be wary of at 16.12, but to be observed at 23.3; Herod is tetrarch at 14.1 and king at 14.9. The message of the Tares is that the gospel seed was sown not only in Israel but among the Gentiles, but judgement is coming for all, and baptism is not enough: a proper standard of ethics is required too – converts guilty of ἀνομία will be burned as tares. Matthew is forever reassuring

---

[4] At 28.17–20 Jesus commissions the Church to preach to all nations, but the Church comprises not only the Eleven, who worship him in faith, but also others (οἱ δέ) who doubted. Cf. also 25.31–46, where the missionaries to the nations are spoken of as 'the least of these my brethren' – cf. the 'little ones' of 10.42.

his Jewish-Christian congregation that observance of the Law is still important.

The Gentile mission was fine then – what Christian could fail to accept it in view of its amazing success? But this did not resolve the question of the Law: how much of it was incumbent on Gentile converts? For the Jerusalem leadership the Torah was the ordinance of God, and that was the end of the matter.[5] For Paul things were not quite so easy. If his Gentile churchmen had to keep sabbath, for example, they were likely to lose their jobs, and starve; and this would be a discouragement to the Gentile mission, which was also the ordinance of God, and laid on him in particular. Paul tries a number of different approaches to the problem. At first he took the line, 'Not beyond what is written', the Bible and the Bible only (1 Cor 4.6) – no 'interpretations' by Jewish Sages, which are merely 'taught words of human wisdom' (1 Cor 2.13); later he took a harder position, the Law was itself the old covenant and a dead letter (2 Cor 3).[6]

Matthew was a moderate, and he saw the Church as bound by the Law, like James. His Jesus says, 'Think not that I came to destroy the Law or the Prophets: I came not to destroy but to fulfil [i.e. to prescribe not just the actions but the attitudes which lead to them]. For truly I say to you, till heaven and earth pass away, not one iota or one letter-crown shall pass away, till all come to pass [i.e. every detail is valid till Judgement Day]. So whoever looses one of the least of these commandments and teaches men so [St Mark, for example, whose Gospel Matthew is rewriting because it contains a number of lamentable errors of this kind],[7] shall be called least in the kingdom of heaven [though he will get in, just]' (5.17–19). Matthew sees the Church as sailing between the Scylla of Law-

---

[5] Cf. n. 3. It may be thought that after the compromise of Acts 15 the Jerusalem leadership was merely concerned that Paul might not be teaching *Jews* to keep the law; this is said in Acts 21.17–21. But right at the end of Paul's life the apostle has still to resist pressure to circumcise his Gentile converts (Phil 3.1–4.1); it is difficult to believe that so persevering a movement could continue without official backing, and James enjoyed a high reputation with the Pharisees (Josephus, *Ant.* 20.9.1; Hegesippus, in Eusebius, *Hist. Eccl.* 2.23.4–16). There is also the problem of the antipathy of Mark and John to the Jerusalem leadership, mentioned above.

[6] See my 'Σοφία in 1 Corinthians', *New Testament Studies* 37 (1991) 516–34. The first problem over the Law was with the meat eaten at eucharistic suppers (Gal 2.11–14), since Jews might be law-breakers if it was not kosher; and Paul hoped to resolve this by arguing that kosher butchers and cooking rules do not come in Leviticus but in the rulings of the Sages ('the words of the Wise'). But when the issue broadened to working on Saturdays (Rom 14), Paul was plainly defying the Bible, indeed the Ten Commandments; so he is driven to a more radical line. In Galatians he tries several other implausible defences.

[7] Matthew is often thought to be opposing people who said 'We have faith but not works', as in James 2.14. But we can actually watch Matthew correcting various points in Mark where the earlier evangelist goes against biblical food and sabbath laws. There is no evidence that Matthew had a version of Mark different from ours.

lessness, represented by the ultra-Paulines, and the Charybdis of legalism, the loveless, joyless, oppressive, hypocritical 'righteousness of the [unconverted] scribes and Pharisees' (5.20), currently leading the reform of Judaism at Yavneh.

Matthew could not accept Paul's distinction between the Law, 'what is written', and the halakha, its practical exposition, the 'taught words of human wisdom'; in real life one has to know how to apply the Bible. So he says, 'The scribes and Pharisees sit on Moses' seat: all therefore that they tell you, observe and do' (23.2f); as in matters like tithing mint, anise and cummin, even though they miss judgement, mercy and faith, 'these [last] things you should have done, and not leave the other [tithing] undone' (23.23). Matthean Christians keep the full Jewish 'way'.

The practical application of these principles may again be seen by comparing Mark's text with Matthew's. Paul's wealthiest converts were often Gentiles, so the church would meet in their houses, and they would provide the Saturday night church supper; so the meat might be bought in the market, and might not be kosher. This meant that Jewish Christians would have either to 'eat with the Gentiles', stifling their consciences (Gal 2.11f), or they would have to stick to a vegetarian diet and resent it (Rom 14). Mark wants to make it clear that Jesus took the liberal, Pauline line: 'There is nothing from outside a man going into him which can defile him; but it is the things which come out of a man which defile a man' (7.15). Non-kosher food cannot make you unclean; it is thoughts of lust and greed and envy which make you unclean – in fact, Jesus said this 'pronouncing all food clean' (7.19). Bacon, lettuce and tomato sandwiches are quite all right.

Now Matthew knows that Jesus said nothing of the kind[8] – well, perhaps something of the kind, but Mark has got the emphasis wrong. So he leaves out the damaging phrase, 'pronouncing all food clean', and he makes the whole discussion a question of whether one should wash one's hands before eating (15.2). So 15.11, 'It is not what goes into the mouth which defiles a man, but what comes out of the mouth . . .', means 'It is [evil talk] which defiles a man, but eating with unwashed hands does not defile a man' (15.20). Matthew is very good at this kind of adjustment: the quickness of the pen deceives the ear. In Mark it was quite clear that Jesus abrogated the sabbath: the Pharisees criticized the disciples for plucking and 'grinding' corn on the sabbath, but Jesus said, 'The sabbath was made for man, and not man for the sabbath' (Mark 2.27). Here is another verse which Matthew drops; and he opens the story by saying, 'His disciples were hungry' (12.1) – poor chaps, they had been fasting for a fortnight.

[8] If Jesus had said all these liberal things about the food-laws, how comes it that Peter took the conservative stance *against* the liberal position maintained by Paul at Antioch?

So Matthew is more conservative than Mark: he is loyal to the Jerusalem leadership, and thinks the Church will be ruined if it does not stick to the Word of God. This raises the awkward question of what line he would take on circumcision, since this was the issue that had nearly wrecked the Pauline mission in the 50s (Galatians; Romans; Phil 3). Of course, Jesus does not speak on such a matter in the Gospel, and we are left wondering. On the one hand, Matthew often speaks approvingly of the Gentile mission; but on the other hand, the Bible prescribes circumcision as the sacrament for joining the people of God (Gen 17; Exod 12.49), and on every other issue Matthew follows the Jerusalem leaders, and backs the Torah. If we are in two minds, how much more will the evangelist have been! He probably adopted the prudent policy of keeping his fingers crossed and hoping the problem would go away. His Gospel gives us the impression that his church members were almost all Jews. Normal synagogue policy was to accept uncircumcised Gentiles as 'God-fearers', and expect them to go the whole hog (so to speak) in time. So here is a second matter in which Matthew had a vision for the Church: a Church mainly of Gentiles, all of whose men had been circumcised. But this was, as he knew, a vision for many days.

IDEALISM AND ETHICS

So far, it might appear that Matthew was not just a conservative but a diehard, a fully paid-up, card-carrying Cephasite. But if he had been, his Gospel would never have made the grade into the Canon, since the NT books were selected by the Pauline churches, and consist largely of letters by Paul, or supposedly by Paul, and books by his friends Mark and Luke, and his incarnationalist follower John. Matthew is in fact an admirer of Paul also, and his Gospel achieved pride of place, both in canonical order and in use, because it combined Pauline insights with Jerusalem traditionalism. Matthew aspired to make a bridge between the two wings of the Church; to accept Mark's Gospel as the base for his own work, combining as it did old pro-Peter material with Pauline theology.

Mark's reader is surprised how little mention there is of love; it is confined to the little piece on the Great Commandment. Love had been the centrepiece of Paul's view of Christian living, and that is where it is for Matthew also. Paul had said, 'He who loves has fulfilled the rest of the Law. For, Thou shalt not commit adultery, Thou shalt not murder, Thou shalt not steal, Thou shalt not covet, and any other commandment, is summed up in this word, Thou shalt love thy neighbour as thyself' (Rom 13.8f). In chapter 5 Matthew wishes to contrast the Christian way with the righteousness of the scribes and Pharisees, and he does it first by setting out something like these commandments – murder, adultery, divorce, false oaths, an eye for an eye, loving one's neighbour and hating one's enemy – as the basis of Judaism. In each case that was what was given at Sinai, but Jesus requires something more. That something is the inclination of the heart, not just the action; and Paul's condemnation of anger, lust, divorce, returning evil for evil, and hatred shows the way. 'Bless those who persecute you; bless and curse not . . . returning to no one evil for evil . . . if your enemy is hungry, feed him . . . be not overcome by evil, but overcome evil with good' (Rom 12.14–21): here is the substance of Matthew's 'But I say unto you . . .' in the sublime eloquence of the Sermon on the Mount.

Paul was made uneasy by Jerusalem Christians who claimed to be 'perfect' (Phil 3.12–16; 1 Cor 2.6); here again Matthew wanted to bridge the gap. His vision of the Church includes saints, and he is at his most moving when he demands the highest: 'You shall be therefore perfect, even as your Father in heaven is perfect' (5.48). But these words are spoken to the Apostles, and the wise pastor knows that not every believer can aspire to perfection. So the Matthean Jesus says to the rich man, 'If you wish to be perfect, go sell your possessions . . .' (19.21): perhaps there are those in the evangelist's pews who would like to enter the kingdom, but do not mind not being perfect. Paul had spoken of his own continence over sexual relations, but others were not so gifted, and if so it was better to marry than to burn (1 Cor 7.9). Matthew makes the same point. With the Church to run (Matt 18), and no release once marriage is undertaken (19.1–9), the Apostles say, 'If that is so, it is not sensible to marry' (19.10). Jesus replies, 'This rule is not for everyone, but for those to whom it is given'; some people voluntarily accept celibacy for the sake of the kingdom – let those who can manage it manage it (19.11f). In this way Matthew shows himself in fact very Pauline: the two of them are the partnership which has sponsored the two-tier ethic which has dominated the Church ever since – perfection for the 'religious', realism for the rest. Only Paul is nervous of the arrogant overtone of perfection, while Matthew welcomes its challenge.[9]

Paul found a persistent problem with his Jewish-Christian (Cephasite) counter-mission in their charismatic excesses (1 Cor 12–14; 2 Cor 11.16–12.13). It was not just 'tongues' consuming the precious time of church worship, but visions which purported to carry angelic instructions and to give 'knowledge' (2 Cor 12.1–4; Col 2.16–18), healings and other such signs (12.12). Paul felt he could hold his own when it came to tongues

---

[9] Religious movements with high aspirations are bound to meet this tension; the higher the aspirations, the fewer the aspirants. Something similar is found in the Qumran community where the word *tamim* was used for the fully committed; and the 'goodmen' among the Cathars in fourteenth-century France were called *parfaits*. The word does not unfortunately imply moral perfection: Bélibaste, for example, was a *parfait* but also a scamp (E. Le Roy Ladurie, *Montaillou* [ET London: Penguin, 1980]).

(I Cor 14.18), but he had never had a vision carrying him to heaven (2 Cor 12.1–5), and his 'signs' had been his endurance of hardship (12.12).[10] However what distressed him was that love, the fruit of the Spirit, was being overlooked in the zeal for these gifts of the Spirit.

Matthew is with him all the way. The road to salvation was that laid down in the Law and the Prophets (5.17), but observed from the heart in the spirit of love (5.21–48); and he closes the Sermon on the same note, 'All then that you wish men to do to you, so do you too to them; for this is the Law and the Prophets' (7.12). But this is a narrow gate and an overgrown way which few find. There are false prophets to lead us astray, whose lives display no fruits [of love]; they say 'Lord, Lord', but do not do the Father's will; they 'prophesy', and cast out demons, and perform many miracles in Jesus' name, but in the end the Lord will say to them, 'I never knew you' (7.15–23). These false prophets are the *epigoni* of the anti-Pauline charismatics of the Corinthian letters. Their religion is all froth and no fruit, and their end is perdition to Paul, hell to Matthew. The evangelist is pretty discouraging about claims to have been ravished to heaven, too, for a vision of God or of Christ: 'No one knows the Son except the Father, nor does anyone know the Father except the Son, and him to whom the Son wishes to reveal him' (11.27). It is the same anti-visionary emphasis which we find so regularly in the Fourth Gospel: 'He that hath seen me hath seen the Father' (John 14.9). The humble Christian, the νήπιος, can come to Jesus and know all that he needs about God.

Paul gives two lists of the gifts of the Spirit in I Cor 12, first the Corinthians' list in verses 8–10, and then his own list, with suitable changes of substance and order, in verses 27f: but both lists specify miracles and gifts of healing, and Matthew is with him here, too. However he thoughtfully implies a restriction of these powers to the Twelve, for it is in the Mission discourse, addressed to them, that Jesus says, 'Heal the sick, raise the dead, cleanse the lepers, cast out demons' (10.8). It is difficult to think that other church leaders of the second generation did not have the same difficulty as Paul in performing impressive healings. No doubt such marvels were experienced in the heady charismatic excitement of the 30s, but the evangelist, like the apostle, seems to be making terms with a soberer reality.

The same limitation may apply to the so-called 'itinerant radicals'. Matt 10 follows Mark 6 in giving instructions to the Twelve to go

---

[10] In 2 Cor 10–12 Paul is answering Jewish Christian allegations that he has no spiritual power – as a person, as a speaker, as a visionary, as a healer. These accusations were largely true (or they would not need answering – 'boasting', 'as a fool'). Paul, with some fast footwork, takes the higher ground: his 'signs and wonders and miracles' had been his 'endurance' – of hardships, as in 2 Cor 6.4 and 11.23–33. Standard interpretations, that Paul had in fact done many [healing] miracles at Corinth, ignore the force of 'in all endurance'.

preaching without provision of food, clothes or money; to cast themselves entirely on the charity of those who hear them; and to get no gold, silver or brass into their purses. Paul used to earn his living by his trade so as not to impose on his converts, but the Jerusalem pillars sent out envoys who did expect the local church to support them, and who furthermore said that Paul was not a proper apostle as he did not claim this right (1 Cor 9; 2 Cor 11.7–15). However Matthew is clearly not supporting Jerusalem against Paul here, for he limits the instruction to the Palestinian mission, 'the cities of Israel' (10.23; cf. 5f). The idea that ordinary Christian converts were expected to go off in pairs and conduct their own private mission is a chimera, at least in the 70s. No doubt gifted leaders (prophets and saints, 10.41) spread the word in Judaea and Galilee in the same way that Stephen, or Paul and Barnabas (prophets and teachers, Acts 13.1) did in Samaria and Galatia; and no doubt they took an assistant along with them (a little one, Matt 10.42; John Mark, Acts 13). But there is no evidence of widespread private missions. The suspicions of the Didachist a century later begin with doubts over the visiting preacher's [Pauline] orthodoxy (*Did.* 11.1), and the passage should be understood as an instruction to Pauline pastors to resist Jerusalem emissaries. The same context is likely for the 'false prophets who have gone out into the world' [from the Jerusalem leadership], and who 'do not confess [give worship to] Jesus', separating him from the divine Christ (1 John 4.1–3).

Something similar is probably true over the thorny question of possessions. Jesus' own mission was supported by a common purse (Luke 8.3), and the primitive Jerusalem church had everything in common (Acts 2.42–45); but in time this led to financial problems (Gal 2.10). Paul encouraged open-handed generosity, but he was insistent that Christians should keep working, and be responsible for their own families (1 Thess 4.9–12; 2 Thess 3). This involved a departure from the radical Jerusalem policy – indeed the suppression of it in 2 Thess 3.

In the Sermon Matthew seems to take the Jerusalem side. The Christian's loving heart, so finely evoked in 5.21–48, is to express itself in its attitude to possessions: 'Do not treasure for yourselves treasures on earth . . . but in heaven . . .'. This is nothing but a generalized form of Jesus' word to the rich ruler. We are to have the generous (ἁπλοῦς) eye: no one can serve two masters, both God and Mammon. So we are not to worry about food and clothing, but to seek God's kingdom first, and all these things will be added to us. Perhaps it is even suggested that we should not work, like the birds and the lilies – and Paul's difficult converts in 2 Thessalonians! They sow not nor gather into barns, they toil not neither do they spin: your heavenly Father knows that you have need of these things before you ask.

We may wonder, however, which side Matthew is really on. In the last resort he is committed to a black and white theology of judgement. The ultimate issue is simple: either we shall enter the joy of our Lord or we shall be weeping and gnashing our teeth – it will be either the Messianic banquet or outer darkness. Matthew is clear that an invisible line divides the Church between those being saved and those moving to damnation. Faith is necessary (8.9, 9.28f), but it is not enough. The King's servants bring in to his marriage feast all whom they find, both bad and good (22.10); and the 'bad' is then revealed by his not wearing a wedding garment (22.11; cf. 'the righteous acts of the saints', Rev 19.8). Ten bridesmaids were awaiting the heavenly groom, but five were not ready, and were shut out (25.1–13). So Matthew is committed to a believable standard of righteousness. He does say that few will find the narrow gate, but they will indeed be few if St Francis's Lady Poverty is so absolutely to be the rule. Also, those who are familiar with such communities know that sanctity and love are not the invariable consequences of selling all that one has and giving to the poor.

It is best then to see Matthew once more as forming a bridge between the conservatism of Jerusalem and the liberalism of Paul. He has Jesus address his disciples (again) in the Sermon (5.1f), in terms recalling the purity of the early Jerusalem church. Then Christians shared all they had, and trusted God, and they had enough. But the crowds are listening to the Sermon too (7.28f); so what was the vocation of the Apostles might be their vocation also. Like other wise preachers, Matthew leaves the conclusion to his audience. A Pauline believer may hear a call to generous giving, to detachment from money, to faith in the divine providence. A Petrine or Jacobite Christian may catch the resonance of treasures in heaven, and the challenge to give up toil and anxiety, and trust that where God guides He provides – to give all he has to support the Church's poor, and live from the common purse.[11] But the evangelist does not want to tell the loyal Pauline that he is consigned to outer darkness unless he takes the Petrine interpretation. It is he who has inserted the condition at 19.21, 'If you wish to be perfect . . .'. Two-tier Christianity is a Matthean invention. So once more pastoral realism is in tension with selfless aspiration. Matthew's vision is of a Church full of saints, perfect, giving all to the Lord, devoting themselves to the mission alone; but he can see the Son of Man just about to descend on his cloud, and his care is for the little ones who believe, lest they perish.

---

[11] The sharing of possessions is evidenced in the 'pillars'' request to Paul for money for the Jerusalem church's poor (c. 48), and in the Thessalonian church whose members gave up work (c. 50). The successors of the Jerusalem Christians called themselves Ebionites ('Poor'), and told Epiphanius that this derived from their fathers' practice in Acts 2 (Pan. 30.15.4). The Epistle of James (cf. also Bauckham below) seems to be written for a community in acute poverty, perhaps arising from the same cause; its unfortunate recipe is more faith and prayer.

BIBLIOGRAPHY

There are several short outlines of Matthew's theology available:

Ulrich Luz, *The Theology of the Gospel of Matthew*. Tr. J. B. Robinson. Cambridge: Cambridge University Press, 1993.

Margaret Davies, *Matthew*. Sheffield: Sheffield Academic Press, 1993.

John Riches, *Matthew*. New Testament Guides. Sheffield: Sheffield Academic Press, 1996.

A fuller account of my own perspective, not limited to Matthew, is *A Tale of Two Missions*. London: SCM Press, 1994.

A useful book of essays on Matthew is Graham Stanton, *A Gospel for a New People*. Edinburgh: T. & T. Clark, 1992.

For a full commentary on the Gospel one cannot do better than Ulrich Luz, *Matthew. A Commentary*. Luz is a Swiss, and three volumes of the projected four (up to ch. 25) have appeared in German in the EKK series. Vol. 1, on chapters 1–7, is available in English (Edinburgh: T. & T. Clark 1990), and a second volume on chapters 8–20 (Hermeneia, Philadelphia: Fortress Press, 1995).

3

Mark's Vision for the Church

MORNA D. HOOKER

A^N invitation to write about Mark's vision for the Church seemed akin, at first sight, to a request to make bricks without straw. Mark's attention is focused throughout his story on the figure of Jesus; he makes no reference to the Church. One does not naturally associate this breathless story-teller with any kind of 'vision' for the future. Does Mark deserve his place, then, in this collection of essays?

Yet Mark was clearly writing with a purpose: his book is not a simple record of what took place in the past, but a challenge to those living in the present. Though Mark's attention is focused on Jesus, Jesus is seen as the nucleus of a community – a community that consists of those who are 'about him' (3.34; 4.10), who belong to his company.[1] The Gospel appears to have been addressed to those who were already Christians rather than to outsiders, and thus to be a challenge to deeper commitment. Such a challenge implies that the author has a vision of what might be, if only men and women respond.

What Mark hoped (and feared) for in the Church at large would have grown out of his experience of a particular Christian community (or communities). His Gospel was probably written in the first place for one such community, and with the needs and shortcomings of that community in mind. That does not mean, of course, that his 'vision' for what we call the 'Church' would not have included all Christian believers; it means simply that the Christian gospel is always formulated in terms that relate it to the evangelist's own experience, and addressed to some particular situation. But where and what *was* this particular community? And what were its problems? There is little agreement among scholars – except in the belief that it was predominantly Gentile in composition.[2] Whether it was located in Rome or Syria or elsewhere we

---

[1] According to H. C. Kee, the question of its own identity was in fact the primary issue for the Markan community, and questions about messianic titles were secondary to this (1977:107).

[2] See, e.g., the explanation about what 'the Pharisees and all the Jews' do in Mark 7.3f, which suggests a Gentile readership. The interpretation of Jesus' teaching in 7.14f, given to the disciples in private in 17–19, draws out the implications for a Gentile Christian community. Similarly, in 10.10–12, in a footnote to Jesus' teaching about divorce, reference is made to a wife divorcing her husband – something that was

do not know. Nor do we know what its problems were: the frequent references to suffering, for example, have often been seen as an indication that the community was being persecuted for its beliefs, and have been understood as encouragement to endure; but these references are equally appropriate if Mark's church was, like that in Corinth, under the illusion that commitment to the Christian gospel was an invitation to an easy life.

But we may be reasonably certain that wherever it was situated, and whatever its particular problems, Mark's church was, like all Christian communities, a mixture of eager response and dire failure, of enthusiasm and cowardice, of joy and fear, of insight and incomprehension. It was, in other words, a community that would see itself reflected in Mark's portrait of the disciples. If we want to discover Mark's vision for the Church, it is no good looking at the disciples! Yet the suggestion that they are meant to represent 'opponents' of the gospel or 'false teachers'[3] is a gross exaggeration. What the disciples represent is the typical human response to the gospel – enthusiasm for the good news, yet an inability to comprehend the ways of God; joy at what is offered, but reluctance to pay the price. Behind their inadequate response, we glimpse the Christian community of Mark's own day – and of every day, for the disciples behave very much as Christians always behave. If we want to discover Mark's vision for what the Church might be, we need to look first of all at what he tells us about Jesus himself, since the community is centred on him; and secondly at what Jesus *demands* of his disciples, but which they fail to give: a radical commitment to his gospel, even to the extent of literally taking up the cross. This is the demand that is addressed to everyone who would follow Jesus, and this is Mark's 'vision' for the community that consists of all who respond to Jesus' call.

CHRISTOLOGY

Mark's attention is focused on Jesus. The material he offers us is primarily christological. Yet all the 'titles' he uses of Jesus imply the existence of a community. This is hardly surprising, since titles express relationships. If Jesus is the Messiah, the Son of David and the King of Israel, the community concerned is clearly Israel. So, too, with the title 'Son of God', which in its Jewish context is appropriate either to the king or to Israel herself. That Jesus is all these things is clear, though the manner of

---

impossible under Jewish law. On both occasions, this teaching is said to have followed the public teaching, and to have been given to the disciples 'in a house': both passages reflect the application of Jesus' teaching in later situations.

[3] As argued, e.g., by T. J. Weeden, *Mark – Traditions in Conflict* (Philadelphia: Fortress, 1971).

revealing them is somewhat unexpected. It is not until Jesus nears Jerusalem that he is referred to openly by any of these titles. As he approaches the city he is hailed by blind Bartimaeus as 'Son of David', and he enters Jerusalem as king, to the plaudits of the crowd, who (unwittingly) welcome him as David's successor; the last event before the Last Supper is another meal, at which Jesus is anointed by a woman, an act which is said to point forward to his burial, but which in Mark's story serves also to anoint him as king, since it is as a king that Jesus is arraigned before Pilate, and it is as 'the King of the Jews' that he is crucified.

The phrase that Jesus himself is said to have used of his own ministry, 'the Son of man', and which Mark treats as a title, also points to the existence of a community. Though all Mark's references to the Son of man clearly concern Jesus' own role and destiny, they nevertheless have implications for the community of believers.[4] The authority of the Son of man to forgive sins was almost certainly an authority being exercised by church leaders of Mark's day (2.10); it is the behaviour of Jesus' disciples that is justified by his appeal to his lordship over the sabbath (2.28). The Son of man must suffer, but so, too, will those who have the courage to follow him, a point that is underlined by Mark in the *pericopae* which follow the first and third passion predictions.[5] The Son of man will be vindicated, and be enthroned at God's right hand, but his faithful followers will share his vindication.[6] What the Son of man does affects the lives of those who belong to his community – above all, by his action in giving his life as a ransom for many (10.45). But the relationship between the one who is the Son of man and his followers is best described as a call to be like him: what he is, they are to be. He calls them to follow him by doing what he does – denying himself, and taking up the cross. They are to serve others, as he has done; they are not to seek for status, any more than he has done. This is why they share his authority, and will be acknowledged as belonging to him. Mark's vision for the community is essentially of a community that is like Jesus.

JESUS' MISSION

Jesus, Mark tells us, proclaimed the gospel of the coming of God's kingdom, and called on everyone to repent and believe this good news

---

[4] Cf. M. D. Hooker, *The Son of Man in Mark* (London: SPCK/Montreal: McGill, 1967).

[5] Mark 8.31–8; 10.32–45.

[6] Mark 13.26f, and, by implication, 8.38. The idea is missing in the third 'eschatological' reference, in 14.62, perhaps because, by that point in the story, Jesus' followers have all forsaken him. The story is juxtaposed with the account of Peter's denial of Jesus, 14.66–72. Nevertheless, the Risen Jesus acknowledges his disciples, and specifically Peter, in 16.7; those who have failed Jesus are forgiven and restored, and the company of disciples is acknowledged by Jesus as his own.

(1.15). But the *beginning* of the gospel was John the Baptist, who prepared the way for Jesus by baptizing in the wilderness.[7] John's dress and food mark him out as a prophet, and his baptism would have been understood as a prophetic action, pointing to another, more significant event:[8] this is the baptism with Spirit which is going to be carried out by his successor, a baptism which is going to purge as well as renew, and so regenerate God's people. Mark emphasizes the fulfilment of John's mission in his apparently hyperbolic language: the whole Judaean region and everyone from Jerusalem flocked to him and was baptized; if all have been baptized with water, all will be baptized with Spirit, whether for judgement or renewal. The opening paragraphs of Mark, then, tell us not only who Jesus *is* – namely, the Son of God who is well-pleasing to God – but what he will *do*, which is to recreate Israel. This is why Jesus comes into Galilee, announcing that the time is fulfilled and the kingdom of God is at hand.

This purpose is confirmed in Jesus' appointment of twelve men, who are chosen 'to be with him' (so forming the nucleus of the new community) and to proclaim the gospel. The symbolism of the number twelve, representing the twelve tribes of Israel, is obvious. Even though a mission beyond the borders of Israel is not specifically excluded, as in Matt 10.5f, it is clear enough that the ministry of Jesus and his disciples is confined to Israel during his lifetime. Gentiles who appear in the story are an anomaly; most notably the Syro-Phoenician woman, whose faith wins her a 'crumb' from the children's table (7.24–30).[9]

But though crowds flock to hear him, Israel as a whole fails to respond: the people fail to see and hear the significance of what is taking place (4.10–12). Jesus' message is rejected in his own home town (6.1–6), and his disciples can expect the same fate (6.11). The religious leaders refuse to acknowledge Jesus' authority: he is opposed by scribes and Pharisees throughout his ministry, and at the end the priests and scribes engineer his death. But those who reject the gospel are themselves rejected (4.12; 6.11); it is those with faith who are healed (5.34). The note of judgement is sounded in the final chapters, in a series of images which imply the

[7] John's baptism has sometimes been interpreted as an adaptation of proselyte baptism, sometimes as a rite similar to the lustrations that took place at Qumran. If the rite of proselyte baptism already existed, this would suggest that Jews were being treated as though they were Gentiles, needing to take a deliberate step if they were going to be included in the 'new' Israel. If the background is to be found in the kind of lustration that took place at Qumran, this again would be a preparation for entering the community. Its origin may in fact be much simpler, and lie in the demand of the prophets to 'wash and be clean'; see Isa 1.16f; cf. Ps 51.7, 9f; Ezek 36.24–27.

[8] I have discussed this idea in my *The Signs of a Prophet* (London: SCM Press/Valley Forge, PA: Trinity Press International, 1997).

[9] It is possible that Mark understood the demoniac in 5.1–20 to be a Gentile, but he does not say so. He is, however, the one person in the story who is told to 'go and tell his people what the Lord has done for him'. Is this a hint of a future Gentile mission?

judgement of the nation: the fig tree is cursed (11.12–14; 20–24); the temple will be destroyed (11.15–17; 13); the vineyard will be taken away from the wicked tenants (12.1–12). Beyond it all, however, there are hints of something new. In chapter 13 we learn of a fig tree that produces new shoots (13.28). At Jesus' trial and crucifixion, we learn that he is accused of claiming that he would destroy the temple and build another in three days (14.58; 15.29), and though the charge is a false one, we recognize the truth behind the distortion: a new community will emerge with the resurrection. The vineyard will be taken away from the wicked tenants and given to others (12.9).

And there are hints, too, that the new community will include Gentiles: the temple is intended by God to be a house of prayer *for all the nations* (11.17), and if it is not, then it will be replaced by a temple 'not made with hands' (14.58); if the vineyard is taken away from its original tenants and given to others, then by Mark's day these 'others' certainly included Gentiles; even before Jerusalem is destroyed, 'the gospel must be preached to all the Gentiles' (13.10); the unknown woman's action in anointing Jesus, an action which signifies Jesus' death and messiahship, will be remembered wherever the gospel is proclaimed, which means 'throughout the whole world' (14.9); and finally, the first human to confess Jesus to be Son of God is his executioner, a Gentile centurion (15.39). The Syro-Phoenician woman, whose faith was rewarded by Jesus, was an anomaly only because she came to him 'too soon'. The mission to the Gentiles belongs, not to Jesus' ministry, but to the time beyond Jesus' death and resurrection: the 'temple' must be destroyed before it is rebuilt 'without hands' (14.58; 15.29),[10] allowing others to worship; the stone (another anomaly: the image of the vineyard has merged with that of a building) must be raised to become head of the corner before the vineyard can be given to 'others' (12.11); Jesus must die before the gospel can be proclaimed throughout the world (14.9); and only when his disciples share his sufferings will it be preached to all the nations (13.10).[11]

THE COMMUNITY

Although Mark focuses our attention on Jesus, the vital question which confronts us is the response that men and women make to him: this

---

[10] Though Mark does not indicate that the accusation of Jesus' enemies referred to 'the temple of his body', as does John (2.21), it is likely that he interprets the saying as an unwitting reference to Jesus' death and resurrection. The death and resurrection of Jesus seal the fate of Israel, and make the destruction of the temple inevitable; by his death and resurrection, the Son of man, now on trial before Israel's high priest, becomes the heavenly judge who will condemn those who rejected him.

[11] This will take place before the temple in Jerusalem is destroyed, but after Jesus himself has been killed and raised.

Gospel is therefore a book about discipleship. Jesus' first action after proclaiming the gospel is to call four men to be his disciples (1.16–20). His last is to send a message to his disciples to follow him back to Galilee, where he first called them to follow (16.7). The book breaks off at the end of the next verse, leaving us wondering why the story is apparently incomplete: why does Mark not tell us what happened next? Intentionally or not, this abrupt end has the effect of presenting the reader with a challenge: are *you* prepared to complete the story yourself, by following Jesus into Galilee? Are *you* prepared to 'return to Galilee', to reread the story, and to hear in his call to the first disciples his call to you to be his follower? If so, then hear what he demands of his followers, and learn from the mistakes of the first disciples, for you can so easily repeat them.

Jesus' initial commission to the first four disciples is to abandon their fishing-nets and catch people instead of fish. Later, he appoints the Twelve 'to be with him', and so that he can send them out to preach and to exercise the authority to expel demons (3.14f). In other words, they are to share his ministry. When, later on, Jesus sends them out, they preach repentance, expel demons and heal the sick (6.7–13).

'Being with Jesus' is an essential part of this commission; for it implies learning from him what his proclamation of the kingdom means. Since God does not reign in a vacuum, his kingdom – or kingship – implies a community of people who acknowledge his rule. Love of one's neighbour is an essential corollary to love of God, to such an extent that when Jesus is asked which is the greatest commandment, he refuses to separate the two. Mark's vision for the Christian community is thus of a community bound together by love. If we look more closely at the teaching Jesus gives to his disciples, we see a little more of what that means. It means a community whose members forgive one another, and do not harbour grudges against one another (11.25). It means a community whose members are not concerned about questions of status or precedent, and who regard it as a privilege to serve one another (9.35; 10.35–45). In this community, human expectations are turned on their heads. The behaviour Jesus envisages is quite unlike that found among the Gentiles – and not only there! But the reference to the Gentiles (10.42) is a clue that Jesus is addressing those who are called to be the true Israel, the true people of God. In this community, love of neighbour means serving that neighbour, not exercising authority over him.

The call to discipleship, then, though it is a call to follow Jesus, is not a call to be alone with him. Is it accidental that in Mark the first disciples are called in pairs (1.16–20), appointed in a group of twelve (3.13–19), and sent out in pairs (6.7–13)? Mark would surely have agreed with John Wesley's comment that 'Christianity is essentially a social religion'.[12] It is

[12] John Wesley, Sermon on the Mount, Discourse IV (*Forty-Four Sermons*, XIX.I.1).

certainly no accident that there is so much 'community' language in Mark, for Jesus' mission is to recreate Israel, and his call is to join the community of those who acknowledge God as King and who await his salvation. The Exodus imagery reminds us that a new Exodus is taking place: God's people are being fed in the wilderness (6.32–44; 8.1–10); the waters of the sea are in his control (4.35–41; 6.45–52); a new covenant is being made (14.24). Jesus is the shepherd of a flock, and like a shepherd he will lead his flock into Galilee after the resurrection (14.27f; 16.7). The flock is scattered and reformed, but something even more drastic happens to the temple, the vineyard and the fig tree. Yet these images imply the continuity between the old community and the new: Israel is recreated, not destroyed. And Mark's community would see itself as part of that new community, as the legitimate tenants of the vineyard. They, and not his natural kin, were the members of Jesus' new family (3.31–35). And as they gathered together in a house to hear Mark's story, the teaching which Jesus had given 'in a house' would no doubt seem immediately relevant to them.

The fact that this new community was the continuation of the old meant, of course, that it had inherited the tasks given to Israel. Mark's vision for the Church is thus of a community that will succeed where Israel had failed, and that will be all that Israel was not. If Israel was condemned for being barren (11.12–14, 20), the new community must take care to bear fruit (11.21–24); if Israel's behaviour prevented the Temple from being a house of prayer for all nations (11.17), the new community must be the means whereby the Gentiles are brought to worship God (13.10); if the leaders of Israel were unworthy tenants of the vineyard, the new tenants must prove worthier (12.1–12); above all, if Israel rejected the one who was Messiah and Son of God (12.6–8; 14.61–65; 15.6–15), the new community is made up of those who are committed to him (8.27–9.1).

THE WAY OF THE CROSS

Jesus' call to discipleship is a radical one. He expects those whom he calls to abandon old family ties and possessions, as he himself has done (1.16–20; 3.31–35; 10.17–31); he commends the woman who gave her last penny to God, and the woman who showed her love for him in a wildly extravagant gesture (12.41–44; 14.3–9). He calls on his disciples to sacrifice everything, as he is willing to do, for the sake of winning the kingdom (8.31–38; 9.43–48). In his teaching on the Law, he is equally radical; God's command is that men and women should love their neighbours *as themselves* (12.31); divorce is contrary to God's purpose in creation, and should not be permitted (10.2–12). On the big issues Jesus makes radical demands, but on the small issues, he sits light. There are other principles which are more important than the sabbath laws and the regulations about purity (2.23–28; 3.1–6; 7.1–23). Saving life is important (3.1–6), but so are acts of kindness (9.41) and caring for the well-being of parents (7.9–13) and children (10.13–16). Those who truly love God and their neighbour should be able to distinguish the important from the trivial.

The radical nature of Jesus' call is summed up in the use of the term 'the way', for the way Jesus walks is the way of the cross. In Acts, the word is used as a synonym for the Christian movement,[13] and it seems to have something of that sense in Mark after Caesarea Philippi. Jesus pursues his way to Jerusalem resolutely, but those who follow him are uncomprehending (9.33f) and afraid (10.32). In contrast to their repeated failure, blind Bartimaeus believes, receives his sight and follows in the way (10.52). That the way of discipleship may mean suffering and death has already been made plain (8.34–38), but it is spelt out again by Jesus in chapter 13, in what is in effect his 'Farewell Discourse' to his disciples. The predictions in verses 9–13 'echo' some of Jesus' own sufferings in the passion narrative which follows. The community that is left must continue to walk in his way of suffering. It will continue Jesus' work, for at the Last Supper Jesus' actions signify the creation of the new community: in sharing the bread, they take on his task; in drinking the wine, they accept God's new covenant, sealed in Jesus' death.[14] Like the Passover offering of long ago, his self-offering becomes a means of redemption 'for many' (10.45). The new community that is now formed inherits the role of Israel and the task of Jesus.

It is no surprise, then, that many of the commands given to the disciples echo the actions of Jesus himself. Jesus, we are told, went away to a solitary place to pray (1.35; 6.46); on the night before his death, he went to Gethsemane to pray (14.32, 35, 39). His disciples, too, ought to pray (9.29; 11.24f); he urges Peter, James and John to pray with him in the Garden (14.38). They are commanded here also to be vigilant (14.34, 37), as in 13.33–37. There are also frequent commands to 'watch out' (βλέπειν, 4.24; 8.15; 12.38; 13.5, 9, 23, 33).

The verb βλέπειν means also 'to see', and it is only one of several verbs with this sense used in Mark. The idea is an important one, because 'seeing' implies far more than physical sight, just as 'hearing' implies more than physical hearing. The deaf man whose ears are opened (7.31–37) and the blind man who is given his sight (8.22–26) are symbols of those who hear and see the truth, and begin to understand who Jesus is (8.27–30).

The 'seeing' and the 'hearing' refer, however, to spiritual truths, and require that men and women look beyond what is taking place in Jesus to

---

[13] Cf. Acts 9.2; 18.25; 19.23; 24.22.

[14] See David Stacey, 'The Lord's Supper as Prophetic Drama', *Epworth Review* 21 (January 1994) 65–74, and M. D. Hooker, *The Signs of a Prophet*, 48–54.

the power of God working through him. He refuses to perform a 'sign' to convince his opponents of his authority (8.11–13). Those with eyes to see and ears to hear should be able to discern the Spirit of God at work in what he says and does (3.22–30), and realize that his authority comes from God (11.27–33). The disciples are castigated because they so frequently fail to see and hear the truth (4.13; 8.14–21); they lack faith (4.40), and are urged to have it (11.22–24). Others, however, are commended for their faith (2.5; 5.34; 10.52).

Faith is required from all who come to Jesus for help (5.36; 9.23f): we recognize the characteristic, even when the word is not specifically used (7.24–30; 2.12; 3.5).[15] This is hardly surprising, since faith in the good news is what Jesus demands at the very beginning of his ministry (1.15), and it is what those who reject him fail to have (6.1–6). It is faith that characterizes those who belong to Christ (9.41f).[16]

The fact that the disciples frequently fail to respond to Jesus as they should does not mean that Mark intends to depict them as opponents of the gospel: in spite of their fear and incomprehension, they do follow Jesus in the way. In their weakness and fallibility, the disciples typify ordinary believers – the Church as it was in Mark's day, and as it has been ever since. The mistakes the disciples make serve to underline the kind of community that the Church *should* be (9.33–37; 10.35–45). The fact that Jesus still acknowledged them as his disciples, even after their apostasy (14.27f; 16.7), offers a message of hope to the community: for those who are willing to set out once again on the road of discipleship, there is forgiveness instead of rejection (8.38).

In contrast to the failings of the disciples, there are other characters in the story who point us to something better: men and women who do what the gospel demands, and so typify what the Church might be. Almost without exception, they are people without status (because, for example, they are women) or who find themselves outsiders. There is Peter's mother-in-law, who serves Jesus and his disciples (1.31; cf. 10.45); there are the men who find themselves excluded from 'the house', and force a way in for their friend (2.1–12). There is the leper, an outcast from society, who comes to Jesus and asks to be cleansed (1.40–45), and the woman who, because of her illness, was permanently 'unclean', but who had the faith to break the taboos and come to Jesus for help (5.25–34). There is the Gentile woman from Syro-Phoenicia, who persists in her demands that Jesus heal her daughter (7.24–30). There is blind

---

[15] Neither the paralytic nor the man with a withered arm could have obeyed Jesus' command without faith that he had already effected a cure.

[16] By putting the sayings in vv. 41 and 42 together, Mark shows that he has understood the 'little ones' of v. 42 to be Christian disciples. Cf. M. D. Hooker, *The Gospel According to St Mark* (London: A. & C. Black/Peabody, MA: Hendrickson, 1991) *in loc.*

Bartimaeus, hailing Jesus as Son of David, whose faith is rewarded by the gift of sight, and who follows Jesus 'in the way' (10.46–52). There is the woman in the temple, who throws all her money into the treasury (12.41–44), and the woman who spends a vast sum on perfume, which she lavishes on Jesus in the house of Simon the leper (14.3–9). Finally, there are the women who have served Jesus in Galilee, followed him to Jerusalem, and who, alone among his followers, watch his death and burial; it is they who come to perform the last service for Jesus, by anointing his body, on Easter Sunday morning (15.40f, 47; 16.1–4): only at the end of the story, confronted with the stupendous news of the resurrection, are they, too, overwhelmed by fear.

The most remarkable feature of this list is the fact that it consists largely of women! In first-century Palestinian society, women perhaps found it easier than men to accept the life-style demanded by Jesus: serving others, not looking for status. For Mark, it is these humble women who represent the ideal of Christian discipleship. This is the more remarkable in view of the fact that those who were commissioned by Jesus as apostles[17] were all men. In the social conditions of the day, this was, of course, inevitable: women would not have been heeded as emissaries of the kingdom, nor would a woman have been counted as a valid representative of one of the twelve tribes. Mark's insistence on their response to Jesus is therefore all the more remarkable. Notable, also, is the fact that some of the men and women who respond with faith to Jesus are 'outsiders'. The clearest examples of this are the woman with a haemorrhage and the Syro-Phoenician, but there are hints of the same idea elsewhere: the crowd prevents the four men from approaching Jesus, and they have to break into the house; Bartimaeus, also, has to defeat opposition from the crowd in his attempt to be heard by Jesus. The fact that outsiders respond to Jesus accords with the fact that so much of his ministry is to outsiders: he touches a leper (1.41), eats with tax-collectors and sinners (2.15–17), heals those with unclean spirits (5.1–20),[18] welcomes children (10.13–16), and is found at supper in the house of Simon the leper (14.3).[19] The new community of believers, consisting of those who respond to Jesus, embraces those who had previously been on the fringes of society.

Mark's vision for the Church, then, is quite simple. It is a vision of a community that is all that God intended Israel to be – a community that

[17] Mark rarely uses the term ἀπόστολος, but he does use it in 6.30, to refer to the Twelve when they return from their mission; it is possible that he uses it in 3.14, where many MSS read 'and he named them apostles', but this is probably a gloss. Nevertheless, its occurence in 6.30, and the fact that the Twelve are appointed 'to be sent' in 3.14 (cf. 6.7), means that this is an appropriate word to describe their function.

[18] The unclean spirits drove the man to live among unclean tombs; when they left him, they moved into a herd of unclean swine.

[19] It is possible that Jesus had healed Simon of his leprosy. Nevertheless, the description reminds us that Jesus mingled with 'outsiders'.

accepts his reign, as it was proclaimed in the ministry of Jesus, and is obedient to the divine command to love God and to love others. The community that believes in Jesus as Messiah and Son of God will do these things, and so follow faithfully in the footsteps of its Lord.

BIBLIOGRAPHY

Best, E. 1981. *Following Jesus: Discipleship in the Gospel of Mark.* JSNTSup 4. Sheffield: JSOT Press.

Best, E. 1986. *Disciples and Discipleship: Studies in the Gospel according to Mark.* Edinburgh: T. & T. Clark.

Hooker, M. D. 1983. *The Message of Mark.* London: Epworth Press.

Kee, H. C. 1977. *Community of the New Age.* London: SCM Press.

Marshall, C. D. 1989. *Faith as a Theme in Mark's Narrative.* SNTSMS 64. Cambridge: Cambridge University Press.

Tannehill, R. C. 1977. 'The Disciples in Mark: The Function of a Narrative Role'. *JR* 57:386–405. Reprinted in W. Telford, 1995.

Telford, W. (ed.). 1995. *The Interpretation of Mark.* 2nd edn. Edinburgh: T. & T. Clark.

4

Luke's Vision for the Church

DAVID SECCOMBE

CHURCHES in every generation need a vision for their life which touches the imagination and inspires the zeal of their contemporaries. However, because churches are fundamentally a divinely ordained phenomenon rooted in God's plan for the salvation of the world, they fail to be Christian – indeed they lose their claim to be the Church of God – unless they are faithful both to how the churches conceived of themselves at the beginning and to the original transforming vision which guided them into their mission to the world.

Luke's writings chart both the primal impulse which originated in the ministry of Jesus and the resulting movement which burst forth in the formation of churches around the Mediterranean world. It was not his purpose to develop a full doctrine of the Church. His major concern was to present Jesus and his kingdom as God's answer to the hopes and aspirations of OT Judaism. However, the form which the divine plan took in its progress from the human life of Jesus to the ultimate 'restoration of all things' was the apostolic mission, whose offspring in Luke's day was churches which continue to our own time. These needed to be explained to inquirers, justified to critics and given direction and vision for believers. All three challenges are met by Luke and his answers provide us with formative insights for a contemporary vision for the Church.

As then, so now, any vision for the Church must arise from an understanding of what it is. Luke's method is not to expound his understanding with a series of propositions. Instead he lets the story disclose its own meaning. It is possible to be sceptical and deal with him as a speculative theologian, propagating his own novel views through the medium of a semi-fictitious story. If so, we must also accredit him with a remarkable genius he would probably have denied. His work bears the impress of a fervent conviction that history is the *obvious* medium through which to expound an understanding of the Church, precisely because the Church is a work of God which predates any theological understanding of it. The frustrating absence of obvious church teaching in the Gospel might itself be thought to speak eloquently against his having fabricated sayings and events to suit his own philosophical purposes. The first church appears suddenly and unexpectedly in the early chapters of Acts and it is something of a puzzle to discover the lines of connection with what preceded it.

Of course, as a purely human social development the appearance of the first church is not difficult to account for. Jesus' untimely execution left his many followers bitterly disappointed in their expectation that he was the coming King-Messiah. But then, renewed in hope through his reappearance, they naturally sought one another out. The form of their association and its developments are known to us as the Christian Church. This is history and it could be seen as essentially accidental.[1] However, if the whole movement is seen as the working out of a divine plan, then we are justified in seeking some fundamental thought lines connecting the ministry of Jesus and the appearance of the Church.

THE CHURCH IN THE GOSPEL OF LUKE?

Reflection on the gospel story reveals an obvious reason for the invisibility of the Church. John the Baptist's call for repentance could easily have led to a 'Church' for the simple reason that his baptism visibly divided Israel into two groups. The intended effect of John's ministry was to create wheat and chaff, which the Coming One would deal with appropriately. Jesus, however, stepped back from judgement and announced God's acceptance to the whole people.[2] He forewent any mark of conversion which would inevitably have been read as a symbol of belonging. The Gospel of Luke portrays a constant movement within the crowds towards and away from Jesus with no attempt on his part to freeze them into membership of his group.[3] Although he is not unmindful of the response of individuals, he appeals to the nation for its decision on him. The kingdom of God is present with him and salvation is there for Israel's enjoyment so long as it is received along with the Son of Man who announces it. The alternative of which Jesus often warns is national judgement.[4] Thus if one were to speak of the Church in this period it would be co-terminous with the nation. Of course, it would be a Church containing many nominal members, but the distinctive feature of this

---

[1] Loisy's famous dictum: Jesus preached the kingdom, and what appeared was the Church. Conzelmann sees it this way and credits Luke with the genius of having created a theology to fix the Church within the plan of God.

[2] At Nazareth Jesus announces God's acceptance of his covenant people (Luke 4.18–21).

[3] For example, see how Jesus speaks to crowds and people in the Sermon on the Mount (Luke 6.17–20, 27, 46–49).

[4] The judgement which threatens in Luke 12.54–13.9; 13.34–35; 19.41–44; 21.5–24 is the destruction of the nation.

period is Jesus' deliberate postponement of any separation of the people into the accepted and the rejected. The door of repentance which might lead to national salvation is kept open until the last moment.[5]

In Luke's telling of the story Israel's restoration is postponed by the nation's refusal of its divine visitor,[6] and the death, resurrection and ascension of Jesus lead to a new phase in the plan of salvation.[7] The restoration of all things now lies in the divinely-appointed future and Jesus instructs his apostles to invite people (individuals and families) near and far to believe in him and become part of the community of his kingdom. Thus is the Church born as an entity distinct from Israel.

However, unexpected as Jesus' rejection and the non-appearance of the promised kingdom was to the disciples, according to Luke it came as no surprise to Jesus. It was implicit in the way he was treated all along the way, from the circumstance of his birth, to his near lynching in Nazareth, to the refusal of Galilee to repent, to his rejection by the Samaritans, and so on to Jerusalem. Although no doors are finally closed during this period, Jesus and his disciples are gathering people from the realm of darkness into the little flock for an as yet unrevealed future, which is neither Messiah-less nor the world-to-come.[8] So there is already a looking forward to a continuation of history in which Jesus' disciples will need to wait, serve, suffer and support one another in the midst of hostility and trials. Jesus thus prepares his followers for their life as his people in the midst of the world. It is this that justifies our looking to the Gospel as well as to Acts for our vision for the Church. It also accounts for Luke's large collection of dominical teaching, particularly the block of almost half the Gospel found in his central section. Luke clearly saw much of Jesus' teaching as suitable, if not intended, for the Church.

THE COMMUNITY OF THE RISEN CHRIST

The community which we meet in the early chapters of Acts – the Jerusalem followers of Jesus gathering in homes and at the temple – is a community without name. From our vantage point we recognize it immediately as the Church of Jerusalem, the original Christian ἐκκλησία, but Luke does not say so. Instead he uses every art to avoid

---

[5] The vineyard owner pleads for another year's grace for the fruitless fig tree: Luke 13.6–9.

[6] Luke 19.41–44 signals the withdrawal of the kingdom's blessings. Israel has had a visitation of mercy in the person and ministry of Jesus. His rejection brings on the gruesome alternative of national destruction.

[7] Acts 1.6–8 announces the purpose of the post-resurrection, pre-restoration period.

[8] In Luke 11.14–23 Jesus portrays himself and his followers 'gathering' people out of Satan's kingdom. 'Gathering' is a significant pre-ecclesiological theme to which we should connect Luke 5.10; 10.20; 14.16–24.

the word. The gathered believers are designated 'all those devoting themselves with one accord to prayer', 'the brothers', 'all those together at the same place', 'all who had believed to the same place', 'those being saved to the same place', 'their own people' and 'the community (πλῆθος) of those who had believed' (Acts 1.14, 15; 2.1, 44, 47; 4.23, 32). The difficulty the copyists had with 2.47, inserting ἐκκλησία in a variety of combinations, and with 2.44, where the difficult reading of Vaticanus (πάντες δὲ οἱ πιστεύοντες ἐπὶ τὸ αὐτό) is probably original (the ἦσαν of the majority of manuscripts being an early attempt at improving the sense), is testimony to the difficulty Greek readers experienced with the awkward way Luke uses ἐπὶ τὸ αὐτό, and alerts us to the fact that he was deliberately avoiding using ἐκκλησία, at the same time as he wished to stress the close association of the believers. It appears he wishes us to see the community as it was, unprejudiced by a name which by the 60s had become a symbol of conflict and misunderstanding. So what is this anonymous entity that comes before us in Acts 1–4?

The new community is defined fundamentally by its adherence to the risen Messiah Jesus. Peter's Pentecost sermon unveils Jesus as the divine king ('Lord and Christ') and it was around this banner that the first believers and subsequent Christian communities rallied. It was when a person believed that the crucified Jesus was 'both Lord and Christ' (Acts 2.36) that he crossed over from 'this crooked generation' to the number of the saved, and received the distinguishing sacrament of baptism and the inward baptism of the Holy Spirit. The ecclesiological meaning of adherence to Christ is explained by Peter when he informs the people that Jesus is the prophet promised by Moses, whom to disobey entails being cut off from the people (λαός) of God (Acts 3.23). Thus Luke portrays the new community as the continuing λαός of God, and the heir of the blessings covenanted to Abraham (Acts 3.25–26).

That such a fundamental defining characteristic must needs form part of Luke's vision for the Church hardly needs to be argued. It is the purpose of Luke's Gospel to lead us to and establish us in this faith. Without faith in Christ there is no membership of the people of God, though there may be baptism and membership for a while of a local church (Judas, Ananias and Sapphira, Simon Magus). Paul, in his final words of exhortation to the elders of the church at Ephesus, reminds them repeatedly how he 'testified of faith in our Lord Jesus Christ', of the ministry given him by the Lord Jesus 'to testify to the gospel of the grace of God', and how he 'preached the kingdom' (Acts 20.21, 24, 25). It is in this address as well in his description of the Jerusalem church that Luke brings to clearest expression his vision and concerns for the Church. His desire is that the elders of every church should see to it that the proclamation of Jesus and the kingdom should continue. Fierce wolves will ravage the flock, and 'from among your own selves' men will arise seeking to draw disciples after themselves (a further reminder of members who are not members). Part of the task of the shepherd-guardian is to resist all attempts to re-centre the faith of the Church anywhere but on Christ himself (Acts 20.28–30).[9] Paul's letters contain all the evidence we need of the urgency of this concern in the 50s and early 60s. Acts closes with him in Rome 'preaching the kingdom of God and teaching about the Lord Jesus Christ' (28.31). The proclamation of Jesus as Lord and Christ is the major theme of Luke and Acts and can never be forgotten without disciples ceasing to be Christians and churches losing contact with the Church.

THE CHURCH AND THE HOLY SPIRIT

The primary spiritual distinctive of the new community is its possession of the Holy Spirit. The 'times of refreshment' which will accompany the return of Christ still lie in the future (Acts 3.19–20), yet the age of the Holy Spirit has dawned. The foundation group is dramatically and miraculously baptized with the Spirit and the promise of the Spirit is extended to all who will believe (Acts 2.1–4, 7–18, 33, 38; 4.31; 5.32). The community enjoys the grace of God (4.33) displayed in periodic mani-festations of the Spirit (4.31) and dwells consciously in the awesome knowledge of the Spirit's presence amongst them (5.1–11). The Holy Spirit continues to make his presence felt throughout Acts as the driving force of the mission and the gift for those who believe in Jesus.

How then may we conceive of the Spirit in terms of a vision for the Church? For Luke his presence is inalienable. The new age is the age of the Spirit's outpouring, and the last days have come (Acts 2.16–21, 33). When disciples are discovered who have not heard of the Holy Spirit something is clearly wrong. They are still part of the old order and need to be baptized in the name of the Lord Jesus and received into the fellow-ship of the new community (Acts 19.1–7). For Luke the Spirit is God's gift to all who believe in Christ. No other transaction is necessary to ensure receiving him than faith and baptism (Acts 2.38–39). The apparent exception in the case of the Samaritans appears to be a deliberate with-holding of the Spirit until the leaders of the Jerusalem church acknowl-edged the Samaritans as fellow believers. This was essential to their full membership, but their incorporation into the Christian community is not complete until they too receive the promised Spirit.

From all this we may surmise that Luke expected that the Spirit would be present wherever there are believers in Jesus Christ and might manifest himself in their common life in a staggering variety of ways. The 'great grace' which was upon all the members of the Jerusalem church is but an

---

[9] ἀποσπᾶν τοὺς μαθητὰς (Acts 20.30) may indicate an attempt to carry off the whole Church in a false direction (Giles 1995:81).

alternative way of speaking of this presence of the Spirit which makes itself felt in mighty winds, tongues of fire and 'other tongues' (2.2–4), preaching (2.14ff), prophesying (2.17), 'cutting to the heart' (2.37), calling (2.39), signs and wonders (2.43), generosity and fellowship (2.44ff), praise (2.47), boldness (4.31), judgement (5.1ff), etc. The Spirit is the purveyor of God's manifold grace to his people as well as the driving power of the mission into the world. Thus, whereas one or another of his mani-festations may form part of a programmatic vision for the churches (we will consider some of these in due course), the actual presence of the Spirit is not so much a matter of ambition or vision, but of recognition, enjoyment, thanksgiving and co-operation. The prayer for the Holy Spirit which Jesus enjoins on his disciples (Luke 11.13) is better understood in its Gospel context as a prayer for the coming of the kingdom (when the Spirit would be poured out) than as a prayer for the Spirit to fill an individual believer. It is a prayer which was answered at Pentecost.

Some of the outward manifestations of the Holy Spirit's presence which Luke highlights as characteristics of the new community are its dedication to the apostles' teaching, its prayers and praise, its life of fellowship and breaking bread, and the miracle working of the apostles (Acts 2.42–47). We shall consider these as possible components of his vision.

A TEACHING CHURCH

The new believers 'devoted themselves to the apostles' teaching . . . and the prayers' (Acts 2.42). The apostles did likewise, for when a diversion threatened they re-affirmed their commitment to what for them was clearly the central task: 'preaching the word of God' (Acts 6.2), and 'the ministry of the word and prayer' (Acts 6.4). The association of preaching and prayer in these two contexts suggests that Luke has the com-munity's prayers in mind. The apostles in Jerusalem are teachers and leaders of the church's prayers. We may guess that this accounts for most of the agenda of the large daily gatherings at the temple and points the direction for later church life. The sheer quantity of apostolic instruction that Luke has succeeded in incorporating in Acts is itself testimony to the importance he gave teaching in the ongoing life of the Christian movement. The bulk of preaching in Acts falls into the category of proclaiming the gospel, but not all. Instruction went on after people were converted. In Ephesus Paul taught daily for a space of two years (Acts 19.8–10). The several references to Paul and his compatriots 'strengthening the churches' are best understood as referring to teaching and exhortation (Acts 14.21–23; 15.41; 18.23; 20.2, 7). Luke's Gospel was in part born out of the dissatisfaction he evidently felt with Mark as a medium of church instruction, for he amplifies it to double its length primarily with dominical teaching.

The task of teaching soon extended itself beyond the apostolic band. Luke names five 'prophets and teachers' in the church at Antioch (Acts 13.1) and alludes to a great many others (Acts 15.35). Once Apollos has been properly instructed by Priscilla and Aquilla, he too begins to teach (Acts 18.24–28). Teaching is clearly an activity in which any appropriately gifted person who understands the faith may engage. Its urgency beyond the apostolic age comes to clear focus in Paul's discourse to the Ephesian elders. Paul does not expect to see them again, and evidently Luke does not expect that he will either. The church and its elders are therefore on their own for the future. They are impassioned to shepherd the Church for which Christ died and Paul has laboured so hard and shed so many tears. The vivid description of Paul's ministry of preaching and teaching, publicly and from house to house, leaves no doubt as to what shepherding means. The Church is to be nourished, guarded, built up, and brought on its way to 'the inheritance among all those who are sanctified' by means of 'the whole counsel of God' (the full revelation of God's character and will and plan; Acts 20.17–35).

Clearly this is an important concern of Luke. It stems from the strategy enunciated by Jesus to build the kingdom of God, not by military conquest, but by means of the broadcast word (Luke 8.1–15). Kinship with King Jesus is not a matter of blood, but of hearing the word of God and doing it (Luke 8.19–21). A church which is loyal to the primal vision will be teaching and defending the apostolic faith.

A CHURCH OF SIGNS AND WONDERS?

'Fear came upon every soul and many signs and wonders were done through the apostles' (Acts 2.43). Luke emphasizes the miracle working which took place in the first church. Is it part of his vision for the Church, or does it serve some other purpose? Unlike teaching it does not appear to be communicable. Apart from the apostles, only Paul, Stephen and perhaps Philip are associated with miracle working. The prominence of Paul as a miracle worker and the well-known similarity of his miracles to Peter's appears as Luke's attempt to demonstrate the legitimacy of Paul's ministry. The argument would have no force if Luke understood miracle working to be shared by many in the churches. In Ephesus God worked 'extraordinary miracles' (δυνάμεις τε οὐ τὰς τυχούσας; Acts 19.11) through Paul. Such an expression forbids us to think such things were commonplace even in the early Church. Just as Joshua was demonstrated to be Moses's successor and Elisha Elijah's, the apostolic miracles were to legitimate the message and ministry of the first generation of leaders and to prove God's ownership of the new community and the presence of the Spirit in its midst. When Paul hands on the baton to the elders in Ephesus there is no mention of miracles, but only of teaching, humility, tears, trials, imprisonment and affliction, and toiling to help the weak (compare the Pastoral Epistles). It is a strange parallel between Paul's ministry and Jesus' that their miracle working appears virtually to cease when they enter into the period of arrest and trial.[10]

A COMMUNITY OF FELLOWSHIP

Luke gives special emphasis to the outstanding degree of fellowship and sharing that marked the early movement. They devoted themselves to fellowship and the breaking of bread, opened their homes to each other and ate together, and contributed money and possessions for the apostles to distribute to the needy. The twin descriptions of the community's common life underline its importance for Luke (Acts 2.42ff; 4.32ff). They contain several Greek proverbs which express an idealized notion of true friendship. 'Friends have everything in common', 'one soul', and 'nothing one's own' (see Acts 2.44; 4.32) were common friendship slogans in Greek literature. They do not necessarily indicate a formal community of possessions in which private ownership is abolished, but an outstanding degree of openness to and sharing with others.[11] Luke wants to convince his Hellenistic readers that the grace of God brought about a quality of life amongst the first Christians which answered even to the ideals of their own world. He was after all, a Hellene writing to Hellenes.[12] He speaks of fellowship (κοινωνία) rather than friendship (φιλία) presumably only because the concept of friendship had become debased by the patronage system.

Thus, the spotlight on the degree of fellowship enjoyed by the Jerusalem community has an apologetic motive rather like the emphasis on signs and wonders, but there is also evidence that it was much more.

In the Parable of the Unjust Steward Jesus counsels his disciples to 'make friends with the mammon of unrighteousness so that when it fails they may receive you into the eternal tents' (Luke 16.9). In the context of the parable Jesus is urging his hearers to take seriously the approaching end of this age, involving as it will 'the failure of mammon', and to act prudently by converting their wealth while it still has value into

---

[10] Jesus' healing of a severed ear and Paul's survival of snakebite are the exceptions; they do not take away from the remarkable fact that neither employs miracles to impress his captors or to avoid the hardships of arrest.

[11] Peter's words to Ananias show that private property was still respected (Acts 5.4). See further, Seccombe 1982:200–09.

[12] Luke's eye is also on his Jewish readers. When the word of God is first received in Antioch, Barnabas arrived and 'saw the grace of God'. We are not told what he saw that signalled to him that grace, but it was demonstrated to the Jerusalem church by the generosity with which the Antiochenes sent relief to Jerusalem in the famine (Acts 11.22–30). Luke would like the Jewish critics of the Church in his own day to acknowledge this evidence of God's ownership of the Gentile churches.

something which will count in the new age. It is interesting that he puts his finger on 'friends' as one commodity that forms a bridge between the present and the coming kingdom. It suggests that the early disciples' commitment to fellowship may have had a conscious kingdom rationale and have been seen as a real anticipation of the fellowship of the new age.

This impression of an eschatological motive for fellowship is reinforced by the observation that the common life of the first church carries on the pattern of open sharing between Jesus and his disciple band and also Jesus' free socializing with 'sinners' and social outcasts, and would therefore seem to have belonged to following him as a disciple. The Gospels interpret Jesus' meals with his disciples as celebrations of the new age when the bridegroom is united to his people, and his friendship towards 'sinners' in terms of God accepting them into his kingdom (Luke 5.33–39; 15.1–32). The saying about new wineskins suggests that such convivial association will be a continuing practice of those who live in the knowledge of Christ's coming. The curious expression ἀφελότητι καρδίας ('simplicity of heart') in the description of how the disciples ate their food (Acts 2.46) may refer to their deliberate lack of scruple about the cleanness or otherwise of whom they ate with. For the strict Jew every shared meal involved discrimination, but Jesus, in imitation of God, had shown an undiscriminating acceptance of all who would come.

Jesus' encouragement to those who entertain to include the beggars and handicapped at their table, which is also an expression and anticipation of God's activity in the new age (Luke 14.12–24), is another example of a revolutionary form of hospitality which the Jerusalem church took very seriously and which Luke hoped would characterize the life of all subsequent Christian fellowships.

Thus, Luke's depiction of the community serves both an apologetic and an emulative function. It is a manifestation of the grace of God which proves his presence in the community as well as being of the essence of a church life which is in true relationship to God and his kingdom.

CHURCH

In Acts 5.11 the community is named for the first time. But why ἐκκλησία? In Luke's time it had come to have a special meaning denoting Christian gatherings, and distinguishing them from synagogue meetings. It was a term of contention. Luke did not invent the term, but it is charged with significance for him. He avoids it, then tentatively introduces it (5.11), then gives it a theological identity (7.38), and, having established for his readers what he sees as its correct association, makes liberal use of it from 8.1 onwards.

Given its strongly Christian significance it is therefore strange to find that Luke can use the word in a purely secular context, to describe both the official Ephesian assembly and the unlawful protest gathering of Demetrius and the silversmiths (19.32, 39, 41). Clearly the word has not lost its plain meaning of a gathering or meeting, to become a purely technical term like our word 'church'. One expects then that even in its Christian use it will retain some connotation of gathering. Luke will never use ἐκκλησία to mean 'Christianity', nor does any NT writer. With two or perhaps three significant exceptions (7.38; 9.31; 20.28), he always uses it of a local entity. With one significant exception (9.31), he never speaks of multiple congregations as 'the Church', but always as 'churches'.

This creates the impression that for Luke, assembling together is an important, conscious component of his understanding of the Church. Especially this is so when ἐκκλησία is considered along with the idiomatic expression ἐπὶ τὸ αὐτό which he uses four times in the early chapters of Acts (1.15; 2.1; 2.44, 47) and never again once the word ἐκκλησία has been introduced. In the LXX it means 'together' (Deut 22.10f: the ox and the ass must not plough *together*; Deut 12.15: the clean and the unclean may eat meat *together*; etc.). Paul uses the expression twice of the Church coming together (1 Cor 11.20, 14.23). C. K. Barrett (1994:172) suggests rendering it 'in church', L. T. Johnson[13] as 'in community'.

It is not just the occurrence of this togetherness idiom which is striking, but the odd combination in which it appears: in Acts 2.47 'day by day the Lord added *together* (or *into community*) those who were being saved'. When all this is added to Luke's observation that the disciples 'devoted themselves to . . . fellowship and the breaking of bread', and to what we have already surmised about the eschatological understanding of friendship, we may hazard that association to fellowship in the name of Christ was for Luke a 'mark' of the Church.

AN ANCIENT CHURCH

Given Luke's twofold use of ἐκκλησία, for a secular meeting and for a Christian assembly, we could perhaps read Acts 5.11 not as the dramatic appearance of the Church, but as its tentative introduction in an ambiguous context. It could be fear throughout the whole Jerusalem church which is being described or fear falling upon the meeting in which Ananias and Sapphira died. Stephen's speech then becomes the first unambiguous use of ἐκκλησία in a Christian context, the significance being that here what is primarily in view is the Church that gathered with Moses at Sinai to hear the words of the Angel of the Presence (Acts 7.38). However, the unmistakable parallel Stephen draws between the rejected Moses, whom God brings back as 'ruler and deliverer' and who gathers

[13] Cited by Giles 1995:261 n. 9.

the people in assembly at Sinai, and the rejected Jesus who is raised up to be 'Leader and Saviour' (Acts 5.31), who is also responsible for the new community in Jerusalem, makes it clear that he is deliberately associating the assembly at Sinai and the Christian ἐκκλησία.

But what is the point of the association? The ἐκκλησία at Sinai was the constitutive assembly of Israel. The whole people gathered before their God to hear him own them and instruct them. Their identity as his covenant nation derived from that occasion. They did not remain in assembly, but could look back to 'the day of the ἐκκλησία – qahal' (Deut 9.10; 18.16), and from time to time the whole community would gather to form 'the great assembly' (Ps 22.25). It was the united character they drew from those assemblies that made it appropriate to name them a congregation even when they were not assembled. If Jesus was the prophet promised to succeed Moses, his community could not be a different one. If Moses declared excommunication upon all who would not follow this prophet, then Jesus and his followers must be the legitimate continuation of the Mosaic community. We have already seen that Luke calls them λαός; ἐκκλησία represents another step. Now they are seen as a people whose essential character is determined by some form of assembly. But presumably they did not call themselves ἐκκλησία solely with reference to the assembly at Sinai or they would have continued with συναγωγή.[14] Nor would the fact of their frequent meetings establish an obvious theological link with the church of Sinai. Frustratingly Luke does not inform us exactly how they came to see themselves as the continuing Israelite assembly – a reminder that he is not expounding a new doctrine of the Church, only reflecting an existing understanding. But if we may divine that understanding from Hebrews and Matthew, their ecclesial nature was derived from the reality of their being gathered as the family of God into the presence of God and his Messiah. It is possible perhaps to see the assembly focused on Jesus, since it is *his* Church (Matt 16.18), he is in the midst of it when it meets in local assembly (Matt 18.20), he stands in the midst of the great assembly (Heb 2.12), and one comes to him when one is enrolled in the church of the firstborn (Heb 12.18–24). However, given the way it is most frequently named 'the Church of God', it must also have been conceived as a community gathered in God's presence. All this being so, it is probably a significant pointer to the coming Church when the Gospels depict Jesus and his

---

[14] Presumably Christian meetings began as synagogues (glaringly absent from Luke's list of community titles), but very early felt the need of another name and chose ἐκκλησία. Martin Hengel suggests it was Stephen and the Hellenists who were responsible, at the time when it became necessary to adopt a Greek nomenclature to match the concepts of Jesus and his Aramaic-speaking disciples. In addition to distinguishing church and synagogue, he thinks it stresses the Church's eschatological claim (1983:27).

disciples as gatherers of the scattered people of God (Luke 5.10; 11.23; John 11.52). The way the early Christians understood themselves at the point of fulfilment of God's foreshadowed purposes makes it probable they would have understood the messianic ἐκκλησία to embrace within it the OT assembly, much as a first-built room which acts as a shelter for the builders may be incorporated in the finished house, though the cornerstone and plan of the whole house is determined by the later structure.

The question now arises why Luke identifies the Church in the way he does, if his purpose is not to develop a full doctrine. From Acts 8.1 on Luke uses ἐκκλησία freely of Christian assemblies and it is difficult to resist the conclusion that he has avoided naming it until its connection with the Sinai church is clear because of misunderstanding or misrepresentation in his own day.

In the middle years of the first century Christianity was dismissed by many Jews as a 'sect' or 'party' (αἵρεσις), a term which denotes a particular school of opinion, and in a pejorative sense, a breakaway group. This was a sensitive point to Luke, because it implied a break with God's eternal purpose (Acts 24.5, 15; 28.22). He retaliates with the counterclaim that the Church is in direct continuity with the Sinai church and that it is the Jews (or at least the Sadducees and Pharisees) who are party movements (Acts 5.17; 15.5). Though the Church was undoubtedly new in form, Luke contends that properly understood it is an ancient foundation. Were it not so, it would hardly have been taken seriously by first-century inquirers as a divine entity.

For the most part in Acts, churches are city congregations. What we have just outlined may help us to understand the two passages in Acts where ἐκκλησία denotes something bigger.

In Acts 9.31 we read, 'the ἐκκλησία throughout all Judaea and Galilee and Samaria had peace, being built up, and, going in the fear of the Lord and the encouragement of the Holy Spirit, it was multiplied'. The use of the singular to describe what must have been many churches, though it looks innocuous to the modern reader, is unusual for Luke (and indeed for the NT). Nowhere else is 'church' used as a collective to describe many churches. It is unlikely that Luke is thinking of the Jerusalem church in dispersion. They would not then be at peace throughout Judaea, Galilee and Samaria, but returning to Jerusalem. He must have in mind that ultimate assembly in the presence of God and his Christ of which local churches and in this case a network of churches are the visible expression. In the light of a dominical promise to build *his* Church and not allow the powers of death to overcome it (Matt 16.18), it is interesting that the context of this unusual use of ἐκκλησία is the first attempt to annihilate the Christian movement, which only results in its being 'built up'.

The other non-local use of ἐκκλησία is found in Acts 20.28 where the context is also helpful to us establishing the relationship in Luke's mind between the messianic Church and local churches. Paul, addressing the elders of the church in Ephesus, urges them to 'take heed to yourselves and to all the flock, in which the Holy Spirit has made you overseers to shepherd the Church of God, which he bought by his own blood'.

It is not impossible to take ἐκκλησία here in its local sense as a reminder to the elders of the great cost at which God had purchased *their* community, but it is natural to see a more transcendent meaning. The startling assertion that God has purchased the Church with his own blood (διὰ τοῦ αἵματος τοῦ ἰδίου)[15] emphasizes his ownership of the Church, its preciousness to him, and the means by which he made it his. The divine Son of God shed his blood to purchase a people for God whom he is gathering and assembling in his Father's presence. The elders at Ephesus are to see their church as nothing less than that Church manifested locally in their city. There is nothing to suggest that Luke sees them as a component part of the larger Church and therefore not fully the Church. Such a notion occurs nowhere in Acts nor in the NT. They are to regard their church as the Church as it is at Ephesus and lavish upon it care commensurate with its value to God.

A JEWISH OR A GENTILE CHURCH?

The Church as we have traced it so far is Jewish. Luke regards it as the Israel of God of the last days. There is not the slightest indication that he sees it as a replacement of Israel, or 'the new Israel' as it is termed in much present-day theology.

Acts tells the story of how a totally Jewish movement threw itself open to the Gentile world. The churches of the early chapters of Acts are 100 per cent Jewish; thirty years later churches of mixed Jewish and Gentile character were springing up around the Mediterranean. However, much controversy accompanied this transformation. Many Jews inside and outside the churches viewed it with alarm and did what they could to oppose it. The issue was not the presence of Gentiles at church meetings. Synagogues of the diaspora had a well-established precedent of allowing God-fearing Gentiles to attend their meetings. The offence was caused by according recognition to uncircumcised Gentiles as full members of the people of God and accepting them into table fellowship. Such acceptance implied either that they were Israelites, albeit uncircumcised, or that God was accepting other nations into the covenant community as equals with Israel. The only way for a Gentile to enter the community of God's

[15] It is possible to translate this as 'with the blood of his own Son' where 'Son' is understood, but if this is what Luke intended he must also have intended the ambiguity.

people, according to Jewish belief at that time, was to become a proselyte by accepting circumcision and submitting to the Jewish law. Many Jewish Christians held to this belief and were offended by developments in the Pauline churches.

Luke's defence of Paul is an apology for Pauline Christianity and particularly his practice of declaring Christian Gentiles equal members of the people of God. Paul's vision was for churches in which Jews and Gentiles ate together without scruple. A step in this direction had been taken in the non-discriminatory table fellowship practised in the Jerusalem church, but the Gentile line is not crossed until the incident of Cornelius. Peter's thrice repeated vision announces the decontamination of the Gentiles. As the story progresses it becomes clear that this means more than God's extending to them the gift of salvation. Peter is going to enter the house of a Gentile and share his food. As he ponders the meaning of the vision Cornelius' Gentile servants arrive and the Spirit tells him he is to go with them not discriminating (μηδὲν διακρινόμενος, Acts 10.20; 11.12). He then invites them in to be his guests (εἰσκαλεσάμενος οὖν αὐτοὺς ἐξένισεν, Acts 10.23), and later becomes a guest himself in the centurion's home. It is interesting to compare this case with that of the centurion who called on Jesus for help in Capernaum. He would not trouble Jesus actually to come to his home, presumably because he understood that for Jesus to do so would have been a serious breach of Jewish custom, if not of the Law (Luke 7.1–10). Peter reminds Cornelius that it is not lawful for him associate closely (κολλᾶσθαι) with a foreigner (ἀλλοφύλῳ) except for the fact that God has bidden him otherwise. Presumably Peter would have been within his rights as a Jew to communicate with Cornelius outside his home in a way which did not involve table fellowship – otherwise how could any proselytes have been made? A startling feature of the story, then, is not just God's dramatic acceptance of Cornelius and his household, but Peter's willingness to remain with them, accepting their hospitality for some days. It is this which brought accusations against him in Jerusalem (11.3). It infringed the holiness of the chosen nation. Cornelius' house is not a 'church' (though what goes on within it is not too far removed), but an important precedent is set for the churches nonetheless.

The Jerusalem church's custom of breaking bread together now becomes the pattern of the mixed Jewish and Gentile churches, no distinction being made on the basis of circumcision or non-circumcision (Acts 20.7; 15.9). Luke wants us to understand that the Church is a community in which Jews and Gentiles share in brotherly partnership and that churches should reflect this in non-discriminatory fellowship.

A question has been raised, however, as to whether Luke did not see Jewish membership of the churches as a temporary phase of Christian development. It is argued that one of Luke's purposes was to signal the end of any mission to the Jews, their final judicial rejection by God, and the opening of the curtain on Christianity as a Gentile movement of essentially Gentile churches.[16] Along with this, Luke is charged with being anti-semitic. This is both curious and alarming, a matter of more than scholarly concern. For when a scholar seizes the moral high ground and alleges anti-semitism on the part of a biblical writer, he or she ought to be aware that the proving of the case may unleash the very evil the scholar purports to oppose. For Luke and Acts are canonical Scripture, establishing for much of the Christian world the mind of God. Christians, by and large, will pay less attention to the moralizing of a scholar than to what they see as the teaching of Luke and the other biblical authors. If someone convinces them that Luke is anti-Jew, they are likely to follow Luke!

In any case a growing number of scholars have argued (demonstrated, in my view) that far from rejecting the Jews, Luke is more gentle towards them than most of the NT writers.[17] The radically conflicting opinions arise from statements relating to the judgement of Israel being taken as anti-semitic. If they are, then consistency would require that Matthew, Mark, John and Paul also be charged, along with Moses, Hosea, Amos, Isaiah, Jeremiah, Ezekiel, etc. – and Jesus himself can hardly be excluded. All of these speak and warn of Israel's judgement. Surely, then, some better explanation than 'anti-semitism' must be found.

In Luke and Matthew (Q) John the Baptist pictures the Coming One arising with fiery judgement for the unrepentant of Israel. Jesus draws back from such an undertaking, but does not deny that God's judgement is a threatening possibility. It is postponed rather than cancelled, in the hope of a last-minute national turning to God (Luke 13.6–9; 12.57–59). When this is not forthcoming in Galilee Jesus concludes that the kingdom of God has been refused and turns to Jerusalem (Luke 10.13–15; 9.51–10.12). A week before his crucifixion he weeps over Jerusalem and solemnly predicts its destruction 'because you did not know the time of your visitation' (Luke 19.41–44). Some of these elements are Lucan, but the general picture is not unlike that in the other synoptic Gospels (see Matt 21.33–43; 24.1ff; Mark 12.1–11; 13.1ff).

This depiction, which is not dissimilar to the situation of Jeremiah's warnings to the nation, could be construed as anti-semitic only if it implied a final total rejection of Israel as the people of God without hope of remnant or redemption, or if Luke were to call people to anti-Jewish behaviour. Neither is the case. Jesus is set 'for the falling and rising of many in Israel' (Luke 2.34) and salvation is consistently seen to be for

---

[16] E. Haenchen 1982:102. J. T. Sanders 1987 argues the case in detail.

[17] Jacob Jervell 1972 has led the case for Luke's sympathy towards the Jews. For a collection of essays for and against, including contributions from Sanders and Jervell, see Tyson 1988.

Israel as well as for the nations.[18] The cataclysm of judgement of which Jesus forewarns is not final and everlasting; though they must needs pay the last penny, a final release is envisaged (Luke 12.57–59). Israel will be trodden by the Gentiles, but only until the times of the Gentiles are fulfilled (Luke 21.24).

Nowhere in Luke or in any of the Gospels is there a trace of any incitement to persecution of, or antisocial behaviour towards, Jews. One might infer from John the Baptist's fiery predictions that Jesus' stance towards unrepentant Jews would be hostile. Instead he announces 'the acceptable year of the Lord' (the time of God's acceptance). Jesus' warnings of judgement against Israel might lead us to expect a negative stance towards Jews in the opening stages of Acts. Paradoxically, God's arms are still wide open to his people (Acts 3.25–26). J. T. Sanders explain this as the Jews' last chance because they killed Christ in ignorance; if they then reject the Gospel they will be finally rejected.[19] Certainly Luke sees a person's response to the Gospel as determining his destiny for salvation or judgement. He also views the failure of the rank and file of Jews to heed Jesus' call to repent and the rejection of him by the Jewish leaders as sealing a judgement of Israel as a nation. But does he extend this to a moratorium on mission to the Jews, remove them from their elect status as the people of God and cut off from them the hope of salvation?

In fact, as often as the warning of judgement is heard, so is the appeal for repentance and the hope of salvation renewed, albeit for individuals. The preaching of the gospel in Jerusalem is followed by Stephen's stinging condemnation of the Jewish leaders (Acts 7.51–53), but the saving of Jews goes on. Indeed one of the very men who sat and heard Stephen's charge of hard-heartedness and consented to his death is raised up to proclaim the name of the Lord Jesus 'before Gentiles and kings, *and the sons of Israel*' (Acts 9.15). The Jews in Pisidian Antioch are judged 'unworthy of eternal life' and Paul turns to the Gentiles, yet this is followed by fresh preaching to Jews in Iconium and more Jews won to the faith (Acts 10.46; 14.1ff).

In Rome the Jews are again charged with hardness of heart and Paul announces again that he is turning to the Gentiles, yet this occurs in a scene in which some Jews believe, and is followed by the statement that Paul continued his preaching of the kingdom welcoming all who came to him (Acts 28.23–31). It is not necessary to translate Paul's words about turning to the Gentiles (αὐτοὶ καὶ ἀκούσονται) in the adversative way they often are: 'They will listen!' 'They too will hear' is as good a translation or better (it does not ignore the καί).

[18] Luke 1.54–55, 68–75; 2.32; 10.21; 24.21, 47; Acts 1.6–8; 2.39; 3.20–21, 25–26; 5.31; 9.15; 13.23, 38; 15.16–17; 26.23.
[19] Tyson 1988:51–75.

In some ways Acts is in startling contrast to the harsh expressions of national judgement found in Luke's Gospel. Not once in Acts is Jewish hostility met with a warning of general national judgement, a sure indication that these warnings belong to the historical Jesus and not to Luke. Nowhere does Acts even remind us of Jesus' prophesies of destruction for Jerusalem. Nowhere is any withdrawal of Israel's elect status intimated, nor any final rejection. Instead there is a consistent tone of appeal to Jews to believe and not to harden their hearts. This, I would contend, is how the conclusion of Acts should be understood. If Luke's vision was for the final triumph of the Gentile Church over the Jewish synagogue one would expect the Church to be visible and prominent at the end of Acts. The 'brethren' come to meet Paul as he approaches the city, but Luke has all his interest focused on the Jews, calling their leaders, consulting them, laying his gospel before them, converting some of them, and, yes, also speaking in the severest terms to those who refused his message. But this is the pattern of preaching to Jews throughout Luke and Acts (and many times in the OT). The charge of hardness of heart functions to explain the reaction of the majority of Jews who do not believe: far from their being an argument against the truth of the gospel, they are acting exactly as Isaiah foresaw that they would.[20] But the charge of hardness is also a passionate appeal to the hearers *not* to harden their hearts. Jesus follows a similar description of Jewish hardness, which he too explains from Isa 6.9, with the appeal, 'Take heed then how you hear' (Luke 8.10, 18). Thus, I would contend that the finale of Acts, far from being a final rejection of the Jews, is rather an urgent appeal to them and to their sympathizers not to harden their hearts.[21] Luke the evangelist at the close of his two-volume work betrays that his interest is more for these lost sheep of Israel and their God-fearing associates than for those Gentiles who were already in the fold.

UNDERSTANDING LUKE'S VISION FOR THE CHURCH

Luke's vision through all this is for a truly multiracial Church, which is Jewish in foundation and Jewish in its foundational membership, but which welcomes people of all nations. These are not required to abandon their own cultural heritage and be circumcised; nor must they practise the cultural provisions of the Mosaic Law. Yet they share with Jews in intimate table fellowship without discrimination or scruple. There is little enthusiasm in Luke–Acts for anything like an exclusively Gentile congregation.

---

[20] See V. Fusco 1996:1–17.

[21] H. van de Sandt (1994:341–58) thinks Acts 28.28 alludes to Ezek 3.6, and like Isa 6 represents reproof and strong warning to Israel, but not final rejection.

How shall a vision like this be honoured in what are now in many parts of the world exclusively Gentile churches? Firstly, by seeking to include people of other cultures both in the church congregation and in the circles of friendship and hospitality which continue to express the ecclesial nature of the Church even when it is not assembled. Secondly, by extending fellowship to Jewish people in a way that does not imply that they need to abandon their Jewishness and adopt Gentile Christian customs. Thirdly, by welcoming the growth of indigenous Jewish churches which may have very different cultural patterns to those in predominantly Gentile churches.

BIBLIOGRAPHY

Barrett, C. K. 1994. *The Acts of the Apostles*. Vol. 1. Edinburgh: T. & T. Clark.

Carson, D. A., ed. 1987. *The Church in the Bible and the World*. Exeter: Paternoster/Grand Rapids: Baker.

Chance, B. 1988. *Jerusalem, the Temple and the New Age in Luke-Acts*. Macon: Mercer University Press.

Conzelmann, H. 1969. *The Theology of St Luke*. London: Faber.

Dupont, J. 1979. 'The Salvation of the Gentiles'. In *Essays on the Acts of the Apostles*. New York: Paulist Press.

Esler, P. F. 1987. *Community and Gospel in Luke-Acts*. Cambridge: Cambridge University Press.

Fitzmyer, J. A. 1989. 'The Jewish People and the Mosaic Law in Luke-Acts.' In *Luke the Theologian: Aspects of His Teaching*. New York/Marwah: Paulist Press.

Flew, R. N. 1943. *Jesus and His Church*. London: Epworth.

Fusco, V. 1996. 'Luke-Acts and the Future of Israel'. *NovT* 38:1–17.

Giles, K. 1995. *What on Earth is the Church?* London: SPCK.

Haenchen, E. 1982. *The Acts of the Apostles*. Oxford: Blackwell.

Hengel, Martin. 1983. *Between Jesus and Paul*. London: SCM Press.

Jervell, J. 1972. *Luke and the People of God*. Minneapolis: Augsburg.

Jervell, J. 1984. 'The Mighty Minority'. In *The Unknown Paul*. Minneapolis: Augsburg. 26–51.

Kaiser, W. C. Jr. 1977. 'The Davidic Promise and the Inclusion of the Gentiles'. *JETS* 20:97–111.

Lohfink, G. 1975. *Die Sammlung Israels: Eine Untersuchung zur lukanischen Ekklesiologie*. SANT 39. Munich: Kösel.

Matera, F. J. 1990. 'Responsibility for the Death of Jesus according to the Acts of the Apostles'. *JSNT* 39:77–93.

Sanders, J. T. 1987. *The Jews in Luke-Acts*. Philadelphia: Fortress.

Sanders, J. T. 1991. 'Who is a Jew and Who is a Gentile in the Book of Acts?' *NTS* 37:434–55.

Seccombe, D. P. 1982. *Possessions and the Poor in Luke-Acts.* SNTU. Linz.

Tyson, J. B. 1984. 'The Jewish Public in Luke-Acts'. *NTS* 30:574–83.

Tyson, J. B. 1988. *Luke-Acts and the Jewish People.* Minneapolis: Augsburg.

van de Sandt, H. 1994. 'Acts 28.28: No Salvation for the People of Israel?' *ETL* 70:341–58.

van Goudoever, J. 1966. 'The Place of Israel in Luke's Gospel'. *NovT* 8:111–23.

Weatherley, J. A. 1989. 'The Jews in Luke-Acts'. *TynB* 40:107–17.

Wilson, S. G. 1973. *The Gentiles and the Gentile Mission in Luke-Acts.* Cambridge: Cambridge University Press.

5

Q and the 'Church': The Role of the Christian Community within Judaism according to Q

CHRISTOPHER M. TUCKETT

JOHN SWEET has been an inspiring teacher of the NT. It was he who initiated me into the richness of NT studies as my first NT teacher. My very first essay, written for him some twenty-five years ago, was on the way in which the gospel tradition circulated prior to the writing of our present Gospels. It may then be appropriate to return to my own roots and offer to him a very small token of the deep appreciation and debt I owe to him in this essay, attempting to show how one strand of the pre-synoptic tradition struggled to hold firm to its vision of the place which Christian followers of Jesus should seek to occupy within a wider social and religious context.

INTRODUCTORY ISSUES

This essay concerns the Sayings Source Q. Inevitably the constraints of space in an essay such as this mean that it is impossible to stop to justify in full every position taken in relation to Q studies in general, or in relation to some key aspects and individual texts and their wording.[1] Thus the present essay must proceed on the basis of a number of pre-suppositions which will be assumed here, without any detailed defence or argumentation. I assume here, for example, the existence of a Q source lying behind our Gospels of Matthew and Luke: the body of agreements between Matthew and Luke, which are not explicable as due to dependence on Mark, are to be explained by common dependence of Matthew and Luke on a body of material, 'Q', to which they both have access. Further, I am assuming that the evidence of the texts of Matthew and Luke is best explained if Q were a written text, not just a body of oral tradition, and a text probably written in Greek, rather than in Aramaic

---

[1] For some attempt at such a fuller justification, see Tuckett 1996. This essay presents some of the results of the final chapter of that study, in slightly amended form.

(though the question of Q's language probably does not affect the argument of the rest of this essay in any significant way). Certainly the agreement of Matthew and Luke in the relative order of the Q material they share is at times striking and seems to demand a written source to explain it.

Given this essentially source-critical theory, it may then be appropriate to ask, as in 'redaction'-critical study in general, what if anything can be discerned of a possibly characteristic or distinctive outlook of this Q material, and what we may be able to deduce about the person/people who preserved this material and handed it on. Such an enterprise in relation to any text is, of course, fraught with many methodological problems, and, in the case of Q, the nature of our evidence for Q adds yet more difficulties. For example, we do not have a copy of Q itself extant. Our knowledge of Q is at best indirect, being only deducible from the texts of Matthew and Luke. We cannot therefore be certain about the precise extent of Q; nor, conversely, can we be sure about what was not in Q. So too, as with any text, such as Q or a Gospel, giving information about events prior to its own time of composition, there is the problem of knowing whether and to what extent the ideas preserved in the text reflect the views of the people who preserved and handed on the tradition. Some of the ideas preserved may be in line with the views of the people concerned, some may not be. Some of the views and beliefs of the Christians who preserved Q may not be directly reflected in Q at all. Further, to think of 'the people who preserved Q' may be to think in too monolithic terms. At the very least, we should perhaps distinguish authors/editors from readers/audience: thus some traditions in Q may have been preserved by some Christians to speak *to* others, rather than simply to mirror the common views of all concerned in any dialogue.

Yet without wishing to deny the serious nature of these problems in relation to the whole enterprise of trying to write about the Christians who preserved Q, some general points may be made. With regard to the problem of the extent of Q, a comparison of the extent of Markan material in Matthew and Luke may help. The fact that Matthew and Luke between them preserve virtually all of Mark makes it unlikely that any substantial amount of Q material has been omitted by both of the later evangelists. Such a possibility cannot, of course, be ruled out of court completely, but it seems reasonable to take as a working hypothesis that Q is preserved fairly fully by Matthew and Luke. (For the problem of possible Q passages preserved by only one of Matthew and Luke, and omitted by the other, see Tuckett 1996:92–96.)

In what follows, I shall therefore be assuming that the Q material preserved in Matthew and Luke gives us a fair approximation to the whole of Q. Moreover, I shall focus on the Q material as a whole in the rest of this essay. Although a very influential body of Q scholarship today (much of it based on the work of John Kloppenborg: cf. Kloppenborg 1987, 1990) would see this Q material as capable of being divided into identifiable literary strata (a 'Q¹', 'Q²', 'Q³', etc.), I would argue that such theories are too hypothetical to be useful or usable. Undoubtedly individual traditions in Q have their own (possibly very complex) tradition histories, some of which we may be able to trace on the basis of our available evidence; but whether we can identify the literary history of the *document* Q in the same way seems to me more doubtful. I therefore confine attention here to the Q which is discernible to us in the form in which it was available to Matthew and Luke.

The problem of how far Jesus traditions preserved by one writer, or one group of Christians, reflect the views of that writer/group is clearly at one level ultimately intractable. It seems however implausible to conceive of a writer or editor preserving traditions that were positively uncongenial to him/her. Such a possibility again cannot be ruled out (and one has only to think of, for example, Matt 10.5–6 or Matt 23.2–3 within Matthew's Gospel); but the assumption that traditions were preserved because they were broadly in line with the views of those who preserved them seems not unreasonable. Certainly it is the basic assumption of so much form- and redaction-critical study of the whole of the gospel tradition, not just of Q studies.

What else Q Christians might have signed up to, apart from the Q material itself, is again impossible to say. It is equally dogmatic to deny that they affirmed anything beyond Q as it is to affirm what they 'must have' believed (e.g. some saving significance of the cross, despite the apparent lack of a passion narrative in Q). Some absences from Q may be purely fortuitous; some *may* be significant (cf. below for discussion of one such absence in Q), but the nature of the evidence inevitably means that we cannot be certain.

With all these caveats in mind, we may reasonably ask what the Q material, as evidenced in Matthew and Luke, may tell us about the group of Christians who recorded it. That there were such Christians responsible for the preservation and dissemination of Q to a wider audience seems to me undeniable. Whether though it is justifiable to talk of a 'Q community' in this context, as is done by many today, is one of the assumptions which this essay seeks at one level to challenge.

THE 'JEWISHNESS' OF Q

On almost any showing, Q is one of the most 'Jewish Christian' strands of the whole gospel tradition. For example, Q evidently has a somewhat conservative attitude to the Jewish Law. There is nothing which explicitly questions observance of the Law in any way (in contrast with the picture in Mark, which certainly can be, and has been, interpreted as presenting Jesus as at times critical of the Law: cf. Mark 2.23–3.6; 7.1–23; 10.1–12). In fact there are one or two hints that Q was at least aware of tendencies that might give rise to such questioning, and was concerned to nip such tendencies in the bud quite firmly.

For example, the saying in Q 16.17[2] about the permanence and abiding validity of the Law seems in part intended to counter any possible implications of the verse which may have immediately preceded it in Q, viz. Q 16.16, to the effect that 'the Law and the Prophets were [only] until John' and were now no longer valid in the post-Baptist era. By contrast, then, Q 16.17 asserts that the Law is still valid right down to the smallest detail of a jot or a tittle.[3] Moreover, the arrangement of the material here may well be editorial (or 'redactional'), so that the concern to promote obedience to the Law reflects the views of the Q editor quite as much as that of earlier tradition.

There is too, the note at the end of Q 11.42 to the effect that, however much more important the great principles of justice and the love of God may be in relation to the practice of tithing, nevertheless the latter 'should not be left undone'. Further, the note has all the hallmarks of a redactional addition to an earlier version of the saying lacking the phrase. Obedience to the Law is thus heavily emphasized, not only by Q's tradition but also by the editorial work of the Q compiler.

The same motif comes through strongly in Q's account of the temptation narrative (Q 4.1–13), where one powerful element in the story is to stress the fact that Jesus is obedient to the words of scripture. Jesus here says nothing that is not a citation of scripture; the story shows above all Jesus' obedience to the Word of God as given in scripture, and his refusal to disobey in any way. Whatever the precise significance of the temptation narrative in relation to the rest of Q, and the degree to which the 'temptations' here are regarded as specifically 'christological', or as paradigmatic for other Christians, it seems impossible to deny that, at least in respect of Jesus' positive use of scripture, a model is being proposed for the followers of Jesus as well. (I have tried to justify this in more detail

---

[2] As is standard now in discussions of Q, I give the references to Q verses by their chapter and verse numbering in Luke's Gospel (without in any way intending to prejudge the issue of whether the Matthean or the Lukan version is more original). Thus 'Q 16.17' refers to the Q verse appearing in Luke 16.17 and its Matthean parallel (here Matt 5.18).

[3] It is possible that the final phrase in Matthew's version of the saying ('until all is accomplished' Matt 5.18d) may indicate an awareness that a jot or tittle might now fall from the Law, if indeed 'all' is in some sense now 'accomplished'. But this phrase is probably due to Matthew's redaction of the saying in Q, and not part of Q itself. The other differences between the two versions of the saying in Matthew and Luke probably do not affect the overall thrust of the saying, asserting the validity of the Law in the present.

in Tuckett 1992.) The horizons of Q, and of the Q Christians who preserved this tradition, seem thus to be firmly fixed within the bounds of Torah-observance.

A similar picture emerges from an analysis of attitudes to Gentiles and the Gentile mission in Q. The situation regarding any possible Gentile mission in Q is much debated. Several have pointed to a number of apparently approving references in Q to Gentiles (cf. the centurion in Q 7.1–10, Tyre and Sidon in Q 10.13–14, the Queen of the South and the people of Nineveh in Q 11.31–32, those from the east and the west in Q 13.28–29; see Manson 1949:20, and others). Yet, as others have pointed out, nearly all of these refer to the distant past or the eschatological future (cf. Hoffmann 1972:293). The only exception may be the centurion of Q 7.1–10, but even here there is nothing to suggest that he is anything other than an exceptional case. Nothing indicates that the centurion stands at the head of a long line of Gentiles who are responding positively, either to Q's Jesus or to later Q Christians. Q may be aware of the existence of perhaps isolated Gentiles who have responded positively to the Christian message. Q may even be aware of the existence of some kind of Gentile mission elsewhere in Christian communities. But for the most part, this is only used as part of the polemic against other Jews who are failing to respond to Q's Jesus (cf. Q 11.31–32; 13.28–29; see Meyer 1970). Further, there seems to be no awareness at all of any problems that such a Gentile mission might create in relation to the Law, in particular of the question of how far Gentile Christians are expected to obey the Jewish Law. Certainly the question is not raised in any parts of what may confidently be restored as Q's version of the mission charge of Q's Jesus to his followers. (One exception might be Luke 10.8b ['eat whatever is set before you'], which some have argued might be part of Q; but there is no explicit Matthean parallel, and hence an origin in Q must remain doubtful.) Any 'missionary' activity in Q seems confined to Judaism. This is reinforced by Q's passing references to Gentiles in Q 12.30; Matt 5.47.[4] Such language clearly implies an 'us/them' or 'in-group/out-group' mentality. But the way in which the 'out-group', or 'them', can be referred to quite casually as 'Gentiles' (alongside 'tax-collectors' in Matt 5.46; again, Luke's 'sinners' here is probably secondary) suggests that the Q Christians regarded themselves primarily as Jewish and constituting (at least part of) Israel.

POLEMIC IN Q

At first sight, some of the fierce polemic which characterizes much of the Q material might suggest a different picture. Q is full of tirades by Jesus

---

[4] Matthew's reference to 'Gentiles' in Matt 5.47 is universally recognized as more original than Luke's more general reference to 'sinners' in Luke 6.33; thus Matt 5.47 almost certainly preserves the Q wording.

against his Jewish audience, with the fierce denunciation of 'this generation' for failing to respond to the message of Q's Jesus and the prophets before him (cf. Q 7.31–35; 10.13–15; 11.37–51, especially vv. 49–51; 13.28–29; 13.34–35, etc.). Some have therefore deduced from this that Q reflects a situation where the Christian community has become irrevocably separated from Judaism and the Jewish community, both socially and 'theologically'. Q has given up all hope for Israel and simply offers dire warnings of eschatological punishment: for Israel there is now no hope, and only judgement remains. (See Lührmann 1969:93, Kloppenborg 1987:167, and others.)

Such an interpretation of the fierce language in Q probably misinterprets the nature of such polemic, and indeed of the nature of eschatological language in general. As with all eschatological or apocalyptic language, predictions of future events may function quite as much to exhort people to act differently now (and hence avert the predicted future) as to state what is going to happen come what may. As John Sweet has reminded us, the importance of a prophetic prediction of the future in the Jewish eschatological or apocalyptic tradition lies as much in the analysis of the present situation and the claims about the true nature of that situation in relation to God as in any 'fulfilment' of the prediction (see Sweet 1990:2–3). The same almost certainly applies in relation to Q. The aim of the Q Christians, articulated through the preaching of Jesus (and probably John the Baptist as well) preserved in Q, was to change Israel, to make their Jewish contemporaries aware of the disaster that was threatening them if they did not 'repent' (cf. Q 3.8; 10.13; 11.32). Hence the aim of the polemic was not to gloat ghoulishly over a catastrophe that was inevitably coming. Nor was it necessarily all directed at the Christian group by way of defining the boundaries around the community, demarcating Christians more clearly from others (i.e. Jews), and reinforcing a sense of group identity (so Kloppenborg 1987:167–68). As we have seen, if there is any group identity and awareness of an 'us/them' distinction, it is much more in terms of Gentiles, rather than other Jews, being the 'them', or 'not us', in such a polarity. The aim then of the polemic seems to be to try to *save* Israel from the threat that is perceived to be coming. Perhaps too, there is even a note of hope of possible success in a saying such as Q 13.35, where the reference to Ps 118.26 seems to be positive and not negative (cf. Uro 1987:237).

Q AND ISRAEL

What then was Q's attitude to Israel/Judaism? And what was the hope and the vision of the Q Christians for the future? How did Q Christians regard themselves in relation to their Jewish contemporaries? How much separation had occurred – at both the social and the ideological levels?

With regard to the degree of separation presupposed, such questions raise enormous conceptual problems. Further, answers given are often heavily dependent on who is giving them. Clearly, any group of Christians within early Christianity must have appeared, both to themselves and to outsiders, as in some sense a group distinct from their Jewish neighbours in concrete social terms and also in terms of elements of their ideology. At the social level, any form of group meeting would have served to accentuate the distinctiveness of the group; and in terms of ideology, the positive attitude to the person of Jesus and his teaching must have marked off the Christian group from others. On the other hand, any Christian group would also display elements of continuity: at the ideological level Christianity, with the exception of Marcion, has never cut its roots from Judaism; and at the social level the fact that Christians and non-Christian Jews lived alongside each other inevitably entailed a degree of social overlap and relationship. Further, the very existence of hostility reflects an element of social and religious identity between the two groups as perceived by both parties concerned. From the Jewish side, the 'persecution' of the Christian movement can only really be seen as stemming from a belief by non-Christian Jews that the Christian movement constituted a threat from within to Judaism's self-identity. If Christianity had been perceived as a religion quite separate from Judaism, then Jews would presumably have ignored it completely. Moreover, as sociological studies have indicated, it is likely that the extreme nature of the hostility indicates (almost paradoxically) the closeness of the relationship between the two groups: it is the closeness of the factions that exacerbates and magnifies the hostility engendered (Coser 1956:67–85). Thus, the existence of the (at times) very harsh and fierce polemic in Q against non-Christian Jews, and the belief that Jews are 'persecuting' the Christians (cf. Q 6.22–23, 27–35; 11.47–51; 12.4–5, 11–12; 13.34–35),[5] probably indicates a large measure of social and ideological overlap between the Christian group and their non-Christian neighbours.

What is perhaps striking in Q is the way in which, from the Christian side, there seems to be a conscious effort to minimize the social rupture which the existence of the Christian claims has engendered. This has been shown recently in the work of David Catchpole in his study of some parts of the Q material (see Catchpole 1993 on the Great Sermon [pp. 79–134], and on 'Reproof and Reconciliation' [pp. 135–50]). Catchpole has shown very clearly the way in which the exhortation in Q 6.31–35 on love-of-enemies is influenced and shaped by the command to 'love your neighbour as yourself' in Lev 19.18 (Catchpole 1993:115). What is

[5] However, see Tuckett 1996:296–323, for doubts about how much active persecution of Q Christians there may actually have been. So often, the polemic in Q seems to be seeking to confront a situation of dull apathy, rather than direct, overt physical and active persecution of the Q Christians.

dominant here is the exhortation to 'love' (Q 6.32 picking up the previous teaching given under the general rubric of 'love your enemies' in 6.27). In the rhetorical questions of Q 6.32–33, the clear implication is that there is a community consciousness; but also that community is clearly Israel. Those addressed see themselves as an 'in group'; and the 'out group', from whom the addressees naturally distinguish themselves, are 'Gentiles' (cf. above on Matt 5.47). What is in mind is thus a national self-consciousness, and the 'nation' concerned is precisely Israel herself. Catchpole also refers to the key position of the Golden Rule in Q 6.31 which sets up the self and the self's wishes as one of the criteria by which to judge ethical action. These three elements – love, Israel, self – all then come together in the key text Lev 19.18 ('you shall love your neighbour as yourself'), where the 'neighbour' is clearly primarily one's fellow Israelite. Thus, Catchpole concludes that in this Q sequence,

> the persecuted ones are thus addressed along the lines of the ancient text, interpreted strictly in its own terms. Of any preoccupation with defining, still less with redefining, the neighbour, there is not the slightest trace. The community to which the editor and his audience belong is therefore not so much a Christian church as Israel . . . Every effort is made therefore to be faithful simultaneously to the confession of Jesus and the command of Moses. (Catchpole 1993:115–16).

Some of the consequences of this for concrete social relationships are then spelt out in the following section in Q 6.36–38. Q 6.36 should probably be taken as a heading for what follows, rather than as a summary of what precedes, and exhorts the hearers to show 'mercy'.[6] Such language evokes the idea of the covenant relationship between Yahweh and his people (cf. Exod 34.6; Deut 4.31; Ps 103.8, etc.). What this means in practice is spelt out in what follows in Q 6.37–38. Q probably contained the double command here expressed in both negative and positive terms: do not judge or condemn; rather, forgive and give generously.[7] If so, then the emphasis should probably (as usual) be taken as falling on the second half of this antithetic parallelism. Thus, the stress in Q seems to lie on the positive side of the double saying, and this in turn expounds further the exhortation to show mercy (6.36). Thus, the Q unit exhorts its hearers to show the same mercy that is characteristic of the God of Israel and to do this by exercising compassion, forgiveness and generosity to others. Further, these exhortations develop the earlier appeals to give generously (6.30), to forgive by refusing to answer evil with evil (6.29) and above all to love one's enemies rather than let hate overrule the relationship.

[6] Matthew's parallel here, which speaks of being 'perfect' (Matt 5.48), is almost certainly redactional, so that Luke's version probably preserves Q's wording here.

[7] The positive exhortation in Luke 6.38, with the vivid imagery of folding a garment to hold grain, looks to be peculiarly Palestinian and unlikely to have been invented by Luke: hence it was probably in Q.

These rather general exhortations are then given more concrete application in the sayings that follow concerning reasoning and reproof,
especially in the saying about the mote and the beam in Q 6.41–42. Here
too, Catchpole's other chapter becomes relevant in highlighting further
evidence from other non-Christian Jewish texts to illustrate the pattern
of teaching to be found in a number of Q sayings. The often-noted
parallel to the mote/beam saying in *b. Arak.* 16b suggests that the context
for the saying is to be located in a situation of reproof and correction of
one party by another. Now reproof implies an attempt to reconcile, to
overcome divisions that arise, to nullify enmity and discord, and to create
community. Thus the saying about the mote and the beam should
probably be seen in conjunction with other sayings in Q about the
importance of forgiveness and reconciliation, especially Q 17.3–4 (on the
importance of unlimited forgiveness, even if there is no repentance on
the part of the offender: this is probably the significance of the reference
to the sevenfold sinning) and 12.58–59 (on the need for reconciliation).
The significant overlap between Q 17.3–4 and 6.41–42, as well as the
evidence from 12.58–59, shows the importance of the theme of personal
reconciliation for the Q Christians in their environment. Catchpole also
points to the common use of the term ἀδελφός in Q 17.3 and 6.41, and
refers to the fact that probably underlying all these passages is the
command of Lev 19.17 (in the immediate context of the love command in
Lev 19.18) to ensure that one does not 'hate' one's 'brother', but instead
one should 'rebuke' one's neighbour. The context and parallelism here
makes it quite clear that 'brother' means fellow-Israelite (Catchpole
1993:145). Thus, the community consciousness behind these sayings is
exclusively and precisely Jewish: the community addressed is not a
Christian 'Church' separate from Judaism, but Israel itself in its totality.
Thus what Q pleads for in all these instances is that forgiveness, love and
compassion be shown to one's 'brother', that is, one's fellow Israelite. The
horizon is entirely intra-Jewish; but equally it is no less than fully Jewish.
There is in Q a sense in which some Jews are threatened with final and
definitive rejection (cf. Q 12.10; 13.28–29, etc.): yet perhaps this is only a
threat of what might happen if nothing is done, and the assumption
seems to be throughout Q that the appeal to Jews must be maintained
continually. Despite the hostility experienced, attempts must be made to
heal the rifts in the community. Forgiveness and reconciliation must be
attempted before it is too late, just as the very existence of Q suggests a
conviction that the plea to the Jewish audience, despite its failure to
respond positively so far, must be sustained before it is too late.

If the above argument is correct, then it suggests that the divisions
between the Christians behind Q and the Jewish community were not
that deep. Certainly there was hostility, though the very existence of
hostility itself indicates a – possibly considerable – degree of positive

overlap between the two groups as well as the negative difference which becomes overt in the hostility. At least from the Christian side, it would appear that any split was still not that severe at the social level. It would seem that the Q Christians had not given up hope for Israel; and they did not think of themselves as a separate community. Obviously at one level there is separation: those who support the Christian cause are distinguished from those who do not – the non-Christians are not Christians! But in terms of the self-understanding of the Q Christians, the important social divisions appear to be primarily those separating Israel as a whole from Gentiles, and the Q Christians are, at least in their own estimation, within that boundary alongside their fellow Jews.

Further, we hear nothing in Q suggesting boundary creation by separate social or cultic practices. It is not clear if John the Baptist's rite of baptism is to be repeated by the later (i.e. later than John the Baptist) Q Christians. It would in one way be surprising if it was not, yet the fact that this is not spelt out *may* indicate the relatively low significance that baptism has in relation to boundary formation in sociological terms. It may also be significant that there is apparently no reference to the Eucharist in Q. Q's Jesus does not institute a new cultic act, which clearly in some way would serve to separate Christians from those who do not belong to the group and thus who do not share in such cultic actions.[8] Any argument from silence is obviously fraught with danger, especially when, as in the case of Q, one is trying to discern a Christian group's self-understanding in such an indirect way, viz. by looking only at the traditions about Jesus which they have preserved, and moreover only those to which we have access via Matthew and Luke. Nevertheless, it may not be entirely without significance that the tradition about Jesus' institution of the Eucharist was not one preserved in Q (or at least the form of Q to which we now have access, albeit indirectly). There is thus no indication that Q Christians are being encouraged to separate themselves from the social and religious life of their Jewish neighbours. Indeed, as we saw earlier, some parts of Q suggest that, in relation to tithing practices and Torah-observance in general, the opposite is the case. There is thus little evidence of a specifically Christian community consciousness or social self-awareness. In terms of nomenclature used by others, the Christians of Q are striving to be 'Christian Jews', not 'Jewish Christians'. (The terminology is sometimes used in Johannine studies, and amongst students of Jewish Christianity, to distinguish different stages, or degrees, of separation of Christians from Jewish institutions.) As 'Christian Jews', the Q supporters are 'Christian' sympathizers striving to stay within the boundaries of Judaism and with no apparent awareness yet (or at least an unwillingness to acknowledge) that those boundaries might be too

[8] See Meeks 1983 for the social significance of such cultic practices as baptism and the Eucharist for the Christian communities.

restrictive to contain both themselves and their Jewish contemporaries. (I leave aside the vexed question of how appropriate it is to use the term 'Christian' in this context. All I mean here by 'Christian' is one who regards Jesus and Jesus' teaching positively.)

Whether others in the contemporary situation would have seen things in the same way is, of course, another matter. Some have argued that Q Christians were facing intense persecution, perhaps being excluded from Jewish social and/or religious gatherings. If that were the case, it would imply that perhaps the non-Christian contemporaries of the Q Christians would have regarded them *not* as 'Christian Jews', but precisely as 'Jewish Christians', that is, a group whose distinctiveness from their contemporaries had reached a sufficiently clear form that they should be seen as constituting a separate social, and perhaps even in some sense 'religious', entity. In fact, the so-called persecution passages in Q may reflect a rather less violent situation than is often thought, and the main reaction from Jewish contemporaries may have been one of sullen apathy rather than physical violence (see Tuckett 1996:196–323). In that case, then, even from the non-Christian side, there may have been not very much awareness of the Christian group as socially, or 'religiously', very distinct. Clearly there were differences. But on neither side does there seem to be any evidence that the differences between Christians and others have created hardened – or even hardening – social barriers.

To use more sociological jargon, what I am arguing is that the Christian group reflected in Q may have been trying to be more of a 'reform movement' working within Israel than a 'sect' separated from its Jewish contemporaries by a rigid line of demarcation. (For the terminology, see Esler 1987:47–53.) I am fully aware of all the dangers of using the language of 'sect' in the present context (cf. Holmberg 1990:77–117). The word itself is used in a variety of different ways by different sociologists, and by different NT scholars seeking to exploit sociological insights for NT studies, as well as being used in a non-technical sense in several contexts. So too there is an acute danger in applying the word to an early Christian group in relation to an alleged parent body of 'Judaism': the 'sect' terminology, as used in the classic discussion of E. Troeltsch, was part of a distinction between a 'sect' and a 'church'; hence here the 'Church' would presumably have to be 'Judaism', though we now realize all too clearly how variegated and non-unitary first-century Judaism was. There is no space here to enter into the debate of how one might, or should, seek to define a 'sect'. All I am doing here is to identify in very general terms a distinction between a 'reform movement', working within a parent group, and a 'sect', which sees itself as in some real sense separate from the parent group, with its own clear self-defined and self-asserted boundaries which distinguish it clearly and visibly from the parent. And all I am claiming is that the group of Christians reflected in Q do not yet seem to have reached

that state of self-conscious 'sectarian' differentiation from their neighbours.

In this Q probably represents a stage prior to that of Matthew. For
Matthew, a 'sectarian' model of the Christian community in relation to
its Jewish neighbours is more defensible. (Again I use the word 'sectarian'
in a fairly loose sense.) The precise nature of the split between Christians
and Jews by the time of Matthew is much debated, though it seems
likely that the boundary lines between the two groups have solidified
very considerably. It is unclear how far Matthew holds out any hope for
the majority of non-Christian Jews. Some individuals may still be the
object of the Christian mission. But the main thrust of large parts of
Matthew seems profoundly pessimistic about any rapprochement
between Christians and Jews. Matthew's redactional addition to the
parable of the wicked husbandmen in Matt 21.43 appears to interpret the
parable in national terms ('the kingdom of God will be taken from you
and given to another ἔθνος'); and the well-known (and almost certainly
redactional) verses in Matt 22.7 (the king of the parable of the great supper
burning up the city of the guests who have not responded to the invitation
to the meal) and Matt 27.25 ('his blood be on us and on our children')
seem to underline the guilt and definitive rejection of the Jewish people
by God, while Matthew's own Christian community claims the right to
be the true 'Israel'. So too, the well-known Matthean habit of referring to
Jewish institutions as 'their' or 'your' synagogue/scribes (cf. Matt 4.23;
7.29; 9.35; 10.17; 12.9; 13.54; 23.34) has indicated to many scholars that the
Matthean community is sharply distinguishing itself at the social level by
having rival institutions alongside those of the Jewish community. On
any showing there is clearly an element of self-awareness on the part of
Matthean Christians distinguishing themselves from, and partly distanc-
ing themselves from, their Jewish neighbours. (I am fully aware that such
a description, both of Matthew's ideology and of his social situation, is
heavily debated; but a full discussion is not possible within the confines
of this essay.)

Such a self-awareness does not appear to be present in Q. Clearly there
are tensions. Clearly there are differences. But the aim of the Q Christians
is to seek to bridge those differences, to stay within the broad Jewish
community of which they claim to occupy a part, and not to separate off
into a separate conventicle or 'sectarian' ghetto. For the Q Christians, the
desire is clearly to stay as far as possible within the social and religious
matrix of Israel. Perhaps too, even on the non-Christian side, the desire is
for the same end: hostility, even 'persecution', presupposes a similar
purpose to maintain unity with an awareness of solidarity, the 'persecution' itself being one means to try to reunite into a whole again what
is perceived as threatening to fracture and disintegrate. The vision for the
'Church' then for Q is that the Christian community remain very much

at one with its Jewish parent body, and that it should *not* seek to separate into a self-subsistent organization and become a separate 'Church'. Rather, its vision is one inspired by the message of Jesus involving forgiveness, love and reconciliation.

The separation of Christian communities from their Jewish neighbours, in terms of both ideologies and social ties, was a long and complex one (see Dunn 1991). In Q we see perhaps a relatively early stage in that history. Certainly it is earlier than Matthew. Perhaps it is the tragedy of subsequent history that the efforts of the Q Christians in this respect, and also of their Jewish contemporaries, were ultimately frustrated.

BIBLIOGRAPHY

Very little has been written directly on the topic addressed here. The following is a bibliography of works cited in the essay.

Catchpole, D. R. 1993. *The Quest for Q*. Edinburgh: T. & T. Clark.

Coser, L. 1956. *The Functions of Social Conflict*. London: Routledge & Kegan Paul.

Dunn, J. D. G. 1991. *The Parting of the Ways*. London: SCM Press.

Esler, P. F. 1987. *Community and Gospel in Luke–Acts*. Cambridge: Cambridge University Press.

Hoffmann, P. 1972. *Studien zur Theologie der Logienquelle*. NTAbh 8; Münster: Aschendorff.

Holmberg, B. 1990. *Sociology and the New Testament*. Minneapolis: Fortress Press.

Kloppenborg, J. S. 1987. *The Formation of Q*. Philadelphia: Fortress Press.

Kloppenborg, J. S. 1990. 'Nomos and Ethos in Q'. In J. E. Goehring *et al.* (eds.), *Gospel Origins and Christian Beginnings* (FS for J. M. Robinson). Sonoma: Polebridge Press. 35–48.

Lührmann, D. 1969. *Die Redaktion der Logienquelle*. WMANT 33; Neukirchen-Vluyn: Neukirchener Verlag.

Manson, T. W. 1949. *The Sayings of Jesus*. London: SCM Press.

Meeks, W. A. 1983. *The First Urban Christians*. New Haven & London: Yale University Press.

Meyer, P. D. 1970. 'The Gentile Mission in Q'. *JBL* 89:405–17.

Sweet, J. P. M. 1990. *Revelation*. London: SCM Press.

Tuckett, C. M. 1992. 'The Temptation Narrative in Q'. In F. van Segbroek *et al.* (eds.), *The Four Gospels 1992* (FS F. Neirynck; BETL 100). Leuven: University Press and Peeters. 479–507.

Tuckett, C. M. 1996. *Q and the History of Early Christianity*. Edinburgh: T. & T. Clark.

Uro, R. 1987. *Sheep among the Wolves: A Study of the Mission Instructions of Q*. Helsinki: Suomaleinen Tiedeakatemia.

6

A Vision for the Church: John's Gospel

J. C. O'NEILL

PERHAPS the title for this essay in honour of a prince of teachers who both saw visions and gave his students a vision should be 'Visions for the Church', 'visions' in the plural. My teacher, Ernst Käsemann, used to say that his teacher, Rudolf Bultmann, put the emphasis on the wrong place: not 'And the Word was made flesh and dwelt among us' was the centre of John's theology, but 'And we saw his glory, glory as of the only-begotten of the Father, full of grace and truth'. I do not think that we have to choose between the two parts of John 1.14, but I agree that the second part gives us easier access to what is distinctive in the Fourth Gospel. I shall try to show that the plural *we saw* is a genuine plural that promises that the Gospel will give many visions of many visionaries; that the promise was carried out, for not one author is responsible for the Fourth Gospel and not one visionary saw the visions; that the visions were old visions seen before Jesus was born; that the polemic in the Gospel was not a reflection of the supposed history of a rather distinctive Christian Church in the last sixty years of the first century, but an inner-Jewish polemic against those who did not recognize the Messiah when he came; and that the authors of the various parts that make up the Gospel were preserving the old visions in narratives designed to convert Jews and Samaritans and Gentiles to belief in Jesus as that Messiah.

Let us start with John 1.14b. The simple past tense (aorist) of the verb 'to see' is commonly taken either as a claim by the first eyewitnesses to be giving an account of Jesus as the incarnate Word or as a claim able to be made by any believer, however far distant in time from the event, that in Jesus can be seen the glory of the Son of God, full of grace and truth. Both readings seem forced. The Word that was born as flesh and dwelt among us cannot, by the nature of the circumstances, be seen directly as the only-begotten of the Father; he is not, as incarnate, 'full' of grace and truth. All that the disciples and the crowds were given were glimpses of glory, signs which needed interpretation (John 2.11, 23; 4.54; 6.2; 12.18, 37; 14.9, 26; 20.30). These full attributes of grace and truth can only be seen when the Word has resumed his rightful place at the right hand of the Father. The claim made by the *we* who are speaking is most likely to be a claim to have seen the enthroned Word in his heavenly glory. The speakers are promising to tell what they have seen when they were granted momentary visions of the heavenly glory of the exalted Word.

The first objection this reading of the Fourth Gospel must face is the claim, made in the Gospel itself, that the Beloved Disciple was the author. Both Richard Bauckham and Martin Rese have recently again drawn attention to these claims and argued that the actual author of the Gospel wanted to be taken to be the Beloved Disciple who was uniquely qualified to be the author of the Gospel by his closeness to Jesus, by his steadfastness during the night trial of Jesus, by his courage in being the only disciple to witness the crucifixion – for which faithfulness Jesus made him his brother and committed to his keeping his mother – by his being the first to believe in the resurrection, by his being the first to identify the risen Jesus on the lake shore as Lord. Rese takes John 21.24 as an actual statement by the author of the Gospel that he wrote the Gospel, laughing out of court the modern assumptions that the commentary on Jesus' statement 'If I will that he tarry till I come, what is that to thee?' in John 21.23 implied that the Beloved Disciple was already dead when John 21.24 was written; Bauckham is content to accept John 21.24 as the redactor's guarantee, speaking for the Johannine school, that the Beloved Disciple was the author. Both Bauckham and Rese hold that in John 19.35 the Beloved Disciple spoke of himself in the third person singular (he saw it, he bore witness, he knows that his witness is true) but revealed himself as the author by then addressing the readers as *you*: that you might believe.[1]

Neither Bauckham nor Rese believes that the author really was the Beloved Disciple, but they both argue in different ways that anyone who would understand the Gospel and the real author's intention must start from the fact that the author wanted the readers to think of the Gospel as written by this nameless one whom Jesus loved. Bauckham and Rese are making more pointed and more explicit the assumption by almost every scholar who has written on the Gospel for the last two centuries that the Gospel represents a massive campaign by an individual theologian and the school that he founded to propagate and justify a unique vision of the Christian religion against opponents within Christianity itself. John's Gospel is to be read as ostensibly about Jesus, but really about what the author and redactors took to be false views of Jesus, false views of which they had learnt the force out of the bitter experience of the persecution of their own distinctive community of Christians by those who held those tenets. The besieged Johannine community had in fact, through the

---

[1] Richard Bauckham, 'The Beloved Disciple as Ideal Author', *JSNT* 49 (1993) 21–44; Martin Rese, 'Das Selbstzeugnis des Johannesevangeliums über seinen Verfasser', *ETL* 72 (1996) 75–111.

instrument of the Gospel itself and the related Epistles, triumphed and saved Christianity, so that the Church simply accepted Johannine christology as the proper christology and did not realize what a hard battle it had been. The Fourth Gospel was tamed and domesticated; the true history of the Johannine community's struggles had to wait on the discoveries of modern critical scholarship. For example, Lessing argued that John knew the Hebrew Gospel behind the Gospels of Matthew, Mark and Luke; that this Nazarene Gospel related nothing about Christ that could not have been truly narrated about a mere man; and that the Christianity based on this Gospel would simply have faded away among Jews as a mere Jewish sect had not John taken a hand. He wrote his Gospel and alone gave Christianity its true consistency and ensured that this religion would endure as long as people thought that they needed a divine mediator between themselves and the Deity, 'that is, for ever'.[2] Critics ever since have toyed with similar stories of the history of Christianity, basing that history on what could allegedly be produced by reading between the lines of John's Gospel.

The foundation of the whole structure is precarious. Every part was based on the observation of facts that were perfectly clear to Christians in the second century: that John's Gospel had Jesus say things about himself that revealed his divinity in a way that few, if any, of his sayings in the other Gospels did. The question naturally arose as to by what authority this Gospel reported sayings quite unlike the usual sayings of Jesus in the other Gospels. The Gospel was itself ransacked for evidence, and the idea took hold that the disciple whom Jesus loved, who was lying at his breast during the Last Supper (John 13.23), was the source of these unique words of Jesus. The early tradition of the primitive elders preserved by Clement of Alexandria (Eusebius, *Hist. Eccl.* 6.14.5–7) – that the other Gospels reported the bodily facts about Jesus, but that John, divinely moved by the Spirit, composed a spiritual Gospel – probably even assumed that the reported words of Jesus giving a spiritual insight into his own nature were not actually spoken by Jesus but only discerned by the disciple whom he loved. The story about the authority of the distinctive material in the Gospel arose, therefore, after the Gospel had been in circulation long enough for it to be compared with and contrasted to the other three Gospels.

The lateness of the story is betrayed by the patently additional note embodied in John 20.30–31:

---

[2] G. E. Lessing, 'Neue Hypothese über die Evangelisten als bloss menschliche Geschichtschreiber betrachtet', written in winter 1777–78, incomplete and unpublished by Lessing; K. Lachmann, F. Muncker (eds.), *Gotthold Ephraim Lessings sämtliche Schriften* (Stuttgart: Göschen, 1866) 14:370–91; ET: 'New Hypothesis concerning the Evangelists regarded as merely human Historians', translated by H. Chadwick, *Lessing's Theological Writings* (London: A. & C. Black, 1956), pp. 65–81, §§ 51–56; 62–64.

Many and varied signs did Jesus perform in the presence of the disciples that are not written in this book. But these are written so that you may believe that Jesus was the Messiah, the Son of God, and that by believing you might have life in his name.

This note is fairly late because it was written by a scribe who knew of the existence of other Gospels that reported different miracles of Jesus; the annotator was concerned to defend the relatively small selection of miracles in the Gospel he was transmitting. That Gospel itself seems to have been written without any knowledge of the other collections that were being gathered at various centres: the argument of Percy Gardner-Smith that it is unlikely that anyone would have wanted to differ from his supposed synoptic sources at so many points of no theological significance seems decisive.[3] Compare, for example, the synoptic and Johannine accounts of Jesus' entry into Jerusalem. The details are different for no reason at all.

Here is my crucial move. Our present text of the Gospel of John contains other tiny additions that were made at this late stage when the problem arose as to why John's Gospel was different from the others. The idea that the Beloved Disciple was the author of the Gospel crept into the fabric of the Gospel as we have it, by the activity of scribes and copyists; they exploited stray hints that they believed gave a clue to the true origin of the Gospel.

The starting point was, of course, John 13.23: 'There was reclining on the breast of Jesus [the place of honour] one of his disciples whom he was loving [omitting the second *Jesus* with 69 213].' The imperfect of the verb 'to love' is insufficiently noted, as is the wide range of meanings that the verb possesses; the statement that there was one disciple on whom Jesus had settled his special love would have required an aorist tense, and the verb by no means always applies to settled love. We should translate rather: 'There was reclining on the right of Jesus in the place of honour one of his disciples whom he wanted [on that occasion] to honour' (there is a similar use of the imperfect of verbs in Mark 9.38 where John came to Jesus seeking instructions from the master as to how they were to treat a man casting out demons in Jesus' name although he did not follow Jesus; John said, 'We saw such a man and we wanted to forbid him because he was not wanting to follow us'). A perfectly simple dramatic device has been employed by the narrator in John 13 to preserve the secrecy of the disciples' consternation at Jesus' general statement that one of them would betray him, and to combine the assumption that Jesus in fact did indicate Judas as the betrayer with the fact that the disciples did nothing to try to foil Judas' plans. Peter does not ask Jesus outright, but signals to the disciple who was guest of honour that day, who got another statement of

[3] *Saint John and the Synoptic Gospels* (Cambridge: Cambridge University Press, 1938).

Jesus on the same subject which applied to all those there, including Judas. John 13.26b should be translated, 'So dipping [each] morsel he takes [one] and gives [it] to Judas too.' These enigmatic sayings and actions of Jesus were followed by a command to Judas that none of those reclining there understood. The narrator has skilfully made up a setting for two traditional sayings of Jesus about his betrayer which are also preserved in the synoptic tradition (Matt 26.21; Mark 14.18a; John 13.21; Matt 26.23; Mark 14.20; John 13.26a; cf. Luke 22.21). The device of the unnamed disciple enabled him to sustain the fiction that Jesus did indicate that the betrayer would be Judas, but that although he conveyed this to one of the disciples, that disciple did not understand the sign and did nothing about stopping Judas from going out to betray the Lord.

This starting point gave a handle for the imagination of the early Church to work out a story, from the Gospel itself, about an unnamed disciple who was especially favoured by Jesus who could play the part of the guarantor of the peculiar material to be found only here among the Four Gospels.

There are seven further incidents in the Fourth Gospel that involve an anonymous disciple: the scene involving an unknown second disciple of John the Baptist who perhaps, like Andrew, the other one of the two, might have got his brother and made up the second pair of brothers in Jesus' band of disciples (John 1.35–42; cf. 21.2, the sons of Zebedee); the story of Peter's betrayal when another disciple got Peter admission to the courtyard of the High Priest (John 18.15–16); the incident at the cross where Jesus committed his mother to the care of a disciple (John 19.26); the story of the other disciple who ran with Simon Peter to the tomb and found it empty (John 20.2–10); the story of the disciple in the boat on the Sea of Tiberias after the crucifixion who spotted that the figure on the shore was the Lord (John 21.7); and the story of the disciple who was told to remain until Jesus came (John 21.20–23). A seventh incident, which originally contained no mention of an anonymous disciple, was linked on to that evolving construction to provide the most spectacular example: the incident of the spear thrust (John 19.34–35) in which the presence and witness of the anonymous figure is invoked by a scribe.

Three of the anonymous figures have a foothold in history; two of them are, like the disciple who happened to have the place of honour at the Last Supper, dramatic devices that sprang naturally out of the historical traditions that were available to the compilers; one, the observer of the spear thrust, is the pure production of scribal imagination; and the first, John the Baptist's anonymous second disciple, is the probable origin of the early tradition that the name of the Beloved Disciple was John, son of Zebedee.

I shall comment on each incident except the first, and take them in the Gospel order, except that I shall leave the spear thrust and the comment on authorship at John 21.24 till last.

JOHN 18.15–16

In the Fourth Gospel, Peter has to be let into the courtyard of the High Priest at the behest of another disciple who had no trouble himself in gaining entry. This could be a historical reminiscence or it could have been the artless device of a story-teller who wanted to heighten the drama of the Galilean accent of Peter by suggesting that he would have needed a local even to get him admittance. We have evidence that further scribal embellishment is at work, in the textual evidence. In John 18.15 the words 'but that disciple was known to the High Priest' are omitted by the first hand of Papyrus 66. In John 18.16 the text is very disturbed and one minuscule, 1424, omits 'who was known to the High Priest'. It looks as though all reference to acquaintance with the High Priest is more gilding of the lily. The compiler made up the local disciple, and the scribes concluded that he was known to the High Priest.

JOHN 19.26–27

If indeed Jesus did see his own mother standing beneath the cross with an unnamed disciple into whose keeping he committed her, we could hardly doubt that the disciple was someone of great importance. The trouble is that it would be very unlikely that any women who came in great sorrow to see the crucifixion would be allowed anywhere near the sufferers. Further, it is also unlikely that Mary the mother of Jesus was among the women: Luke knows only a general report that women who had followed him from Galilee were present (Luke 23.49), and that general report has also lodged in Mark at Mark 15.41; Matthew and Mark have another tradition that ascribes names, but not the name of Mary, Jesus' mother (Matt 27.55; Mark 15.40). The names are part of a tendency to give names to the nameless.[4]

When we pay close attention to John 19.26–27 and isolate that as an independent tradition, we find that there is no specific indication that the mother is the mother of Jesus. The article with the word 'mother' can indicate, according to semitic usage, an indefinite mother. There is no

---

[4] See B. M. Metzger's famous article under that title: 'Names for the Nameless in the New Testament: A Study in the Growth of Christian Tradition', *Kyriakon: Festschrift Johannes Quasten* (eds. P. Granfield and J. A. Jungmann; Münster: Aschendorf, 1970) 79–99; repr. *New Testament Studies: Philological, Versional, and Patristic* (Leiden: Brill, 1980) 23–45, including Addenda.

reference to *his* mother in the best manuscripts. The incident could have occurred in Jesus' ministry. Jesus encountered a mother left childless, but in the company of another male disciple. Jesus delivered the mother to this man with the words, 'Woman, behold your son' and to the disciple, 'Behold your mother'. And we read, 'From that hour the disciple received her into his own home.' The words 'whom he loved' are not in L* 346 and were most likely added by a scribe and adopted as the received text, since no scribe would omit 'whom he loved' since the tradition was already firmly established that the Beloved Disciple was the author of the Gospel.

JOHN 20.2–10

The story of the two disciples who ran to the tomb and found it empty was originally, I suspect, a story about two Jerusalemites, not of the inner band of the Twelve – for the Twelve, according to instructions, had gone to Galilee. One of the Jerusalemites may even have been called Simon, and he, of course, became Simon Peter. This becomes clear when we recover the true ending of the story. Our present text reads:

> Then the other disciple who had come first to the tomb entered and saw and believed; for they did not yet know the scripture that it was necessary for him to rise from the dead.

That is pretty obscure. How does the second half of the sentence, 'for they did not yet know the scripture', follow from the first? Fortunately the supplement to the Codex Bezae preserves the original text, and puts a 'not' before the verb 'believed'. The Syriac Sinaiticus preserves another feature of the original and has the two verbs 'saw' and 'believed' in the plural. The original story said:

> Then the other disciple who had come first to the tomb entered and they [both] saw and did not believe; for they did not yet know the scripture that it was necessary for him to rise from the dead.

The two disciples who found the tomb empty and the grave clothes folded could not yet believe the true explanation because they had not been taught to expect the resurrection of the Messiah by the proper interpretation of scripture.

Naturally, the dramatic incident of the physical prowess of the unnamed one, combined with his natural timidity – all features of the original story – prepared the ground for a further imaginative move by a scribe, who had already identified the Simon of the original with Simon Peter: that is, the unknown one would naturally be assumed to believe. Perhaps the 'not' first fell out by mistake; in any case, once gone, who would be eager to restore it?

JOHN 21.7

The disciple in the boat on the Sea of Tiberias who was reported as saying, 'It is the Lord', was originally given the line in order to prompt Peter to dash for shore before the boat could reach it. In the original story, 'It is the Lord' meant simply, 'It is our master' – and 'our' is read by the Codex Bezae and could well be original. Later the words were naturally taken in the sense of a confession of faith in the risen Lord. If 'our' was original, it was omitted. Finally a scribe has taken the device further by identifying that unnamed disciple who made the confession of faith with the Beloved Disciple. Again, these all are grounds for believing that the Beloved Disciple was the product of scribal imagination and not part of the earliest Gospel.

JOHN 21.19b–23

The incident following Jesus' foretelling that Peter would die a martyr's death was once quite distinct. The original beginning was in the command, 'Follow me' (John 21.19b). The distinctness of the incident is clinched if we direct our attention to Peter's strange words in John 21.21: 'Lord, why is this one . . . ?', to give a rather wooden translation of the Greek. We naturally translate it 'Lord, what of this man?' in order to get the words to fit a possible question by Peter about the mode of death of the Beloved Disciple. Originally, however, the question seems to have been about an unnamed disciple whom Peter saw not following them to Jerusalem for Passover. The original force of the rather cryptic Greek was, 'Lord, why does this one [not follow us]?' Jesus had said of him, 'If it is my will that he remain until I come [back again], what is that to you? Follow me'. The saying was, of course, not a straight denial of Jesus' realization that he was likely to die in Jerusalem, simply a sign that all was not settled; as the Gethsemane story showed, the future was open in his mind, and he could have ordered a disciple to stay behind in Galilee and not follow him to Jerusalem. Naturally the saying led to speculations (based on Jesus' prophecy that the End could come within one generation) that this disciple would see both the End and the return of his master before he died.

This reconstruction of the original incident is strengthened when we observe that scribes have added to the original a touch that would destroy its point: they have added the information that the unnamed disciple was following Jesus and Peter as they walked and talked. In John 21.20 the participle, he saw the disciple 'following', is omitted by ℵ first hand, W, the Old Latin ff² and we should accept this shorter reading. Similarly, X and the Syriac Sinaiticus have added the same verb 'following' in John 21.21: Peter seeing this one 'following' says to

Jesus . . . The whole point of the original incident was that the disciple was to stay behind.

JOHN 19.35; 21.24

So far we have found natural explanations as to how the unnamed disciple the narrators sometimes introduced into the story in order to keep the action moving or the unnamed disciple who belonged in the story have become the object of scribal curiosity so that there was a tendency to weave all the incidents involving an unnamed disciple into one story.

The process was completed by the two further examples. These are the spear-thrust tradition at John 19.35 and the last verses of the present Gospel, John 21.24–25.

The spear-thrust tradition was originally part of Matthew's Gospel at 27.49 in א B C L Γ, some manuscripts of the Vulgate and the middle Egyptian Coptic, as well as a part of John's Gospel. Matthew has the incident at a more appropriate time than John, making the thrust of the spear the merciful shortening of Jesus' life. John has tacked the spear-thrust tradition onto another tradition which explains why Jesus' legs were not broken; the juxtaposition is not particularly successful, for if Jesus was dead and did not need his legs breaking neither did he need the thrust of the spear.

Westcott and Hort labelled the longer text of Matt 27.49 a 'non-Western interpolation', that is, it is for them the solitary example in Matthew among cases found otherwise only towards the end of Luke where the Western text was shorter than their Neutral text and so, contrary to their usual general rule of favouring the readings of א and the Codex Vaticanus, to be preferred. Accordingly, the Revised Version and all modern translations follow the Textus Receptus and the Authorized Version here in omitting a passage that has much to be said in its favour. Why? Because they want to preserve the incident as unique to John's Gospel in order to give further verisimilitude to the suggestion that the only disciple who, according to John, could have seen the spear thrust, was the one to whom Jesus committed his mother. No scribe would have added a floating verse about the spear thrust to Matthew's Gospel when the report was already branded as the witness of the Beloved Disciple, the author of John's Gospel.

However, the textual evidence again allows us to see that this idea that the spear thrust is peculiar to the Fourth Evangelist is late. John 19.35 is unlikely to have belonged to an early stratum of the Gospel, since it is omitted by the Old Latin e and one manuscript of the Vulgate. It is hard to imagine that any scribe would have omitted such a note, and easy to see why such a note would be added.

What does John 19.35 mean? Notice that the last clause, 'in order that you might believe', does not follow from its immediate antecedent. It could follow from 'he bore witness' but it can't follow from 'he knows'. It might have followed from λέγει, 'he says' or, better, 'he writes'. The verb λέγω is used of written communication as in Luke 1.63, Gal 5.2, and often. However, as the sentence stands, the last clause must follow 'he knows', and that, as we have seen, is nonsense. Nonnus of Panopolis's paraphrase implied a text that read 'we know' instead of 'he knows', perhaps: καὶ ἐκεῖνος οἴδαμεν ὅτι ἀληθῆ λέγει, ἵνα καὶ ὑμεῖς πιστεύητε, which can be translated, taking ἐκεῖνος as a hanging nominative: 'And as for that one, we know that he writes true things in order that you may believe.' The final clause now follows naturally from 'he writes'. Scribes who did not grasp the construction made the verb 'I know' into a third person singular to agree with its supposed subject ἐκεῖνος and so produced a sentence that has kept scholars busy ever since. The present Majority Text leaves it entirely unclear whether 'that one' refers to the one who had seen, to the author of the Gospel as distinct from the one who had seen, to Christ (as Erasmus, Zahn and Bultmann took it), or to God. If we read 'we know' with Nonnus we see clearly that the whole verse is a marginal note written in the first person plural by the church authorities who vouched for the Gospel. They assumed that the Beloved Disciple was still with Mary, the mother of Jesus, at the foot of the cross, and that he had seen the blood and water flow from the pierced side. They vouched furthermore for the fact that the Beloved Disciple had written not only of the spear thrust but of all the other true things contained in the Gospel. The original Gospel did not actually say that the Beloved Disciple was there and that he saw the blood and water. John 19.35 was, like John 21.24–25, the work of a late commentator.

Scribes who copied Matthew's Gospel did their bit in support of this romantic idea. They knew of the claim in John 19.35 and decided that the tradition of the spear thrust in their manuscripts of Matthew was in the wrong Gospel – since John's Gospel was particularly dependent on a disciple who had stayed to witness the crucifixion, not, like Matthew's Gospel, on a disciple who could only have got the story at second hand, since he had fled. They could regard it as a gloss and exclude it. Better editors saw that the omission was a mistake, but pious tradition was too strong for them; and we moderns have colluded with pious imagination, since no modern translation, to my knowledge, ever includes Matt 27.49b in the text.

The penultimate verse of our present Gospel, John 21.24, is the final example of scribal imagination. It is tacked onto the incident in which Peter asked about the disciple whom Jesus wanted to stay behind and not to follow him to Jerusalem. Our present text of verse 24 is rough:

This is the disciple who bears witness concerning these things – and who wrote these things – and we know that his witness is true.

The present tense of 'bears witness' is strange. It must imply that the *we* who know that the witness of the Beloved Disciple is true are saying that the Beloved Disciple is still alive and that he had completed an account of all the things that he had witnessed. But that present tense is a tell-tale sign that the words 'and wrote these things' are a later addition. It seems that a glossator took the present tense to be a true present. Then he had to wonder how the disciple who was dead, on a plausible reading of the dialogue between Jesus and Peter on the manner of the unnamed disciple's death, could be said to be bearing witness in the present time as though he were still alive. The scribe therefore added a marginal note to the effect that the Beloved Disciple was still bearing witness, though dead, because he had put down his account before he died, and that account is there to be read now. That is how Rese takes it. In fact I suggest that the present tense of the verb 'to bear witness' was properly a historic present. The note originally said:

This is the disciple who used to bear witness concerning these things and we know that his witness is true.

So it came about that a gloss to the more modest original note at John 21.24 finally clinched the tradition that the Beloved Disciple not only left accounts of individual incidents that he saw, like the spear thrust and the conversation between Peter and Jesus, but that he also wrote the Gospel.

The Beloved Disciple is a construct of the curiosity and imagination of the scribes of the Fourth Gospel. They had stories of unnamed disciples to work on, even, as I have argued above, one spectacular story launched by the transposing to the foot of the cross of an incident involving a childless mother and an unnamed disciple, but most of the work was done by scribes who wanted to bolster the authority of the Fourth Gospel. They invoked the unnamed disciple as a particularly privileged observer of critical moments in the story, and two late glosses even suggested that he wrote the whole Gospel. When the Beloved Disciple is left out of the earlier story, we are in a better position to appreciate the true nature of the Fourth Gospel at the early stage when it was used by a church that had no other Gospel – before a comparison with the other Gospels had raised the questions that led, eventually, to the solution that the Beloved Disciple, a mysterious participant at crucial points of the Gospel, was the true author who guaranteed its unique message.

It is very unlikely that one author was responsible for the whole Gospel. Individual scenes, like the story of the Woman at Samaria, or the Man Born Blind, or the Raising of Lazarus are the work of individual authors, but the inept juxtaposition of one incident alongside another betrays the fact that the combination of incidents was later than the composition of incidents. For example, the anointing of Jesus at a meal by Mary is put later than the raising of Lazarus which is introduced by a note that the sister of Lazarus was the woman who anointed Jesus with oil (John 11.2). It is likely that one author would have told things more smoothly and not have needed to add explanatory links like that. Similarly, Bultmann's placing of John 6.1–59 before John 5 really is better, for at the end of chapter 4 Jesus is still in Galilee and could easily be said to go to the other side of the lake there (John 6.1), whereas in chapter 5 he is in Jerusalem and there is no explanation as to how he got back to Galilee for chapter 6. An author would have done better; a collector would have given the blocks of material as they came to him.

No one author, but individual authors produced each block of material. I have already above drawn attention to the artistry of one of the authors in the scene of the Last Supper.[5] The clue to the technique of the school that produced the Gospel is this: one large-scale dramatic scene was woven out of fixed and given traditions – synoptic-type stories, but, above all, traditional sayings. In the Last Supper story, the compiler was bound to weave in two sayings about the betrayer of Jesus, the general saying that one of the disciples was to betray him and the special form of that saying that the betrayer would be one who had shared the same meal as he. The sayings are sacred, but the artistry that sets the sayings in a narrative framework is allowed to be free.

It follows that the peculiar sayings of Jesus in which he openly revealed his true but hidden glory are more likely to have been traditions that the compilers of the stories were bound to weave into their narratives than sayings that they felt free to make up. This conclusion is reinforced by the observation that these revelatory sayings belong to a genre of saying found also in third-person forms and found widely scattered in other Jewish books. The third-person sayings in the Prologue of the Fourth Gospel (John 1.1–18) and in John the Baptist's revelatory discourse in John 3.31–36 are similar in vocabulary, structure and thought to the revelatory sayings of Jesus in the rest of the Gospel. Similar sayings are found in Revelation, such as 'I am the Alpha and the Omega' (Rev 1.8; 21.6; 22.13), in the Syriac Odes of Solomon, such as 'I took courage and became strong and captured the world, and it became mine for the glory of the Most High, and of God my Father' (*Ode of Solomon* 10.4), and in the canonical Proverbs, such as 'By me princes rule, and nobles, even all the judges of the earth; I love them that love me; and those that seek me early shall find me' (Prov 8.16–17).

---

[5] For a more detailed discussion, focusing on the difficult verse, John 13.10, see 'John 13:10 again', *RB* 101 (1994) 67–74.

I argued at the beginning that John 1.14b was a claim by seers to report the words they had heard when caught up into heaven and given the privilege of hearing the heavenly words of the One who sat on the throne with the Father. Sometimes in John's Gospel there are sayings of this revelatory type that betray their heavenly origin and do not quite fit the earthly Jesus into whose mouth they are put, such as when Jesus is made to say, 'I will not leave you orphans; I come to you' (John 14.18). Another example: John 11.25–26 was not written by a theologian in comment on an incident in the life of Jesus and his friends. Martha has just said she believed that Lazarus would be raised on the last day (John 11.24). Jesus is made to add the great 'I am the resurrection and the life' saying. It does not quite fit the situation of Lazarus. Lazarus has not believed; it is his sister who is going to believe (John 11.27). To be sure, the first half of the double promise of John 11.25b, 26a would seem to apply to Lazarus: 'if he dies he will live'. But the second half, John 11.26a, does not obviously apply to Lazarus: 'and everyone who lives and believes in me will never ever die'. The true meaning of the couplet is probably that John 11.25b refers to the general resurrection and John 11.26a to the reward of the righteous who escape the second death (Rev 2.11; 20.6; 21.8). The one who was heard to say, 'I am the resurrection and the life' must origin-ally have been the exalted heavenly Son of God. The whole saying could be attributed to Jesus because the work of the raising of Lazarus he did on earth disclosed the hidden heavenly status that was to be his at his exaltation.

It seems likely to me that the original compilers of the stories and their readers knew that these sayings of the heavenly Christ were not actual sayings of the earthly Jesus. They were sayings conveyed to them by seers who had been given the privilege of access to the heavenly court and heard unspeakable words, which it is not lawful to utter – except to other members of the communities of the sons of the prophets (cf. 2 Cor 12.4).

VISIONS FOR THE CHURCH RATHER THAN A VISION FOR THE CHURCH

The visions were given first to Jewish prophetic communities, who treasured them and, if they believed their Teacher to be the Messiah, applied them to him. These communities then became believers that Jesus was the Messiah, and the sayings were applied to him. Visionary Judaism always believed that God had given to Moses and the prophets secret sayings as well as open sayings (2 Esdras [4 Ezra] 14). John's Gospel is the legacy of these communities. It does not represent a different vision for the Church but preserves visions that arose in the necessary adjunct to the secular Church, the communities of the religious who had never disappeared, from the days of the prophets onwards.[6]

We can read off a picture of a church from the fact that the compilers of the great scenes and dramas that make up John's Gospel incorporated old sayings of the Heavenly Son, and wrote as members of communities privileged to hear and treasure these sayings. It was a church that had special communities of people living lives set aside from normal life, lives devoted to prayer and study. Some of their members were caught up into heaven and heard things that they brought back to their fellow members. These sayings were written down and treasured. Eventually they were worked into stories about the words and deeds of Jesus to make up the scenes that comprise our Fourth Gospel. This Gospel assumed that most disciples of Jesus lived in the world, and it also assumed that Peter and the other disciples were given special responsibility by Jesus to spread the Gospel. What makes John's Gospel unique is not that it represents a different Christianity, born of some obscure struggles between factions in the early Church that labelled each other heretical. What makes John's Gospel unique is that it is made up of long scenes of great artistry, designed to convert Jews and Samaritans and Gentiles to following Jesus as Messiah and Son of God, scenes that revealed the heavenly words of the one who was crucified and raised to his former glory in heaven. The Fourth Gospel embodies visions for the Church, and implies a church that both contained separated communities nurturing seers who were given visions of heaven, and honoured an ordinary hierarchy of apostolic leaders.

BIBLIOGRAPHY

Bauckham, R. 1993. 'The Beloved Disciple as Ideal Author'. *JSNT* 49:21–44.

Brown, Raymond E. 1979. *The Community of the Beloved Disciple*. London: Geoffrey Chapman.

Gardner-Smith, Percy. 1938. *Saint John and the Synoptic Gospels*. Cambridge: Cambridge University Press.

Hengel, M. 1989. *The Johannine Question*. London: SCM Press.

Housman, A. E. 1972. 'The Application of Thought to Textual Criticism'. *Proceedings of the Classical Association*, 18 (1922) 68–69. Reprinted in *A. E. Housman: Selected Prose*. Ed. J. Carter. Cambridge: Cambridge University Press, 1961. 131–50. *The Classical Papers of A. E. Housman*.

[6] J. C. O'Neill, 'The Origins of Monasticism', *The Making of Orthodoxy: Essays in Honour of Henry Chadwick* (ed. R. Williams; Cambridge: Cambridge University Press, 1989) 270–87.

Collected and edited by J. Diggle and F. R. D. Goodyear. Cambridge: Cambridge University Press. 1058–1069.

O'Neill, J. C. 1995. *Who Did Jesus Think He Was?* Leiden: Brill. Chapter 9.

O'Neill, J. C. 1996. '*The Jews* in the Fourth Gospel'. *IBS* 18:58–74.

7

The Johannine Community and the Letters of John

STEPHEN S. SMALLEY

JOHN's[1] vision for the Church in the first century CE can be expressed quite simply. He longed for its unity, based on a commitment to truth and love. That fundamental hope was shaped by the volatile life of his own community. The present essay sets out to test this thesis, by paying particular attention to the corporate and individual dimensions in John's doctrine of the Church. In this way we can both plot the history of the Johannine community, with its need for cohesion, and also draw out the relevance of this teaching for the Church in our own day.

I have always admired John Sweet's vision, and respected his scholarship. This contribution is offered to him now, with great gratitude for his warm friendship and constant encouragement.

I

It will be necessary at the outset to indicate my understanding of the situation which existed in John's church, and also my version of the order in which the documents belonging to the Johannine corpus (which, in my view, includes Revelation) were composed. I assume that there *was* a community around John (see Smalley 1994:17–19), and that its character is clearly reflected in the Apocalypse, as well as in the Johannine Gospel and letters. Moreover, I would argue that Revelation was written first (in 70 CE), followed by the Gospel (*c.* 80 CE) and then the letters (*c.* 90 CE; cf. Smalley 1984:xxxiii; and 1994:40–50). In that case the story of John's community may be traced from Revelation, through the Fourth Gospel to 3 John.

We can begin with the Gospel, and note carefully its balanced view of the person of Christ. The fourth evangelist is insistent that Jesus was in some sense one with God (John 10.30), but also one with humanity (14.28;

[1] 'John' will serve as a description of the author(s) of the NT documents which carry that name, whatever the precise identity of the writer(s). For my own views, see Smalley 1984:xxii; Smalley 1994:37–50, 134–37.

16.28); so that he could be the Saviour of the world (4.42; cf. 1 John 4.14). The reason for this christological equilibrium, to my mind, lay in the problems which were besetting the Johannine church. One group within it probably maintained a balanced understanding of the two natures of Christ. But a second cluster, from a Jewish background, thought of Jesus as no more than a man; while a third party, believers of predominantly Hellenistic origin, were regarding him as little less than God (see Smalley 1978:145–48, and also 246–51 on the question of balance).

These last two sets of believers, with their heterodox tendencies, had presumably begun to 'see' the real identity of Jesus (cf. John 12.45); but neither had comprehended fully the mystery of the Word made flesh. No doubt the result was friction within the community; in which case John's balanced christology, together with his pleas for mutual love (John 15.12, 17) and God-like unity (17.11, 21–23), would be entirely appropriate for this troubled circle.

If we now go back to the Apocalypse, it is possible to see the same problem, in its early stages, being experienced by the Johannine Christians. There the writer is addressing Asian congregations, the members of which were obviously undergoing or anticipating persecution from Rome, but were also beginning to encounter theological difficulties, especially of a christological kind; and these misunderstandings were evidently leading to wrong behaviour on their part.[2] So John the Divine lays before his congregations the crucial importance of maintaining a faith which is christologically balanced (e.g. Rev 3.20–21, where the Amen, who shared in God's creation, stands at the door of the Laodicean church, and promises to the victorious a place in heaven equal to his own). As in other parts of the Apocalypse, Jesus is regarded as being in touch with both earth and heaven (cf. Rev 5.11–14; 13.8;[3] 22.12–13).

The seer of Revelation also addresses a situation in which inadequate or erroneous belief has led to bad conduct, and even immoral behaviour; and such praxis was apparently characteristic of the two incipiently heretical and opposed groups in the Johannine community, ex-Jewish and ex-pagan (cf. Rev 2.14, 20–22; 3.4). As with the fourth evangelist, the writer of Revelation accordingly issues to his adherents, some of whom were on the brink of conflict, a call for love (Rev 2.4–5);[4] and he also

[2] The evidence for this assumption, and for John's answers to the putative problems involved, may be adduced particularly from the letters to the seven churches in Asia (Rev 2–3). But John's teaching throughout the Apocalypse is coherent, and intended for the wider Church as well as for his local congregations (Smalley 1994:132–34).

[3] Translating, 'the Lamb slain from the foundation of the world'; rather than referring the phrase 'from the foundation of the world' to names written in the book of life (so NRSV). See Rev 17.8. Sweet 1990:212 favours the former construction.

[4] The reference to the Ephesians returning to the 'love they had at first' probably includes love for God, even if its primary allusion is to love for others. So also Mounce 1977:88.

produces for them the vision of a completely united church community (7.4–17; 22.1–5, *et al.*), at peace with God and at one with itself. If John's summons to love and unity is less direct in the Apocalypse than it is in the Fourth Gospel, this is possibly because, at the time Revelation was written, the troubles and tensions within the Johannine church were only just beginning to emerge, and the threat of secession had not yet become a reality.

The history of John's community, its life and its problems, is thus reflected at a primitive stage in Revelation, and also, during a hazardous period of development, in the Fourth Gospel. By this time (around 80 CE), the possibility that the community might be torn apart had been brought nearer.

To move from the Gospel to the letters of John is to see that disintegration completed. Obviously, the evangelist's appeal for right belief and mutual respect had fallen on deaf ears. The friction had increased, a polarization of christological beliefs was in progress, and ethical implications had emerged: the 'Jewish' sector was emphasizing law (see 1 John 2.7–8), and 'Hellenistic' believers had become indifferent to right conduct, including love (3.10–11).

In one last attempt to keep his circle together, therefore, John reminds his readers of the basic content of the Christian gospel; he then urges them to receive God's eternal life through his Son, and to follow him by living in the light as loving children of God (1 John 1.1–7; 3.1–3; 4.7, 11, 21; 5.11–13). But the drift had already begun. It is the last hour, and some members (Jewish, as well as pagan, in background) have left the community (1 John 2.18–19). By the time that 2 John was composed, 'many deceivers (of both kinds) have gone out into the world' (v. 7).[5] With 3 John the story comes to an end. Diotrephes, who for doctrinal as well as political reasons fails to acknowledge 'orthodox' authority, is treating 'heresy' as the norm: refusing to welcome true believers into the church, and excommunicating those who wish to do so (vv. 9, 10).

Such an inversion signals the final dissolution of the Johannine community, of which no more is heard. Presumably those from a Greek background became associated with the gnostic systems which flourished in the second century CE, while adherents of Jewish origin would be linked to Ebionitic movements. Finally, those whose loyalty to the apostolic faith was such that they could later be described as 'orthodox' would no doubt have become absorbed in mainstream Christianity (see Smalley 1984:xxx-xxxii; for a less convincing sketch of the situation which developed in John's troubled circle, see von Wahlde 1990, esp. 260–67).

---

[5] The Greek for 'going out' in 2 John 7 is ἐξῆλθον, which may imply that the heretics 'went out' into the world in a missionary spirit, to win over others to their false beliefs. Cf. by contrast John 8.42 (the mission of the Son); 17.18 (that of his followers); but see also 13.30 (of Judas). Note also 3 John 7. See Smalley 1984:328.

II

John's letters, in this reconstruction, represent a point at which the Johannine community seems to disappear; and it has been suggested so far that the history of such a circle can be traced, in reverse, back to the Apocalypse.

But there is a further way of reading the literature in the NT which carries the name of John, from Revelation to 3 John, and that is by exploring the individual and corporate aspects of John's *ecclesiology*. To do so may support the thesis proposed in this article about the nature and development of the Johannine church.

JOHN'S REVELATION

In Revelation, John's teaching about the Church of God is presented in strongly corporate terms. The writer mostly addresses, criticizes and praises the Church as a whole, or portrays his local communities as collective units (so Rev 2–3). Individuals *are* occasionally mentioned, such as John, the prophet-seer, himself (Rev 1.1), and Antipas, the faithful witness (2.13). But the life and (often mixed) character of the Asian churches, at least, is described in predominantly corporate terms.

That collectiveness on earth is reflected in John's vision of the people of God in heaven. Again, some of the supernatural beings appearing there are individual in character: such as God himself (Rev 4.3), the Lamb (5.6), an elder (7.13), and identifiable angels, including Michael (8.3; 12.7).[6] But at the centre of the heavenly dramatic action is the whole company of the new Israel, the members of which worship together and receive salvation through judgement (cf. Rev 21.3–4). Even the heavenly roll-call in Rev 7 is by tribes, rather than by names (vv. 4–8); and the vision in the remainder of that scene is of an innumerable and united multitude of the redeemed (7.9–10).

The corporate nature of the seer's doctrine of the Church in Revelation is highlighted by the biblical concept of the covenant, between God and his people, with which it is associated. Although covenant language is not prominent in the Apocalypse, the idea is consistently present, and associated with God's redemption. Through the redeeming Christ, John shows, it is possible for believers to enter into the *new* covenant, and to be sealed as authentic members of the new Israel (Rev 7.2–3; 10.1–7; cf. 11.19, using '[the ark of God's] covenant'). The climax of this covenantal and corporate relationship between God and humanity, newly and finally

---

[6] The 'woman' who flees into the wilderness at 12.1–6 is probably a representative, rather than an individual, figure (= the community from which the Messiah comes; cf. 12.17). See Beckwith 1919:612–17.

achieved through the Son, is expressed by the final vision in Revelation of 'all things made new,' as God makes his home among mortals in the heavenly Jerusalem (Rev 21.1–5). John's teaching about the Church in the Apocalypse, therefore, is overwhelmingly corporate in its nature.

JOHN'S GOSPEL

It can be argued that the ecclesiology of the Fourth Gospel is less corporate than that of the Apocalypse, and that individuals feature more visibly in its pages. In a famous article, for example, C. F. D. Moule (1962) proposes that the unfolding of the Jesus tradition in St John's Gospel is strongly individualistic in character. Many dominical sayings in the Gospel, he points out, refer to the relationship between individual people and Jesus himself (e.g. John 4.10; 6.44). Four out of seven of the Johannine signs involve particular people;[7] and the most 'representative' of the signs, pointing forward as it does to the resurrection life which Jesus makes universally available, concerns the raising of one man, Lazarus (John 11).

The same individualism seems to characterize John's ecclesiology, in that he uses distinctive ideas to describe the Christ–Christian relationship, such as temple, shepherd and vine, which include an individual dimension: the stones of the temple, the sheep of the flock and the branches of the vine. However, two points can be made in response to this general proposal. First, John's teaching about the Church in his Gospel can in no sense be described as purely individualistic. The images of temple, shepherd and vine, for example, are manifestly collective in their primary reference. Furthermore, the Johannine theme of corporate belonging – to Christ, and to other Christians – complements that of individual relationship.

This idea of collectively belonging becomes focused in the Twelve, who emerge under that title only three times in the Gospel (John 6.67, 70; 20.24), but are present throughout as the nucleus of a new community. The Twelve are called to follow Jesus individually; yet they believe in him together (John 1.43; 17.6, et al.). The disciples of Jesus form a group, not simply a collection of individuals. After the resurrection, moreover, they share corporately the indwelling and activity of the Spirit-Paraclete (John 10.16; 14.16–17; 20.22–23). The Twelve become part of a Church, not a sect.[8]

Second, much recent research and writing on the Fourth Gospel, especially that which adopts a literary and narrative approach to the text,

---

[7] John 4 (the official's son); 5 (the sick man); 9 (the blind man); 11 (Lazarus).
[8] Against E. Käsemann, *The Testament of Jesus: According to John 17* (Philadelphia: Fortress Press and London: SCM Press, 1968) 56–73, esp. 73.

has discovered (or, perhaps, rediscovered) the possibility that many apparently individual characters in John are in fact *representative*.

For example, Brown (1979:192–98) sees Mary, the mother of Jesus, and to some extent the beloved disciple, as symbolic models of discipleship and as representative members of Christ's true family. Brodie (1993:169–70) interprets Nathanael as a representative of Israel alienated from God (under the fig tree), and coming to him by believing in Jesus (John 1.43–51).[9] Brodie (216–17) further regards the Woman of Samaria as an individual person who occupies a role which is representative both of Samaria itself, and of the whole body of believers. A final sample of this hermeneutical method may be found in the work of Koester (1995: 32–73), who understands a whole range of characters in John's Gospel as symbolic and representative figures: from Jesus himself, the representative of God and of his disciples (embodying the new temple, and thus the Christian Church) to Nicodemus, who speaks for all humanity in darkness as in light; to Martha, the paradigm of faith.

None of this implies a denial that these individuals were historical; the interpretative process rather affirms in addition that their personalities are representative, and therefore collective. John's theology of the Church, we may conclude, is balanced between the one and the many; but its dominant character is corporate.[10]

So far we have seen that in the Revelation, as in John's Gospel, teaching about the Church is presented in predominantly corporate terms. (See Rensberger 1989, esp. 15–36.) Even if the seer and evangelist write with a specific and needy congregation in mind, they are sensitive to the existence, composition and activity of the wider Christian assembly. We may now return to John's letters, to see what happens to his ecclesiology in the end.

JOHN'S LETTERS

The Johannine epistles manifest a strong sense of community; but this is not the same, I suggest, as saying that their author is preoccupied with the idea of the Church as a whole. It is the local community which is exclusively in view in the letters. Even when the term ἐκκλησία ('church') itself is used (at 3 John 6, 9, 10), the reference is to John's own circle. This claim is not contradicted, I think, by the fact that the appearance of the word 'church' in Revelation (frequently in Rev 2–3, and at 22.16) is

---

[9] As Brodie himself admits, however, such suggestions about the representative character of Nathanael are not new. See Brodie 1993:168–69.

[10] Smith (1995:152–55) underscores the balance, while emphasizing the essentially collective nature of John's ecclesiology. He also reminds us that, as with the epistles (with the possible exception of the reference to 'elder' at 2 John 1 and 3 John 1), the *organization* of the Johannine churches is scarcely in view.

similarly local in reference; or by the discovery that the term is absent altogether from John's Gospel. For in both documents, as we have seen, a strongly corporate *idea* of the Church is present.

It could be argued from the letters that the Johannine understanding of the community itself is individualistic. John does not use the Pauline, corporate images of 'the body' or 'Israel' to describe his churches, for example; and on the other hand his favourite metaphor of divine regeneration, to describe the believer's reception of new life, is in the first place manifestly individual in character (1 John 3.9; 5.18; cf. John 3.3). However, as Lieu (1991:43, 47) points out, such an experience as 'abiding' or 'remaining' in the Godhead is both individual (1 John 3.6; 4.15–16) and communal (4.13a, which speaks of a *mutual* indwelling, 'we in God, and he in the community of Christ's followers'). Similarly, the Spirit is experienced within the community, where the confession that Jesus is God's Son is both made and tested (4.13b–16).

Nevertheless, focus is given to John's perception of the nature of his community by his description of the practice of love within it. Those within the circle who have been born of God are exhorted urgently to love their fellow-Christians (1 John 3.11–15), and to do so in action and with genuineness (vv. 16–18). I doubt if John is being rigidly exclusive in that passage, or anywhere else in his letters (cf. 2 John 5–6; 3 John 6). Those beyond the immediate Johannine congregations are naturally included in the love command. But the writer's first concern, in a situation of conflict and potential fragmentation, is for the cohesion of his own group (Smalley 1984:181; against Bultmann 1973:53–54).

This exegesis is supported by the assertion at 1 John 3.14 that love of 'the brotherhood' is a mark of having passed from death to life. The phrase, loving 'the brotherhood' (τοὺς ἀδελφούς, lit. 'the brothers [and sisters]'), may carry technical overtones, suggesting the intimacy of a group committed to the spiritual outlook of its leader. In any case, it also implies separation and exclusivism. Shocked by the heretical tendencies and schism within the community, and pressured by the hostile world outside, John's adherents are encouraged to love *each other*. Such a response arises easily from the dualism in John's letters, and from his attitude to the world. The community is a place where love is exercised (1 John 4.16–17, 20); the world (in the sense of those who are worldly: 2.15–17), by contrast, is a source of hatred (3.13; cf. Lieu 1991:68–71).

If sectarian vibrations belong to John's attitude, these are prompted by a situation in which an 'orthodox' community is being described, over against the 'heretics' and the world. He is not distinguishing between the belief and life of his church, and mainstream Christianity as such. John shared the basic kerygma to which, with all the NT writers, he owed allegiance, even if his presentation of the gospel was distinctive (Smalley 1984:189). Nevertheless, his primary task was to hold together a disintegrating community; and it is this, not the Church at large, which informs the fundamental stance of his ecclesiology.

Moreover, this community orientation narrows still further. In 2 and 3 John, where the history of the group comes to an end, and the fragmentation is complete (as we saw above), we are left not with a circle but with individuals: the elder himself (2 John 1; 3 John 1), Gaius and Demetrius (3 John 1, 12), the representatives of orthodoxy; and Diotrephes, the symbol of misused authority and heretical unbelief (3 John 9–10). The representatives of light and darkness remain in unhappy division and stark conflict; even if, given the advent of the word of life (1 John 1.1), we know that the darkness is already fading, and that the real light will continue to shine (2.8).

III

From our study, we may draw three conclusions: one in relation to the Johannine literature as a whole, and two which are relevant to the life of the contemporary Church.

First, we have noticed that John's ecclesiology narrows in perspective as we move from the Apocalypse to the letters. In Revelation, the depiction of the Church is strongly collective. That corporate understanding of God's people prevails in the Fourth Gospel, where the individual personalities belonging to the Jesus narrative are often representative in their appearance. When the epistles were written, and the coherence of the Johannine circle was under serious threat, the survival of the elder's local congregations became uppermost in the writer's mind; and his ecclesiology, while still collective in character, was therefore turned in the specific direction of the Johannine community, rather than that of the Church in general.

As a result, my proposal is that the ecclesiology of the Johannine literature, from its origins in the Apocalypse to its development in the letters, was heavily influenced by the situation from which these documents came to birth. The ideal, corporate conception of the Church of Christ gave way to a 'congregational' understanding only when the plea for unity and love needed to be intensified. At the same time, the study of John's thinking about the Church in his corpus allows us to plot the trajectory of this community's history.

Second, the life and traumas of the Johannine community, particularly evident in 3 John, bid us recognize the constant danger of individualism within the Church. Where isolationist and sectarian movements take over, spearheaded by a leadership which is misled, or where the wrong kind of church planting takes place, problems inevitably result.

In this context, Diotrephes provides us with a solemn warning (see 3 John 9–10). The patent hostility in John's community, between

Diotrephes and the presbyter, may have arisen because of a disagreement over either polity or doctrine. Equally, it could have resulted from a combination of the two. (See further, Smalley 1984:353–58.) Diotrephes was clearly a powerful figure, who had assumed a position of leadership in the congregation because of an egocentric desire for power (he loved 'to put himself first', 3 John 9); and he confused this with zeal for the gospel. In the process, he deviated from the truth, as well as from Christian love; and his behaviour precipitated the dissolution of the Johannine community. The elder was anxious that the influence of Diotrephes should spread no further (v. 11a; cf. 2 John 10–11). But the damage had already been done; and what began as political strife, ended in doctrinal division.

The lessons for today are obvious. The exercise of all authority in the Church, and monarchical claims to leadership, need constantly to be checked against the traditions and experience of the body corporate. Presentations of the Christian message, and the interpretation of Scripture, need similarly to be tested, especially when these appear in an extreme form (cf. 1 John 4.1–3). Diotrephes caused disruption and finally disintegration in the life of the Johannine community, because he provided a focus whereby heterodox beliefs and sectarian tendencies could find their ultimate expression. John's vision, from which we ourselves can learn, was quite different. It was of a community of believers living and walking together, as part of the Church of God, in truth and love (2 John 4–6; 3 John 3–6).

Third, and consequently, the turbulent life and progress of the Johannine circle is a standing reminder of the need in our own day, as in the first century CE, to espouse a faith which is adequate, and in particular to maintain an estimate of Christ's person which is balanced. Whenever in the history of Christianity the christological symmetry of the Church's teaching has been upset, doctrinal and practical errors have been the result (Smalley 1994:174).

Accordingly, if John's early vision of a united Church, committed to a true faith and moral praxis, is to become a reality, we must take seriously his plea for a coherent Christology: Jesus, as the Word made flesh (John 1.14), is both one with the Father and one with us. That equilibrium needs to be maintained, also, if the Christian Church in the twenty-first century is to have a worthwhile contribution to make to the cause of world mission, or to the progress of ecumenism.

The Johannine literature, and the stormy history of John's community to which it bears testimony, affirms the need for ecumenical endeavour, and encourages its development. The lack of unity and love, in faith and praxis, which featured so largely in the Johannine congregations, should stir us now to trust one another in the body of Christ to a greater extent than ever: according to the Benedictine, as well as the biblical, model of mutual obedience and respect. It should also drive us to remove a crucial stumbling-block, standing in the way of complete unity, and to recognize joyfully one another's ministries within the Church of God.

John's vision for the Church of his time, and indeed of all time, was for its unity. He saw this as inseparable from an obedience to Christian truth, and from an active love for others: within his community and beyond. Should that vision remain a dream?

BIBLIOGRAPHY

Beckwith, I. T. 1919. *The Apocalypse of John: Studies in Introduction*. New York: Macmillan. Reprint: Grand Rapids: Baker Book House (1967).

Brodie, T. L. 1993. *The Gospel According to John: A Literary and Theological Commentary*. New York and Oxford: Oxford University Press.

Brown, R. E. 1979. *The Community of the Beloved Disciple: The Life, Loves and Hates of an Individual Church in New Testament Times*. New York: Ramsey/Toronto: Paulist Press/London: Geoffrey Chapman.

Bultmann, R. 1973. *The Johannine Epistles: A Commentary*. Hermeneia (ed.) R. W. Funk. Philadelphia: Fortress Press.

Koester, C. R. 1995. *Symbolism in the Fourth Gospel: Meaning, Mystery, Community*. Minneapolis: Fortress Press.

Lieu, J. M. 1991. *The Theology of the Johannine Epistles*. New Testament Theology. Cambridge and New York: Cambridge University Press.

Moule, C. F. D. 1962. 'The Individualism of the Fourth Gospel', *NovT* 5:171–90.

Mounce, R. H. 1977. *The Book of Revelation*. NICNT. Grand Rapids: Eerdmans.

Rensberger, D. 1988. *Overcoming the World: Politics and Community in the Gospel of John*. Philadelphia: Westminster Press/London: SPCK (1989).

Smalley, S. S. 1978. *John: Evangelist and Interpreter*. Exeter: Paternoster Press. 2nd edn. forthcoming.

Smalley, S. S. 1984. *1, 2, 3 John*. WBC 51. Waco: Word Books/Milton Keynes: Word UK (1991).

Smalley, S. S. 1994. *Thunder and Love: John's Revelation and John's Community*. Milton Keynes: Nelson Word/Waco: Word Publishing (1995).

Smith, D. M. 1995. *The Theology of the Gospel of John*. New Testament Theology. Cambridge and New York: Cambridge University Press.

Sweet, J. P. M. 1990. *Revelation*. 2nd edn. TPINTC. Philadelphia: Trinity Press International/London: SCM Press.

von Wahlde, U. C. 1990. *The Johannine Commandments: 1 John and the Struggle for the Johannine Tradition*. New York: Paulist Press.

8

The Pauline Communities

ANDREW CHESTER

PAUL's vision for the communities that he writes to can be summed up quite succinctly. He sees them as being a new creation in Christ, filled with the Spirit, possessing gifts of the Spirit and overflowing with the fruit of the Spirit, controlled above all by love; they are communities that should be pure and holy, mutually supportive and interdependent, completely united, transcending the oppositions and tensions between different groups within the community, and with every kind of barrier that would divide them in normal society now broken down.

This brief summary may seem over-idealized; it may indeed seem somewhat grandiose and abstract, especially in the light of the occasional letters that Paul wrote to quite different communities, often on very specific and mundane issues. Certainly it is easy to beg questions by extrapolating these themes in this way. At the very least, they need to be related to the particular perspectives of Paul's letters. It also has to be said that theory and practice in any case often fail to coincide, and the way that a particular community lives can be very far removed from Paul's vision of what it should be. Paul himself is made painfully aware of this. Indeed, it is probably true to say that we have a semblance of Paul's vision for his communities, to a large extent, because of the problems that have arisen in a number of those communities and that Paul feels the need to counter. That is, Paul finds himself faced with what he considers false practice, or even a complete negation of his ideal of the Christian community, and hence has to urge those in these communities that he has founded to become what they know they should be, and not remain as they are. But because there are clearly such sharp differences between Paul and some of his communities on this question, he finds himself having to spell out very clearly (at least in general terms) his own understanding of the true nature of the community, so that there can be no cause (or excuse) for confusion.

Hence what I undertake here is (1) to set out more fully the various aspects of Paul's vision that I have outlined above; (2) to consider the issues and tensions that arise from this vision, both in practice, in relation to the harsh realities of the communities, and in theory, in relation to Paul's own ideal and fundamental conception of the community; and (3) to examine the extent to which Paul has a vision which is coherent and sustainable, and to assess its value and validity, both in itself and as far as Christian theology, life and practice are concerned.

1. PAUL'S VISION OF THE CHRISTIAN COMMUNITIES

1.1 A New Creation in Christ

For Paul, this is a collective as well as an individual theme. The idea of being 'in Christ' is fundamental to Paul's whole understanding of the distinctively new Christian existence and identity. It is obviously closely related to Paul's idea of the body, and of corporate belonging. That is, being in Christ represents the specific sphere of belonging for the new community, and its distinctive point of reference.

Paul's usage of 'new creation' (καινὴ κτίσις) does look to be individual in reference (Gal 6.15; 2 Cor 5.17), but even in these two passages there is clearly a collective, communal dimension implied. Thus, in Gal 6.15 Paul is concerned with the distinctive identity of the Christian community as a whole, warning them that circumcision is completely irrelevant for their status as the chosen people or true Israel. At 2 Cor 5.17, Paul speaks in the singular ('Therefore if anyone is in Christ, he is a new creation; the old has passed away, behold the new has come'), but his main concern is the contrast between the old and the new age. It is belonging to this new age, and being reconciled to God, which now characterizes not only the individual but the Christian community as a whole.

More widely as well, this is what Paul implies for the whole Christian community. That is, the community is God's new creation, which is characterized by the new life given at baptism and incorporation into Christ. Baptism for Paul represents specifically entering into the new community and new sphere of existence (as 1 Cor 12.12–13; Gal 3.27–28 and the first person plural usage in Rom 6.3–10 make clear), and it involves a radical rejection of the old world. Hence the Christian community, on Paul's understanding of it, implies belonging to an altogether different world, where accepted standards and practices are no longer taken for granted. With baptism comes receiving of the Spirit and renewal of the whole person. Hence just as baptism for the individual denotes becoming a new person, so for the community it implies the anticipation of a restored world and humanity (Gal 3.27–28; cf. Rom 6.3–10; 8.22–23) .

1.2 A Spirit-Filled Community

Paul's understanding of his communities as filled with the Spirit is central to his vision of the essential nature of the Christian community. Just as the individual receives the Spirit at baptism, so also the community is correspondingly characterized by possession of the Spirit. Paul simply assumes this to be the case (e.g. Gal 3.27), and sees it as a wholly positive phenomenon (e.g. 1 Thess 4.8; 5.19; 2 Thess 2.13), a sign and anticipation of the new age that has already begun.

1.2.1 Spiritual Gifts

For Paul, the community should exhibit gifts of the Spirit in abundance, as a clear correlative of possessing the Spirit. Paul's vision is in no sense narrow here: there is a wide variety of gifts, and all are potentially valuable. Certainly Paul comes close to implying that some gifts are more important and worth having than others, but this is mainly a contingent argument in the particular circumstances of the Corinthian church (1 Cor 12.4–12, 28–31); it should not be taken as detracting from his positive emphasis on the value and sheer variety of these gifts, as far as his overall vision is concerned. Nor does it override Paul's insistence on the importance of each individual to the whole community, and the role that each can play within it. Paul's vision of the community sees spiritual gifts being used to the full, both for the mutual benefit of the community internally and also for the propagating of the Gospel and allowing the community to extend itself and its message to the world around.

1.2.2 Fruit of the Spirit

It is the fruit of the Spirit which, in an important sense, epitomizes Paul's vision of what the Christian community and its true character should be. This vision is only spelt out fully in one place, at Gal 5.21ff, but clearly the theme itself runs through what Paul says throughout. This is so, for instance, at Phil 2.1–11, which culminates in the portrayal of Christ as an example. Here love and, above all, joy are the dominant motifs (along with, implicitly, faith), but there are several other attributes that Paul also includes here in relation to what he calls 'participation in the Spirit'. So also, following the portrayal of gifts of the Spirit at Rom 12.6–8, Paul proceeds to urge his readers to exemplify what effectively correspond to fruits of the Spirit, in 12.9–13 (or perhaps, indeed, the whole of 12.9–21). There is, of course, a very strong ethical element in these passages, and what Paul presents as the 'fruit of the Spirit' can be understood as forming the basis of his ethics, as at Gal 5–6. This is what it means to 'walk by the Spirit'. Paul alludes, briefly but powerfully, to the distinctive qualities of this life that is filled with the Spirit in Rom 14.17; 15.13, and more fully and generally in 1 Cor 12–14.

1.3 Controlled by Love

Love is the supreme gift of the Spirit in Paul's vision of what the Christian community should be like. This is clear from both Gal 5.22–26, where it is set at the head of the list, and also 1 Cor 13 (more precisely, 12.31–14.1), where love is given the central place and controlling function in Paul's long discussion of the gifts of the Spirit in 12–14. In 1 Cor 13, love is not specifically designated as a 'fruit' of the Spirit, and it does indeed come as the climax of Paul's argument, where he speaks of seeking the 'higher gifts'. This shows clearly that it would be wrong to separate fruit and gifts sharply from each other in Paul's understanding; nevertheless, there is an important sense in which love transcends all other gifts in Paul's vision of the Christian community (1 Cor 13.13).

Indeed, the fruit of the Spirit can probably be set higher than gifts in Paul's vision, since it provides the controlling theme and framework for how the community should live and for its essential character. Certainly in its self-giving nature here, love can be seen to represent what Paul envisages as the ideal for his communities to aim for. Love is portrayed in a more profound way than any particular action, so that Paul is even able to claim that no activity whatever is good unless it is controlled by love (1 Cor 13). Nor is it just in one or two isolated passages that Paul shows love to be central to his vision of what the community should become. Thus, for example, in Rom 12.9–13, a passage touched on already (1.2.2), love expresses Paul's understanding of the way the whole Christian community and its way of life can be transformed (Rom 12.1–2 is also comparable in this respect). Here again, in Rom 12, love has the controlling place and is bound up with experience of the Spirit. In Rom 13.8–10, indeed, Paul sets love as the fulfilment of the law and as that which is fundamentally important for all relationships and conduct within the community.

Nor is this merely a vague, abstract concept. In Rom 12.14–21, certainly, Paul does not specifically cite Jesus' command to love one's enemies, and at 13.8–10 it is simply love of neighbour that is referred to. The main thrust of Paul's admonition in Rom 12–13, however, is of love being not just the guiding principle for the community, but also being given practical expression throughout. This theme has already been anticipated in Gal 5.13–14, where again love is set as the fulfilment of the law, and is given concrete expression in serving others within the community. This provides the specific perspective for what is said about gifts of the Spirit. Again, at 1 Cor 8.1 (with which Eph 4.1 may be compared), it is for Paul love that builds up the community; this is precisely what he argues that gifts of the Spirit should be used for, in 12–14. So also Paul demands concrete expression of love at 2 Cor 8.7, 24, and clearly sees it as basic and essential to his vision of what the community should be. It is the same urgent and practical understanding of his vision, governed by love, that

Paul sets out at 1 Thess 3.12; 4.9–12 (cf. 1.3; 2 Thess 1.3). So then, it is love for each other within the community (and beyond) that Paul calls his communities to aspire to.

1.4 A Pure and Holy Community

Fundamental to Paul's vision of the Christian community is the conviction that it should be pure and holy, a shining light in complete contrast to the darkness of the world around. Certainly Paul is under no illusions that at least some of his communities are very far from being holy, but this in no way causes him to compromise the ideal he holds. There is no indication that the community can or should be seen as a 'mixed community' of good and bad (as it appears to be in Matthew 13; but cf. 18.17!), that will only be sorted out at the final judgement. Paul refers to all his communities as 'holy ones' (ἅγιοι), and despite all the imperfections that he recognizes, he clearly does not intend this as a merely formal or empty usage. This is so even in the case of the Corinthian community, where he is appalled to find instances of gross immorality, and invokes the final age and judgement as a necessary corrective to their over-confident, libertarian attitude and way of life. Here, above all and deliberately, he stresses their true calling and character as 'holy ones'. For Paul, the solution to the problem of corrupt conduct is not to tolerate it until the final judgement, but to expel the offender, so that the community can be much more pure and holy, as it should be.

On the other hand, Paul's vision of the community does not envisage it as isolated from the world around. In the case of the Qumran community, where again there is strong emphasis on purity and holiness, it may have been much easier to approximate to the ideal, since it existed as a conclave for the most part cut off from society. The vision that Paul has is quite remarkable, since the communities exist in the urban world of the Roman Empire in the first century CE, and their members are caught up in the everyday life of their respective cities. In 1 Cor 5.9–10, Paul makes it absolutely clear that the community cannot expect to live in splendid isolation from the corrupt and immoral society around; thus the isolated existence of a community such as Qumran is specifically ruled out. Instead, it is those who live in an immoral way who must be refused admission to the community, or ejected if they already belong. 2 Cor 6.14–18; 7.1 appears to present a different vision to that of 1 Cor 5.9–10, and has sometimes been understood as not authentically Pauline, but in fact the main emphasis here is completely consistent with what Paul says otherwise. That is, there should be an absolute difference between the community (on an individual level and also corporately) and the world around, and as a Christian community it should show itself to be completely pure and holy. In the rhetorical stress that he places on this point, Paul does indeed come close to saying that believers should have nothing at all to do with unbelievers. The reality he recognizes, however, is clear from 1 Corinthians: the community does not exist as a compact, physically separate entity, day in, day out, and there is no way in which individual members could avoid all contact with individuals and society around, even if Paul wanted them to. His vision instead is that they should shine in the darkness, and show clearly at all times the absolute difference between themselves and secular society.

Purity for Paul means above all sexual purity. That is especially clear from 1 Cor 5–6 and 1 Thess 4.3–8, but it is in fact a theme that pervades his writings and his understanding of the community. Paul takes a very stringent position, close in many respects to Jewish halakhic requirements. His vision of the community is for it to be free of immoral conduct of any kind. He simply cannot understand how the Corinthian community could allow or condone grossly improper behaviour in the way that it has. There is an enormous divide between Paul and (some of) the Corinthian community on this point; for the Corinthians it is a matter of no great consequence, but for Paul it is a complete negation of what it means to be a Christian community. Yet purity and holiness, for Paul's understanding of the community, are not simply defined in relation to sexual conduct or impropriety. One main thrust of Paul's complex argument in 1 Cor 8–10, on the issue of food sacrificed to idols, is concerned with the community keeping itself pure and undefiled, in relation to idolatry: that is, the worship (either actual or as perceived to be happening) of other 'gods'. Above all for Paul, however, the community as pure and holy means that it must be completely different to the world around, and set in contrast to it, while at the same time remaining firmly set within it. Thus in Rom 6–7, Paul draws an extended and absolute contrast between two spheres of existence: the one is characterized by sin, law and death (including giving in to sinful passion), while the other is characterized by faith, grace and life, and also by sanctification and holiness. This is precisely Paul's point in 1 Cor 8–10 (as also in 1 Thess 4 and Phil 2.2; 3.8–16): that is, the community should have left behind completely the old age, its previous existence and the world around. Now it should be living in a pure and perfect manner, marked out as the holy community that God has called it collectively to be, just as he has called the members individually.

1.5 A United Community, Free from Conflict

Paul's vision is that the community should be characterized by perfect unity and the breaking down of all potential barriers that exist between its members. This means, then, that it should also be characterized by complete equality amongst its members, and the absence of any kind of conflict on any level. The fundamental equality that Paul insists on, despite all the inequalities and differences there seem to be on the surface, derives from the common point of entry into the community that all its members share, their common initiation through baptism and their common experience of receiving the Spirit. All of this is undergirded by the fact that for Paul the Christian community can only be made up of those whom God has called to be members of it. They belong on equal terms, and their belonging is a gift of God's grace; so for Paul, no one in the community has any basis for boasting or claimed superiority. This is absolutely basic for Paul, not as any kind of abstract theology, but as a vital part of what the community is, or should at least become. The essence of this vision is expressed in its most succinct and powerful form in Gal 3.27–28, where the central themes are baptism, the experience of the Spirit, and the breaking down of all barriers. There is a similar formula at 1 Cor 12.13 and, within the Pauline tradition, at Col 3.11.

Paul's vision for his communities is not, however, limited to a few isolated formulae. So, for example, throughout Galatians he argues consistently for a fundamental equality and breaking down of barriers between Jew and Gentile, since observance of Torah can in no sense be a condition of membership. In Romans as well, although Paul's argument is both less specific and more nuanced than in Galatians, he still insists on the essentially equal standing of Jew and Gentile within the community. The way in which Paul envisages the community as a whole transcending all opposition and tensions within it also becomes clear from what he says about the strong and the weak both in 1 Corinthians (8–11.1) and Romans (14–15). His vision, then, is of a community where everyone will be concerned with the interests of others, not themselves. The fundamental equality in the Spirit, at their entry into the community, is reinforced by the fact that there will be no assertion of superiority, or acting in ways that may make other members feel inferior. Paul makes a similar point with his image of the body: there are differences between the members, but there should be no sense of superiority on the part of any.

For Paul, the fundamental problem with divisions and factions within the community (as in 1 Cor 1–4; cf. 11.17–34; Rom 12.3; Phil 2.1–5) lies not in the practical issues that arise but in the fact that these represent a denial of the true nature of the community. So Paul expresses his ideal of the community as a 'seamless whole', bound together in perfect unity, not only through the emphasis on the experience of the Spirit and baptism, but also through language drawn from family relationships (as ἀδελφοί, φιλαδελφία). This unity and harmony should, as Paul sees it, also be expressed in the common meetings and meals that the community shares together. It is again this kind of unity and solidarity that Paul sees as of central importance in binding the community together in the face of threats of suffering and persecution (as e.g. Phil 1.27–30; cf. 1.3–7). It could even be claimed that Paul's approach to the collection that he is organizing for the poor in Jerusalem points to a unity that transcends particular communities and binds them all together on a different level. Certainly Paul (apart from what is found in the Pauline tradition in Colossians and Ephesians) does not for the most part think of the 'Church' as a general or universal entity: he uses ἐκκλησία primarily of the particular community; but in his conception of the collection (as also e.g. in Rom 16.23; 1 Cor 10.23; 15.9; Phil 3.6), he comes close to going further. At any rate, his vision of each particular community is as a paradigmatic perfect unity. So he wants the Roman community, which he has not founded and which exists in different small groups, to be a perfect harmony of Jews and Gentiles, to show that what Paul's mission is concerned to bring about is indeed God's true community of the final age.

1.6 A Mutually Supportive Community

There are several further passages where Paul uses the metaphor of building up (or edifying) the community, and this metaphor is often bound up as well with emphasis on unity and mutual harmony. The thrust of what he says here is closely related not only to the theme of unity, but also to that of the community being controlled by love. Thus, Paul's vision of the community is one in which the members constantly support one another. This is summed up succinctly in 1 Thess 5.11: 'So encourage one another and build each other up, just as you are doing.' Paul's desire to see the community characterized by actions that 'build up' is the controlling theme of 1 Cor 14, as indeed it is implicitly for the whole of 12–14. In this section of 1 Corinthians the point is at least partly that spiritual gifts, above all tongues, should be used in ways that promote the community positively as far as outsiders are concerned, but Paul also clearly wants the life and gifts of individual members of the community to be used for the benefit of all within the community as well. Again, 1 Thess 5.12–21 (directly following Paul's exhortation to 'building up') is very close to this, implicitly recognizing the limitations and problems of at least some gifts of the Spirit (in this case prophecy: vv. 20–21), but wanting all these gifts to be used in the service of the community (so 5.14; 12–13, for example, are also relevant here). Paul also uses the idea of 'building up' or edifying in Rom 15.1–2; here there is a powerful combination of a call to mutual support and concern and a summons to live in harmonious unity. The building up of the community and the breaking down of barriers and tensions within it are separate but closely related themes. It is this mutual concern and interdependence, clearly evident in Paul's developed understanding of the body of Christ and his related argument, that is strikingly present in Phil 2.1–5 as well (thus v. 4: 'Let each of you look not only to his own interests, but also to the interests of others'). As I have noted above, Paul here uses the example of Christ, in a remarkable way, as a paradigm for the way of life of the community as a whole.

Before turning to issues arising, it is worth emphasizing that Paul's vision of the Christian community is not merely abstract. So, for example, in his greetings at the start and especially the end of his letters, he gives vivid expression to the understanding of a community that is mutually supportive, controlled by love and showing the Spirit in action. Here we find (especially, for instance, in Rom 16), again and again, practical and concrete expression of this vision, as it relates to particular communities and specific individuals within them.

2. ISSUES ARISING

2.1 Equality and Unity

I have stressed that it is central to Paul's vision that the Christian community should be characterized by unity, equality and the breaking down of all barriers between its members. The best statement of this is at Gal 3.27–28. Here, however, the question has to be raised of whether this vision of the community is original to Paul, and whether he holds this position consistently in all his writings. It is commonly held that Gal 3.27–28 represents an early baptismal formula, which is simply taken over by Paul but not actually composed by him. Even if this point is conceded, of course, it can still be held that Paul would not take over a position, and use it emphatically, unless he were in complete agreement with it. In this case, then, it could still be seen as an integral part of Paul's vision. There is a further complication, however; Paul uses a very similar formula at 1 Cor 12.13, but here the reference to male and female is completely lacking. In the light of what Paul says otherwise in 1 Corinthians about women in the community, especially at 11.2–16 and 14.33–35, it is quite plausible that he has deliberately omitted any mention of the removal of distinctions between men and women at their initiation into the community through baptism and the receiving of the Spirit.

There can be no certainty on this point, because at Col 3.11, for example (within the Pauline corpus and related to the same basic baptismal tradition), in a longer list, there is again nothing of male or female; in Colossians this is not a particular issue, and it may then be that 'male and female' was a far from fixed part of the baptismal formula. But the suspicion still remains. It is not possible here to provide a detailed discussion of whether a fixed formula ever existed and whether Paul deliberately departed from it. It may be more helpful, however, to consider whether Paul himself gives substance to this aspect of his vision. As I have noted, 1 Cor 11 and 14, and probably 1 Cor 7 as well, cast doubt on whether he really sees all barriers between male and female to be broken down. Similarly, 1 Cor 7.21–24, along with the letter to Philemon, do not suggest that Paul understands there to be any fundamental equality between slave and free. These issues are complex, and these various passages would need much more careful discussion than is possible here. It would appear, however, that it is only in the case of Jew and Gentile that Paul comes close to maintaining, fully and consistently, the position set out in Gal 3.27–28. Even then, he clearly engages in special pleading in a number of cases (especially Rom 9–11; cf. 1.16!). In fact I doubt that these specific instances do compromise Paul's position fundamentally, but it is obviously possible to reach a different conclusion. The question that needs to be raised, then, is whether Paul ever really has a vision of the Christian community as a place where all these barriers are broken down, or whether he begins with such a vision but allows it to be compromised in the course of his ministry and his dealings with particular communities and their problems. It is perhaps ironic that one of the main defenders of Paul, as both holding this vision firmly in the first place and also not conceding any ground on the question of women's basic equality, is Schüssler Fiorenza 1983 in her feminist work on Christian origins. In fact she very much needs to have not only Jesus but Paul as well in support of her position, in her struggle against conservative Catholics on the one hand and post-Christian feminists on the other. Too much of her argument at this point, however, is special pleading, and the question of the integrity of Paul's vision remains open.

There is a further question to be raised here, and that is whether the claimed equality and breaking down of barriers is not in any case set on too limited a scale. So, for example, Theissen 1982 has argued that in 1 Cor 11.17–34, Paul gives the impression of condoning social differences and inequalities, at least as far as the everyday lives and situations of the members of the community are concerned, outside the specific community meetings. He characterizes this as 'love patriarchalism', which means that a limited, and rather patronizing, display of unity and equality takes place within the community gatherings, but outside these, the obvious social differences and inequalities come to the fore again. Hence, on Theissen's argument, it would seem that either Paul's concept of community is too limited, so that too much of life and relationships are left out, or else that Paul does not genuinely have a vision of the community as radically equal or able to challenge the society around it. It is, of course, possible to raise questions about Theissen's thesis, about the social level and composition of the Christian communities, and about the nature and style of their leadership. Nevertheless, the nature of Paul's vision does at least need to be discussed further.

2.2 The Spirit-Filled Community

Paul sees this theme as axiomatic and positive, in principle at least, but clearly his vision of what it means to be a Spirit-filled community does not always correspond to what comes about in a specific situation. This is notoriously the case at Corinth, where the use of some gifts has for Paul grown out of hand, while at 1 Thess 5.19–20 the problem may be the reverse, that the Spirit is not being given free rein. Paul is quite clear about the proper direction and limits of spiritual gifts and related matters (1 Cor 12–14), but there could obviously be very genuine and real differences in the way the experience of the Spirit is understood and expressed, and the extent to which the real force of the gifts of the Spirit is allowed free range. This problem is not limited to Paul's handling of the issue, but belongs to the much larger question of the way in which powerful forces such as the Spirit are understood within religious movements, especially at their inception. Paul's vision involves encouraging the expression of these gifts, but in a controlled manner, and clearly he has to walk a tightrope on this issue. It is very easy for Paul to appear not to have a clear vision, as others do, of what through the Spirit the community might become, and instead to be advocating compromise or effectively suppressing the extraordinary energy and power at work in both the individual and the community.

2.3 Leadership and Hierarchy

Paul's vision may seem blurred on this issue as far as the Christian community is concerned. It is not surprising that the issue of leadership and hierarchy should arise, as very often happens in the case of new religious movements with strong expectations of a final decisive event. Compared with what can be observed elsewhere in the NT, and the rapid developments otherwise in early Christianity, Paul appears not to have a particularly developed or precise view. A few indications are given in Rom 12 and 1 Cor 12. Again, however, the larger questions arise of whether Paul would want effectively to give preference to some kinds of individuals, and whether he is in danger of asserting or imposing his own authority; and in both cases, how compatible this is with his overall vision. Within the Pauline tradition, especially the Pastorals (e.g. 1 Tim 2–6; Titus 1.5–16), there are clear developments that compromise the ideal of Paul's vision and move decisively in the direction of giving superior position to particular kinds of individuals. Hence it needs to be asked whether this represents a perversion of Paul's vision, or a natural and inevitable development.

2.4 Community and Secular Authority

Rom 13.1–7 represents the most famous, or notorious, statement of Paul's understanding of state authority. This passage inevitably raises the question of whether the position Paul advocates can allow the Spirit-filled, holy community to appear sufficiently distinctive, or to represent a real challenge to the world around it and the evil and oppressive aspects of the Roman Empire. Despite attempts to play down its significance,

Paul does in fact lay strong emphasis on state authority and civil law as having divine sanction (so vv. 1, 6). It appears that Paul calls on those he addresses to be good citizens, fully supporting the governing authorities and the existing social order. This tradition is also represented in developments of the Pauline tradition (Titus 3.1; 1 Pet 2.13–17), but not in so full a form (although 1 Pet 2 includes the honouring of the Emperor). The potential implications of Paul's position in Rom 13 are clear, and whatever limitations are set on the interpretation of this passage, the basic question it raises about a sustainable vision of the Christian community as a distinctive entity cannot be avoided.

2.5 Libertine and Legalist

Paul's vision of the Christian community implies that it should be a Spirit-filled community living without rules or constraints, set free to live as the Spirit leads. The transformation that new religious movements and their members undergo has been characterized as a shift from rules to no rules to new rules, where the middle stage is an interim, short-lived limbo state. It appears that in practice Paul's understanding of his communities fits this schema very well, but the crucial question is what precisely Paul holds as his ideal. Certainly it seems, both on the surface and well beneath it, that Paul sees the 'law' and the observances required by it as precisely what are set aside in the new age, and his vision of the Christian community therefore requires it to be set free completely and for ever from these constraints. There are, of course, vastly complex questions involved here about Paul's position *vis-à-vis* the law, and not least whether the law should be understood simply as a set of rules. Yet Paul does appear, at first sight anyway, to be open to the charge that he sets freedom from the law as a fundamental principle of his vision of the new community, and portrays a new life of freedom in the Spirit as the positive counterpart to this; but that he then introduces a new set of rules, closely corresponding to Jewish principles, through the back door. This may be so especially when he sees his vision of the Christian community failing to be lived out in practice, but it is in fact already evident in his earliest writing (e.g. 1 Thess 4.5) There is, then, a clear tension between the apparent pure form of Paul's vision, with its unconstrained freedom, and the impression we are left with, especially from 1 Corinthians (and in some respects Romans), where the position is more complex and the community more regulated.

2.6 Paul and Jesus

In the light of a number of the issues considered in this section, the question can be raised whether, if at all, Paul shares and continues the vision represented by Jesus. This is, of course, an enormous, as well as disputed, issue, and it is not possible to do more than scratch the surface of it here. On the surface, indeed, there look to be considerable similarities, not least in the strong emphasis that both Jesus and Paul give to the imminence of eschatological events. Yet whereas Jesus can be seen as presenting a radical challenge to his contemporary society and those in authority, and as looking for a transformation of values and reversal of roles to be brought about in the kingdom in the near future, these themes are not evident in Paul. As we have seen already in this section, much of what Paul says can be understood as supporting the status quo and state and civil authorities, and making his communities appear less not more different from the world around them. Hence it can be argued that Paul advocates a position that is essentially quietist and conformist, as far as relations between the community and wider society are concerned; this trend is most pronounced in the Pastorals, but it is already evident in letters generally recognized to be authentically Pauline.

3. PAUL'S VISION IN PERSPECTIVE

Paul's vision is thus clearly vulnerable; it appears to be flawed, perhaps seriously, in several places. That does not, however, mean that it should simply be set aside as having nothing to offer. So, for example, quite a lot of the discussion here has (inevitably) related to what Paul says in his letters to the Corinthians. It is, however, questionable to judge him too severely on the basis of his Corinthian correspondence, since so much of it is reactive and defensive, trying to repair damage that has been done and effect workable compromises. Indeed, Paul is constrained by circumstances in all of his letters; this is so even for Romans, where a situation of tax riots and potential civil disobedience may well provide part of the relevant context for 13.1–7.

At the same time, Paul's particular position in Corinthians contains much of what we have characterized as his vision for the community overall. It can thus serve as a starting point for an assessment of whether he has in the end a coherent and sustainable vision at all. One dilemma that emerges for Paul's position is his vision of the Christian community both as characterized by freedom in the Spirit and yet also as the pure and holy community of the final age, showing itself beyond any doubt to be the true people of God. For Paul himself, there is no conflict at all between these two; the Spirit is always manifested in fruit and gifts that in and of themselves demonstrate the true nature of the community. Clearly, however, it does not take much of a shift in the experience and perception of freedom in the Spirit for Paul's vision to appear much less self-evident and cogent.

If the strength of Paul's vision of a Spirit-filled, holy community is also a source of weakness, there is a clear tension inherent in another central thrust of his position as well. That is, Paul comes close to portraying the

Christian community as an alternative society: the community should regulate their own affairs, resolve disputes without involving secular courts, and conduct their own initiation ceremonies, common meetings and meals, all with their own self-evidently distinctive standards and way of life. At the same time, Paul's vision is firmly of his communities belonging within the world around them, and not retreating from it. That does not in itself imply that Paul's vision lacks coherence. On the contrary, it is fully consistent for Paul to envisage his communities as an alternative society that should make an impact on the world around them. There are, however, problems. The concept of the Christian community as an 'alternative society' is open to criticism, in its modern as well as Pauline form. But more specifically, Paul often seems deliberately to move too close to the perspectives and standards of the world around, in the way he develops his understanding of his communities. One obvious danger of this is that his vision of a distinctive Christian community may become less distinctive and coherent.

At this point, in considering whether Paul's position is sustainable, it is necessary to take account of the contingent circumstances that are relevant to the way in which he develops and modifies his vision. So, for example, there are eschatological constraints; the imminent expectation of the end means that, in some respects at least, normal life is set in abeyance (1 Cor 7.29–31), but so also therefore are long-term considerations for the communities and their way of life. Paul may indeed make greater demands because of this (e.g. Rom 13.11–13; 1 Thess 5), but the point is that the main focus of his vision is the immediate future, not the long-term development of the communities. Secondly, there are pragmatic constraints: particular members of the community need to be able to maintain social contacts and credibility, and the community needs to be able to exist without attracting hostile attention. Thirdly, there are missionary constraints: Paul's primary and urgent purpose is to take his movement and gospel onwards, and nothing can be allowed to hinder this.

Despite objections that have been raised, these constraints are real, and clearly affect the way Paul works out his understanding of his communities and their way of life. Yet that does not in itself make it easier to argue for Paul's vision as coherent. That is, if he modifies his vision of the community for essentially tactical reasons, the integrity of the vision clearly becomes open to question. Thus, for example, Theissen's love-patriarchalism thesis holds that Paul's vision for his community works only to a limited extent, internally; in the end Paul effectively favours those with wealth and social position, and prevents himself from creating a radically alternative community at all. Equally, to say that these various constraints prevent Paul from being concerned with specific societal issues still begs the question of what vision Paul really would want to develop, and how it might relate to Jesus' vision of the kingdom being fulfilled.

All this may seem to go further in the direction of the negative considerations set out in section 2. It does indeed appear that, in some respects at least, Paul's position is not fully consistent. Nevertheless, the very real strengths and coherence of Paul's vision should not be set aside too readily. At the very least it can be said that Paul's vision of the Spirit-filled, holy community constituting an alternative society comes as close as anything in his writings to the fulfilment of Jesus' vision of the kingdom on earth. Certainly Paul's vision of the new age seems vague, and scarcely an adequate substitute for what is implied in Jesus' own vision. Yet despite these limitations, it remains in important respects a powerful vision of what the Christian community of the final age can and should be like. It begs a number of questions, and some of the developments from it (particularly in the Pastorals) are potentially disastrous. Nevertheless, it is an impressive understanding and vision of how the distinctive nature of the Christian community can make a difference to those inside and outside it, and how it can in significant ways refuse to conform to the standards of the world around.

Perhaps in the end we are in danger of demanding too much from Paul's vision, especially in expecting the ideal to work out in reality and for Paul to hold on to the ideal in whatever circumstances might arise. It is easy to criticize Paul, for example, for not striving more to achieve genuine equality between men and women or between slaves and free; yet here especially we need to take account of the specific constraints of first-century society. In fact it is a remarkable achievement that Paul holds so resolutely to his vision of the barriers between Jews and Gentiles being broken down. It would be surprising if there were no continuing tensions here, and we are of course left with the question of how far Jews especially would feel fully part of the developing movement. Paul could not allow his vision of a united Jewish–Gentile community to be undermined, and it is clear from Galatians and Romans that Jewish identity and observance were major issues that he had to struggle with.

In the light of our own experience in the twentieth century, however, it is no small accomplishment to have a vision of the overcoming of ethnic and racial divides, and to see at least some realization of this ideal. This may indeed point the way forward for a wider realization of Paul's vision, and if it has to be admitted in the end that Paul's vision is flawed in some respects, and becomes more fragile as it is worked out in particular communities and situations, this should not surprise us. Nor, however, should it cause us simply to give up the vision completely. It may indeed be precisely because we can see Paul's vision as fragile but still alive, in the harsh realities it encounters, that it can appear acutely relevant for the difficult situations of present-day churches, in their own grappling with confusing and recalcitrant realities. Our reading of Paul for the present day needs of course to be more subtle than that, but it affords us at least some perspective for making a rather less presumptuous assessment of Paul's vision. This is so, however much we recognize that Paul's vision is not in the end fully adequate for the Christian community, and needs to be corrected and supplemented from elsewhere within the NT. Paul's vision in the end is of a community that exemplifies God's Spirit in action, and Christ's self-giving love as pervading its whole way of life, in difficult everyday situations. It is a vision that goes deep, and deserves still to be taken seriously by us.

BIBLIOGRAPHY

Banks, R. 1980. *Paul's Idea of Community: The Early House Churches in their Historical Setting.* Grand Rapids: Eerdmans.

Becker, J. 1993. 'Paul and His Churches', in J. Becker (ed.), *Christian Beginnings.* Louisville: Westminster, John Knox Press. 132–210.

Cerfaux, L. 1959. *The Church in the Theology of St Paul.* New York: Herder & Herder.

Meeks, W. 1983. *The First Urban Christians.* New Haven: Yale University Press.

Newton, M. 1988. *The Concept of Purity at Qumran and in the Letters of Paul.* Cambridge: Cambridge University Press.

Schüssler Fiorenza, E. 1983. *In Memory of Her.* New York: Crossroad.

Theissen, G. 1982. *The Social Setting of Pauline Christianity.* Philadelphia: Fortress.

9

Romans 12.1–2 and Paul's Vision for Worship

MICHAEL B. THOMPSON

ANY discussion of Paul's 'vision' for his churches' worship must engage with Romans 12.1–2.[1] There, according to many, the apostle redefines worship in words that draw a sharp contrast between Christian self-offering and cultic worship, particularly that of the Jews. Together with the facts that (1) he rarely elsewhere uses the specific vocabulary of worship and (2) when he does, it is usually with a non-cultic nuance, this interpretation has been taken to demonstrate that Paul rejected his Jewish heritage and saw worship as essentially a life of obedience *rather than* as the primary activity when Christians gathered as 'church' (1 Cor 11.18). I wish to argue, however, that such conclusions are mistaken and rooted in a misunderstanding of what Paul is doing in Romans 12. In addition, I will briefly suggest some contours of Paul's vision for congregational worship.[2]

Interpreters widely agree that Romans 12.1 marks the major hinge in the body of the letter. Paul moves from theology to paraenesis, and begins to describe what the life of Christians should look like. He summarizes the new perspective of humanity in Christ in 12.1–2, before going on to sketch an outline of behaviour in the following verses. The implied motivation for life is thankfulness in response to God's mercies in Christ, described in preceding chapters. This gives a new perspective, as Christians approach all of life as self-offering in Christ. The means by which this is to be accomplished is through an ongoing process of transformation, as thinking (which controls action) is renewed. The goal of life now is an obedience of faith to God's perfect will. So far, so good.

[1] As one of the many former students in whom John Sweet invested so much time, I am delighted to be able to honour my doctoral supervisor with this essay. Always a source of encouragement and wise advice, he has never ceased to amaze me with his grasp of the Greek NT, often quoting long passages from memory. We share a common interest in Romans and liturgy, and I offer this piece in that pursuit.

[2] By 'worship' I mean 'the celebration of God in his supreme worth in such a manner that his "worthiness" becomes the norm and inspiration of human living' (adapted with a minor change from R. P. Martin 1982:4).

121

The problem lies in what we deduce from the appeal for hearers to 'present your bodies as a living sacrifice, holy and acceptable to God, which is your spiritual worship' (NRSV). The words 'present', 'sacrifice', 'holy', 'acceptable', and 'worship' together evoke *cultic* worship.[3] With the addition of the words 'your bodies', 'living', and 'spiritual', and the call to transformation and non-conformity in 12.2, however, Paul makes it clear that his vision for worship is breaking out of a mould. The question is, which mould? Is he using the dead animal sacrifices of Judaism offered in a cultic setting as a foil for Christian worship which is to differ in every respect? Fundamentally, is Paul's purpose in 12.1 to offer a new *definition* of worship?

REJECTION OF JEWISH WORSHIP?

To support an interpretation focusing on a contrast between Jewish and Christian worship, one could cite the immediate context. Paul has just finished discussing the 'problem' of Israel in chapters 9–11, and the only other instance of the word translated 'worship' (λατρεία; specifically [cultic] service rendered to God) in his letters besides 12.1 is in 9.4, referring to Jewish worship. Nevertheless, there are verbal and conceptual links with earlier parts of the letter which are not focused on Judaism. Furthermore, the 'mercies' referred to in 12.1 may well be broader than those recounted in the immediately preceding words. Given the fact that 12.1 marks such a sharp turn in the argument, those mercies probably go back further to the grace seen in earlier parts of the letter as well (e.g. ch. 3; ch. 5; 7.24; 8.34). As we shall see, the immediate context may not be as decisive as the larger structure of Romans.

One could also call upon a reading of Paul (e.g. Lutheran) that emphasizes his conversion to an essentially different religion of grace as opposed to works of the Law. Therefore Paul here would be rejecting his Jewish past; Phil 3.7f, 13 could be pressed into service for support. But the 'new perspective' on Paul as developed persuasively (if needing qualification) by Dunn *et al.* requires us to think again.[4] Paul's problem with Judaism was not with the religion of the Hebrew Bible but with (1) the

---

[3] I follow here W. Eichrodt's characterization of the *cultus* as 'the expression of religious experience in concrete external actions performed within the congregation or community, preferably by officially appointed exponents and in set forms' (*Theology of the Old Testament* [London: SCM Press, 1961] 1:98).

[4] J. D. G. Dunn, *Jesus, Paul and the Law. Studies in Mark and Galatians* (London: SPCK/Louisville: Westminster, 1990). M. Hengel and others have rightly observed that some texts (e.g. 4 Ezra) do indicate the mentality of merit that E. P. Sanders denies as having characterized Judaism in Paul's day (M. Hengel and R. Deines, 'E. P. Sanders' "Common Judaism", Jesus, and the Pharisees' *JTS* n.s. 46 [1995] 1–70). Nevertheless, Sanders makes his point with the majority of texts.

fundamental rejection of Jesus by the Jews Paul sought to evangelize [Rom 1.16; 10.3; 15.19; 1 Cor 9.20] and (2) the insistence by Jewish Christians that Gentiles had to become Jews in order to join God's people. When we find Paul saying critical things about the Law or the Jews, one or both of these two aspects looms in the context.

We cannot be certain that Paul rejected Jewish worship as a whole when he became a Christian. The few clear references to Jewish cultic sacrifices in his letters are not critical, but neutral (1 Cor 9.13; 10.18). Paul's statement that 'our paschal lamb, Christ, has been sacrificed' (1 Cor 5.7) picks up the imagery but does not necessarily reject the value of the original practice. We lack hard evidence that Paul did *not* participate fully in worship at the temple when he visited Jerusalem. In fact Acts 21.15–26 and 24.17f offer evidence to the contrary, if we will allow it; with the gradual rehabilitation in recent research of Luke as a historian,[5] we should consider doing so – especially given its consistency with Paul's stated practice in 1 Cor 9.20. At the very least, the passages in Acts show that Luke had no problem with such a Paul. We do not have to go all the way with F. C. Baur to see that Christians in Jerusalem continued to worship as their ancestors did. Acts makes no effort to hide that fact (Acts 2.46; 3.1; 5.12, 42; etc.; cf. Matt 5.23; 1 Cor 16.8), despite the potential discomfort or embarrassment it might cause to Gentile Christians. Matt 5.23; 1 Cor 16.8 and the traditions about James the Just in Eusebius (*Hist. Eccl.* 2.23.6) offer further evidence of the Jewishness of early Christian worship. Only by its very Jewish practice could the Church in Jerusalem have been allowed to continue to make use of the temple, and to enjoy relative peace, until the two ways of Judaism and Christianity diverged so widely that an irreparable breach occurred. But that is another story.[6]

One more factor makes it unlikely that in 12.1 Paul is advocating a rejection of Jewish patterns (or forms) of worship. In Romans Paul walks a rhetorical tightrope. He wants to show that faith in Jesus means that people do not have to become Jews to be Christians. At the same time, he wants to show the Gentile majority of believers in Rome that they should not adopt a superior attitude to the Jews (cf. 11.13–25). As a growing number of scholars agree, Paul's warning to the 'strong' not to ridicule their weaker brethren in 14.1–15.6 most likely reflects this same concern (see Thompson 1993). If the 'weak' are to be identified as primarily Jewish Christians, are we to assume that Paul begins his discussion of Christian behaviour by rejecting their approach to worship? Although he identifies

[5] See e.g. the work of M. Hengel, C. Hemer, and the multi-volume series *The Book of Acts in its First Century Setting* (Grand Rapids: Eerdmans/Carlisle: Paternoster, 1993–).

[6] See, e.g., J. D. G. Dunn, *The Partings of the Ways Between Christianity and Judaism and Their Significance for the Character of Christianity* (London: SCM Press/ Philadelphia: Trinity Press International, 1991).

with the strong (15.1), Paul does not criticize the weak's observance of days (14.5f) and their avoidance of (ritually) 'unclean' food (14.2f, 6, 14). What is more, he has just insisted that God's gifts and calling to Israel are irrevocable, and that the 'worship' belongs to them (9.4; 11.29). To see 12.1 as a rejection of Jewish worship would be to stand this affirmation on its head.[7]

ANOTHER EXPLANATION

In order to understand what Paul is doing in 12.1–2, we must go back all the way to 1.18–32. We should not be surprised if, in describing the behaviour of humanity in Christ, Paul echoes language he has already used in his description of human depravity. In short, the beginning of the second 'half' of Romans amounts to a call to participate in the reversal of the downward spiral described at the beginning of the first 'half'. This is not a new insight, but only recently has it begun to gain a wider acceptance (Furnish 1968:101–106; Thompson 1991:78–86; Peterson 1993).

Paul began the body of his letter by emphasizing that at the root of the sin which has led to the current revelation of God's wrath (1.18) lies humanity's refusal to *glorify* and *thank* the God to whom they know they are accountable (1.21). To glorify (δοξάζειν) and to give thanks (εὐχαριστεῖν) is essentially to worship, as the terrible 'exchange' in 1.23 and 1.25 confirms. The result of turning away from God did not mean an end to worship *per se*. As a result of withholding praise and thanks, the focus of human worship shifted from the glory of the Creator to images of his creatures, from the truth of God to the lie of idolatry. They *worshipped* (ἐσεβάσθησαν) and *served* (ἐλάτρευσαν) the creature instead of the Creator (1.25).

If Paul frequently used technical terms for worship, the link between the λατρεία of 12.1 and ἐλάτρευσαν in 1.25 might not be significant. But as is well known, the apostle rarely employs such language (see e.g. Marshall 1985). Σεβάζομαι (to 'worship, show reverence to') in 1.25 is a Pauline *hapax legomenon*, as is the cognate σέβασμα in 2 Thess 2.4. Λατρεύω ('to serve' in a religious/cultic context) appears elsewhere in Rom 1.9 (of his own service to God; cf. 2 Tim 1.3) and Phil 3.3 (of serving/worshipping in the Spirit, in contrast to the Judaizers' insistence on circumcision). The verb θρησκεύω ('to practice religious observances, worship') is altogether absent from Paul, and the noun θρησκεία ('worship'; BAGD: especially as expressed in religious service or cult) we find only in Col 2.18 regarding the worship of angels (cf. ἐθελοθρησκία in Col 2.23).

---

[7] For this latter point I am indebted to Markus Bockmuehl.

So far then, it would seem that one could begin to make a case for a contrast between the λατρεία in 12.1 and either the λατρεία in 9.4 (so e.g. Martin 1974:137) or the λατρεύειν of 1.25. But further evidence confirms a connection with chapter 1.

When they refused to offer true worship, Paul says people became futile in their *thinking* (1.21), and their senseless heart was darkened. Although they professed to be wise, they became fools (1.22). A lie replaced the truth (1.25). The failure to see fit to acknowledge (δοκιμάζειν ... ἔχειν ἐν ἐπιγνώσει) God resulted in his giving people over to a debased *mind* (ἀδόκιμον νοῦν; 1.28). The downward spiral results in a state of antipathy to the divine decree (1.32).

In light of these statements, Paul's call in 12.2 to renewal of the *mind* (ἀνακαίνωσις τοῦ νοός) in order to be able to 'approve' (δοκιμάζειν) the will of God begins to make even more sense. The only other occurrences of νοῦς in the intervening chapters are at 7.23, 25; 11.34, none of which shed light on Rom 12. Paul's emphasis on wrong *thinking* in chapter 1 best explains his choice of the word λογικός to describe Christian worship in 12.1. Λογικός is sometimes translated 'spiritual', but 'rational' or referring to that which is endowed with reason is a more common meaning. In his criticism of irrational pagan worship, Paul is drawing positively on a long Jewish tradition (cf. Isa 44; Wisd 13f; *Joseph & Aseneth*; etc.). Thankful self-offering to the true God in response to his mercies is reasonable, right-minded worship, in contrast to the topsy-turvy mentality that withholds thanksgiving and trades truth for a lie (1.21, 25).

There is more. As a result of their rebellion, Paul says God gave people over to impurity (ἀκαθαρσία) and the dishonouring of their bodies (σώματα) in 1.24. In Romans 12, he calls his readers to present their bodies (σώματα) as a sacrifice (the singular here is important, as we shall see), holy (ἁγίαν) and pleasing to God. Many commentators observe that σῶμα here connotes the whole person and not simply the 'body'. That may well be true, but it is striking that virtually every occurrence of the word in Romans up to 12.1 either has the physical body primarily in view or at least includes it (1.24; 4.19; 6.12; 7.4, 24; 8.10f, 13, 23 – 6.6 is difficult). Although he was obviously aware that the adjective 'holy' would normally connote cultic sacrifices, Paul may well be using it with an ethical nuance here. He uses the cognate participle ἡγιασμένη similarly in 15.16, another passage where he applies cultic language in a non-cultic fashion (cf. also ἁγιασμόν in 6.19). In short, Paul calls Christians to glorify God with their bodies (cf. 1 Cor 6.20).

When we summarize the different points of contrast, the strength of the case for a connection becomes more apparent:

Romans 1	*Romans 12*
wrath of God (v. 18)	mercies of God (v. 1)
refusal to honour or thank God (v. 21)	(thankful) pleasing sacrifice (v. 1)
dishonouring the body (v. 24)	presenting the body to God (v. 1)
impurity (v. 24)	holiness (v. 1)
foolish, idolatrous worship (vv. 21–23, 25)	reasonable worship (v. 1)
debased mind (v. 28)	renewed mind (v. 2)
refusal to acknowledge (v. 28)	discernment & obedience (v. 2)
the decree of God (v. 32)	the will of God (v. 2)

Given the position of both texts at the beginning of two major sections of the letter, a contrast seems likely. Other, more remote lines of evidence could be explored, such as the idea that Adam may underlie some of the language in chapter 1, and Christ in 12, or that the situation in 1 characterizes life in this age, to which 12 calls for non-conformity (see Thompson 1991:78–86). But there is enough here to indicate that the correspondences are not coincidental.

What are we to make, however, of the addition of the adjective 'living' (ζῶσαν) to the sacrifice Paul urges in 12.1? Is this not a clear contrast with dead animal sacrifices (so e.g. Delling 1962:11)? Perhaps, depending upon how much weight we give to the reference to 'worship' in 9.4. But we do not find in Romans the same kind of argument that characterizes the letter to the Hebrews. Outside of 1.23 Paul does not refer to (dead) animals or their blood, and as we have seen, his only references to Jewish cultic sacrifices (1 Cor 9.13; 10.18) are neutral.

A more likely explanation of ζῶσαν begins to emerge when we consider the significance of the verb and the noun ζωή ('life') earlier in Romans (especially 5.10, 17f; 6.10f, 13; 8.2, 6, 10). Chapter 6 is particularly crucial. There Paul uses the same words 'present', 'body', and 'living' that we find in chapter 12:

> So you also must consider yourselves dead to sin and *alive* (zw`nta~) to God in Christ Jesus. Therefore, do not let sin exercise dominion in your mortal *bodies*, to make you obey their passions. No longer *present* your members to sin as instruments of wickedness, but *present* yourselves to God as those who have been brought from death to *life* (ὡσεὶ ἐκ νεκρῶν ζῶντας), and *present* your members to God as instruments of righteousness. (6.11–13)

In the light of this text, it seems more likely that Paul is effectively saying in Romans 12: 'present yourselves to God as those alive from the dead (and hence, alive *to* God)'; cf. Gal 2.19; 2 Cor 5.15. Instead of being dead in sin/Adam/this age, they are responsive and obedient to God, available to effect his will.

If the above exegesis is remotely on target, Paul is not trying in 12.1f to contrast Christian worship with Jewish cultic worship; he is reflecting how a right Christian orientation to God contrasts with the foolish idolatry resulting from a refusal to recognize and thank the Creator (cf. 1 Thess 1.9, where Paul puts it in a nutshell). Humanity in Christ is called to do now what humanity originally failed to do – to offer what amounts to appropriate worship to the true God. The worship of the Jews is not primarily at issue here.

A NEW DEFINITION FOR WORSHIP?

Robert Banks concludes from Rom 12.1f that Paul could not hold that Christians gathered primarily to worship (1994:88). Likewise Howard Marshall 1985 argues from the lack of technical terminology for worship in the NT and from the many references to 'edification', etc., that Christians gathered essentially for fellowship and mutual up-building (cf. e.g. 1 Cor 14.26). Continuing this line of thinking, John P. Richardson further asserts that 'The church is not ultimately a "God-*worshipping*" community but a "God-*serving*" community' (1995:216; his italics).

A corollary of our exegesis, however, is that Paul is not intending to exhaust the meaning of the word 'worship' in 12.1. In the first place, λατρεία is only one of several terms referring to particular aspects of worship. Furthermore, the brevity of the reference indicates that worship is not the *subject* in the text; this is no *topos* treating the form, organization and practice of corporate Christian λατρεία. Instead, λατρεία is the *predicate* or better, the *complement*. The apostle urges a way of life as a whole, *identified* as a right-minded worship or service. In doing so, he no doubt expands our understanding of what kind of worship God values. True worship is inseparably connected with Christian behaviour in general. But it is a logical fallacy to conclude from this text that he re-defines worship as, or reduces worship to, Christian ethics – any more than Hosea's commendation of love and knowledge over sacrificial offerings (Hos 6.6) proves that the prophet was calling for an absolute end to form and ritual.

All of life may be 'worship', but all of worship is not simply everyday obedience. The concept of worship is larger than the specific vocabulary that Paul may or may not use in his occasional letters. The absence of systematic instruction about worship can be taken in different ways. Since Paul does not speak of cultic worship, he obviously did not value it – this sort of argument has been used in the past to deny his interest in the historical Jesus. Nevertheless, the adage of archaeologists remains true: absence of evidence is not evidence of absence. One could just as easily argue that precisely because we find so little in his letters, Paul *assumes* a familiarity with the tradition, and does not feel the need to instruct his readers as to how to conduct their worship, except when he is putting out pastoral fires, as in 1 Corinthians. In fact, Paul *does* appear to use a technical term for the worship of God (προσκυνεῖν) with a cultic nuance in 1 Cor 14.25. Marshall 1985:219 seeks to minimize the significance of this verse by noting that it does not describe the action of the Christians but rather that of an outsider, but it would be not a little odd if non-Christians were the only ones to worship at a Christian meeting!

Alastair Campbell has rightly corrected Richardson and Marshall, showing what many will consider obvious – that the early Church did indeed meet for the purpose of worship as well as for upbuilding. He proposes that whereas 'worship' is an appropriate term for 'Godward' activity in Christian gatherings, 'everything that went on in such meetings is consistently *evaluated* by the New Testament writers in terms of its manward [*sic*] benefits (or lack of them)' (1995:139). David Peterson similarly calls edification and worship 'different sides of the same coin' (1992:215).

But this fails to go far enough. A crucial metaphor underlying the language of 'building up' (οἰκοδομή, οἰκοδομεῖν) is that of the Church as a *temple* (1 Cor 3.16f; cf. 3.9–15). We cannot demonstrate that the apostle always had this image in mind when he spoke of 'edification' (see Chester's examples in his chapter in this volume), but Paul saw the Church, the people of God, as the worshipping building of God (Delling 1962:22). It is the temple God indwells (2 Cor 6.16; cf. Eph 2.21f; of the individual: 1 Cor 6.19), present by his Spirit. It is therefore the place of encounter with God and sharing in that same Spirit. The one who worships is struck by the fact that God is truly among his people (1 Cor 14.25). His presence in the community means that the care Christians give to one another when they gather is at the same time a reflection of and participation in the character of the one who indwells the whole. Upbuilding of the community – and mission for that matter – is not an end in itself, but a means towards the goal of enlarging and enhancing a living 'temple' where God is glorified and thanked (2 Cor 4.15) in a worthy fashion.

PAUL'S VISION FOR GATHERED WORSHIP

If Romans 12 does not argue against the form and ritual of Jewish worship, the burden of proof lies on those who would deny that Paul's vision of ideal Christian worship appropriated significant elements of Jewish practice, just as his theology and ethics 'baptized' many aspects of his pre-Christian heritage. Acts tells us that a number of his first converts in different locations were either Jews or Gentiles already attracted to worship in the synagogue (Acts 13.43; 14.1; 16.13f; 17.1–4, 10–12; 18.4, 7,

19; 19.8). Pauline exhortations to forget what liturgical practices and organization they had learned are hard to find. He is certainly critical of the imposition of Jewish ritual law on Gentile Christians, but it is another thing altogether to see Paul as an iconoclast, creating his own religion *de novo*. He preached the same faith he once tried to destroy (Gal 1.23). As Paul's occasional comments elsewhere in his letters show, he assumed that Christians gathered as church for worship. It is to the form and conduct of *that* worship that we now turn.[8]

The chief source for our understanding of Paul's vision for gathered worship is 1 Corinthians (Martin's suggestion, that when arranged in lines 1 Thess 5.16–22 reads as though it preserves an order of service, is fascinating but inconclusive [1974:135f]). The difficulty here is threefold: we cannot say with confidence exactly what Jewish worship was like in the first century (Bradshaw 1992:1–29), we only see Paul correcting that which has gone amiss, and we do not know enough to be able to separate Corinthian particulars from the general contours of any ideal Paul may have had for worship. Nevertheless, we should not forget that his letters were evidently written to be read when the community gathered (1 Thess 5.27; 2 Cor 1.1 [including probably Athens and Cenchreae]); Gal 1.2; Col 4.16; Rom 1.7 [noting the absence of reference to '*the* Church']; and the circular letter Ephesians, if authentic). That reading therefore formed part of the worship itself. What we can do is identify Paul's explicit statements of purpose and draw together inferences from the letters in the Pauline corpus. A useful starting point for detailed study of worship in Paul is Martin 1993; for a survey of research on the NT as a whole, see Bradshaw 1992:30–55.

Paul's vision begins and ends with God, whose mercies in Christ by the Spirit are the ground, motivation, and enablement of praise. That praise is characterized by thanksgiving, and glorying in what God has accomplished (in addition to Rom 1 and 12: Col 3.17; 1 Thess 5.18; 1 Cor 11.26). It includes considerable singing of psalms and hymns (1 Cor 14.26; 14.15; cf. Col 3.16; Eph 5.19); we may have a song fragment in Phil 2.6–11 (although this continues to be disputed); cf. Eph 5.14; 1 Tim 3.16; etc. Prayer is an obvious feature (1 Cor 14.15), including blessings and thanksgivings in the Spirit (with interpretation, 1 Cor 14.16f), supplications and intercessions (e.g. Phil 4.6; 1 Thess 5.17). In particular we find prayer for Christ's return (1 Cor 16.22; cf. Rev 22.20), and in a later letter, prayer for those in authority (1 Tim 2.1ff, 8).

Paul assumes a coming together (1 Cor 11.18, 20) for worship that *remembers* (particularly in the Lord's Supper, 1 Cor 11.24f), that *proclaims* (1 Cor 11.26), and that is *worthy* (1 Cor 11.27–33). The Lord's Supper is celebrated as part of a meal, which is to be entered into with discernment

---

[8] The question of personal/individual devotion in Paul lies outside the scope of this essay.

and consideration for the needs of each other (1 Cor 11.17–34). It is a sharing with and in Christ (1 Cor 10.16, 21f). The frequency with which Paul's churches met and observed the eucharist is uncertain; at any rate, corporate worship was regularly on Sundays (1 Cor 16.2).

Worship is fundamentally *corporate* and *united*. We have already seen this implied in the singular 'sacrifice' (θυσία) of Rom 12.1, and 1 Cor 11.18 makes this explicit. It is *inclusive* of Jews and Gentiles glorifying God with one voice (Rom 15.6, 7–13 – arguably the climax of Romans; cf. 1 Cor 12.13), if *exclusive* with regard to those who cause dissensions in opposition to the teachings received by the community (Rom 16.17; 1 Cor 5.3–5). It is characterized by *uniformity of aim* (Phil 2.2; Rom 15.5) but is wide enough to allow for *diversity of expression* and practice (Rom 14.5f).

Spiritual gifts are to be used *for the common good* (1 Cor 12.7). The gifts to be foremost in worship are the *greater* gifts (1 Cor 12.31), i.e. those which are intelligible and build up the community (Fee 1994:196f; 1 Cor 14.26). Love should *govern* their use (1 Cor 13; 14.1) and is the *goal* of instruction (Phil 1.9; cf. 1 Tim 1.5). Potentially each person has a contribution to make (1 Cor 14.26), although unintelligible speech should be accompanied by interpretation (1 Cor 14.27f), and prophecies should be weighed (1 Cor 14. 29; 1 Thess 5.21). Like synagogue meetings, it probably includes readings from the Old Testament (Rom 15.4; 1 Cor 10.6; cf. 2 Tim 3.16); the reading of Paul's letters has already been noted.

Paul envisions a worship that is 'free', enabled and empowered by an unquenched Spirit (1 Thess 5.19), yet orderly (1 Cor 14.40). This call to order implies local leadership (cf. Rom 12.8; 1 Thess 5.12; Phil 1.1), although some students of Paul see the existence of leaders in worship as a later development. Both sexes played leading roles (women prayed and prophesied, 1 Cor 11; cf. Horbury in this volume), but there were differences and limits as seen to be appropriate (1 Cor 14.34f). Here, as no doubt in many other respects, Paul's vision was constrained by social realities. We may consider him to have been inconsistent in carrying through his declaration of equality (Gal 3.28; see Chester's discussion in this volume), but any failure to eliminate all 'barriers' between men and women was probably rooted in a concern for mission; Paul urged what was 'seemly' in order not to erect barriers to others coming to faith. The same issue of consistency appears in his own policy of being all things to all people, that he might by all means save some (1 Cor 9.22).

For Paul, worship is not simply cerebral but worked out in appropriate postures (kneeling: Rom 14.11; Phil 2.10; cf. Eph 3.14; prostration: 1 Cor 14.25; standing: 1 Tim 2.8), attire (1 Cor 11.4–16) and ritual acts (the holy kiss: Rom 16.16; 1 Thess 5.26; 2 Cor 13.12) which signify and depict theological truths (baptism as a death: Rom 6.3f, and resurrection: Col 2.12; cf. the washing/rebirth in Tit 3.5; eucharist proclaiming the Lord's death: 1 Cor 11.26). It could take particular liturgical forms such as the Amen (1 Cor 14.16) uttered in Christ's name (2 Cor 1.20), the Maranatha formula (1 Cor 16.22), the cry 'Abba' (Rom 8.15; Gal 4.6), confession formulae (Rom 10.10; Phil 2.11), benedictions (Gal 6.18; Phil 4.23; 1 Cor 16.23), doxologies (Rom 1.25; 9.5; 2 Cor 11.31; Rom 11.36; Gal 1.5; cf. 2 Tim 4.18; Eph 1.3), and the triadic blessing (2 Cor 13.14).

Where then would Paul 'go to church' today? Who best reflects his 'vision' for worship? An unspoken assumption in such questions of course is that his vision remained static and never changed. Nevertheless, we can offer a few observations with some degree of certainty. Besides the usual ingredients of prayer, praise and instruction that we might expect, the sort of gathered worship Paul hoped would characterize his congregations featured freedom yet form, unity yet diversity, authority yet mutuality. Gathered worship was not escape from the world where a life of worship is lived, nor an individualistic exercise in piety, nor essentially a one-way flow from a person 'up front' to the rest of the flock. Precisely in his insistence on the use of gifts and mutual ministry (1 Cor 14.26) he summoned his hearers to take risks that many find difficult to accept today. The risk includes the possibility of a genuine encounter with God that challenges, renews and transforms – and potentially embarrasses. The extent to which a church replaces that risk with control reflects its departure from at least a part of Paul's vision.

CONCLUSION

We cannot underestimate the importance of Rom 12.1f. Paul's use there of cultic language in a non-cultic fashion epitomizes what we find elsewhere in Romans (e.g. 1.9; 3.25; 15.16) and in the apostle's other letters (Phil 2.17). But in our text Paul is not so much defining Christian worship over against Jewish worship (he will go on in 14.1–15.7 to urge tolerance of Jewish Christian religious scruples), as offering a vision of the Christian life as a whole. This life is not shut off in a separate compartment from those times and places when 'worship' is offered. Life itself becomes an act of worship – particularly *reasonable* worship in contrast to the idolatry that rejects the Creator. Hence all that is said or done is now to be accompanied with thanksgiving (Col 3.17) to the glory of God (1 Cor 10.31).

For Paul, all of life takes on a holy significance; this is not to deny, however, the value of occasions that concentrate and focus the worship of the community. As Moule pragmatically observes, 'the surest way to profane the whole week would be to try to make every day equally holy' (1983:77). Paul's vision for worship includes more than everyday obedience and self-offering, inasmuch as the experience of 'church' gathers praise and thanks, provides a setting for the use of gifts for transformation and proclamation, and summons the body of Christ to an inter-dependence which reflects the very life of God.

Bibliography

Banks, R. J. 1994. *Paul's Idea of Community*. Revised edn. Peabody, MA: Hendrickson.

Barrett, C. K. 1985. *Church, Ministry and Sacraments in the New Testament*. Exeter: Paternoster.

Bradshaw, P. 1992. *The Search for the Origins of Christian Worship: Sources and Methods for the Study of Early Liturgy*. London: SPCK.

Campbell, Alastair. 1995. 'Once More: Is Worship Biblical?' *Churchman* 110: 131–39.

Cullmann, O. 1953. *Early Christian Worship*. Translated by A. S. Todd and J. B. Torrance. London: SCM Press.

Delling, D. G. 1962. *Worship in the New Testament*. Translated by Percy Scott. London: Darton, Longman and Todd.

Fee, G. D. 1994. *God's Empowering Presence: The Holy Spirit in the Letters of Paul*. Peabody, MA: Hendrickson.

Furnish, Victor. 1968. *Theology and Ethics in Paul*. Nashville: Abingdon.

Hahn, F. 1973. *The Worship of the Early Church*. Translated by D. E. Green. Philadelphia: Fortress.

Marshall, I. Howard. 1985. 'How Far Did the Early Christians *Worship* God?' *Churchman* 99: 216–29.

Martin, R. P. 1974. *Worship in the Early Church*. Revised edn. London: Marshall, Morgan and Scott.

Martin, R. P. 1982. *The Worship of God: Some Theological, Pastoral and Practical Reflections*. Grand Rapids: Eerdmans.

Martin, R. P. 1993. 'Worship.' In *Dictionary of Paul and His Letters*, eds. G. F. Hawthorne and R. P. Martin. Leicester: IVP. 982–91.

Moule, C. F. D. 1983. *Worship in the New Testament*. Nottingham: Grove Books Ltd. One-volume reprint of a two-volume Grove revised version (1977–78) of the original Lutterworth edition (London, 1961).

Peterson, David. 1992. *Engaging with God: A Biblical Theology of Worship*. Leicester: Apollos.

Peterson, David. 1993. 'Worship and Ethics in Romans 12.' *Tyndale Bulletin* 44: 271–88.

Richardson, John P. 1995. 'Is Worship Biblical?' *Churchman* 109: 197–218.

Thompson, M. B. 1991. *Clothed with Christ: The Example and Teaching of Jesus in Romans 12.1–15.13*. JSNTSup 59. Sheffield: JSOT Press.

Thompson, M. B. 1993. 'Strong and Weak.' In *Dictionary of Paul and His Letters*, eds. G. F. Hawthorne and R. P. Martin. Leicester: IVP. 916–18.

The Church in Hebrews

MARKUS BOCKMUEHL

T HE document known as the Letter to the Hebrews continues to tease scholars with rather more questions than answers. Who wrote it, where and for whom? Does it date from before 70, at a time when the Temple in Jerusalem was still standing? What sort of relationship with Judaism may be assumed? Does it address Jewish Christians? Is the theology of Hebrews best understood against a Jewish (e.g. Alexandrian or Essene), a Platonic, or even a Gnostic background? Is Hebrews best seen as a homily to which a covering letter (e.g. 13.22–25) was perhaps only subsequently affixed? Is the writer's primary concern one of doctrine (the high priestly all-sufficiency of Christ) or of moral exhortation (endurance and faith) – or if both are equally important, what is the relationship between them? On these and other issues, critical scholarship is still some considerable way from reaching a consensus.

Our brief here, fortunately, is more limited: we are concerned to ask specifically how this writer views the Church, both as it is and as he longs for it to be.[1] Nevertheless, to address this question we must make a few assumptions about the origins and setting of this homiletical text, without being able to account for them here in detail. In view of the considerable variety of scholarly theories on the setting of Hebrews, it is hoped that the scenario here proposed is sufficiently broad to accommodate a range of views.

A. THE ORIGIN OF HEBREWS

1. Author

Along with a good many writers, we shall assume that the authorship of Hebrews is most plausibly sought in pro-Pauline circles between the 60s

---

[1] Unlike many of the other contributors to this volume, I never studied under John Sweet. Nevertheless, during six years as a junior colleague I learned much from his wisdom and learning, his lively theological engagement and his unflagging commitment to his students and to the Church at large. This essay is offered in gratitude for his constant and eponymous example: *verbum dulce . . . et lingua eucharis* (Sir 6.5).

I wish to thank Dr W. Horbury for his helpful comments on a draft of this chapter.

and 90s of the first century – with no clear preference for a date before 70.[2]

The ancient Church received Hebrews into the New Testament as composed in close proximity to the Apostle Paul. Among other MSS, the Chester Beatty papyrus 𝔓⁴⁶, our oldest extant collection of Paul's writings (c. 200 CE, possibly earlier), includes Hebrews immediately after Romans. Speculations about the name of the author thrive only in the absence of evidence; patristic discussion, at any rate, shows no clear tradition about authorship. We are left having to agree with the famous assessment that the origin of Hebrews, rather like that of Melchizedek, is known only to God (cf. 7.3; Origen cited in Eusebius, *Hist. Eccl.* 6.25.14).

2. Readership

To understand the central concerns of Hebrews, however, a far more important question than that of its authorship is in any case the identity and situation of its readers. Both author and audience clearly belong to the second or third generation of Christians who received the gospel from the apostles (2.3; 13.7); the readers themselves came to faith some time ago (10.32–34; 5.12). Beyond that, however, debate has been keen and protracted.

(a) *'Hebrews'?* The ancient but secondary superscription Πρὸς Ἐβραίους ('To [the] Hebrews') is widely agreed to be already dependent on a particular interpretation of the document. Nevertheless, the letter was thought to address 'Hebrews' rather than 'Jews' or 'Christians of Judaea', thus perhaps indicating an assumed link with Jewish Christians who maintained cultural and linguistic links with Palestine. A specific connection with Palestine and even with the Hebrew language was explicitly affirmed in Alexandrian tradition (cf. Eusebius, *Hist. Eccl.* 6.14.4) and in the subscriptions of some manuscripts (81 'to those in Jerusalem'; A P 'to the Hebrews from Rome'). However, while the Jerusalem church is indeed known in some early Christian sources as 'the church of the Hebrews' (e.g. *Ps.-Clem. Hom.*; cf. Acts 6.1), synagogues 'of the Hebrews' in fact existed in various parts of the diaspora, including Corinth and Rome.

---

[2] No deductions are possible from present-tense verbs relating to the temple cult, since comparable usage recurs in *1 Clem.* (e.g. 41.2) as well as in Josephus (e.g. *Contra Apionem* 2.77), the Mishnah and other post-70 Jewish writings. The first generation of leaders appear to have died (13.7). On the other hand, 10.1–3 could be taken to view the end of the sacrificial cult as a counterfactual hypothesis (so Vanhoye 1985:497), while 10.32–34 and 12.4, if indeed addressed to Rome, might suggest a date between 49 and 64 CE (cf. Lane 1991:lx-lxvi).

(*b*) *Jewish or Gentile?* The substance of Hebrews does at first sight appear easily compatible with a Jewish Christian readership, if not necessarily tied to a particular Palestinian location. The author can evidently assume his readers to be biblically literate and familiar with priestly ritual, especially as it relates to the Day of Atonement. In a context of growing Jewish nationalism before 70 or rabbinic consolidation after 70, it is easy to see how a writer might have wanted to strengthen Jewish Christian readers' loyalty to the new faith and assurance about the all-sufficiency of the atonement accomplished in Christ. Since Y. Yadin and H. Kosmala there have also been repeated, if on the whole unpersuasive, attempts to identify in Hebrews specific attention to Essene concerns, including such subjects as angels, Melchizedek, Jerusalem viewed in analogy to the Israelite 'camp' (Heb. 13.12–13; cf. 4QMMT 32–34, 63–65), and cultic and priestly matters interpreted specifically in relation to the OT laws about the tabernacle rather than to the temple in Jerusalem.

Advocates of this widely supported view of a Jewish Christian reader-ship tend, however, to underrate the importance of careful arguments from Scripture in a variety of writings to early *Gentile* churches who were attracted by Judaizing claims, for example Galatians, *1 Clement* and the *Epistle of Barnabas*. Indeed it is precisely characteristic of such literature that it seeks to establish the legitimacy and sufficiency of Christian faith *from the Torah itself* (and thus the wilderness tabernacle), rather than by appeal to contemporary Jewish practice and tradition.

What is more, the language of 'backsliding' in Hebrews never specifically addresses the problem of a return to Judaism. On the contrary, the doctrinal foundations of repentance from 'dead works' (i.e. sins, cf. 9.14; 4 Ezra 7.119), faith and 'baptisms' to which the writer appeals (cf. 6.1–2) are compatible with the Christian message as it would have been preached to Gentiles as well as to Jews. The text does, of course, strongly contrast the 'old' covenant and high priesthood against the 'new', even to the point of questioning the validity of certain 'old' practices (e.g. 13.9–10; see further Frey 1996). Nevertheless, there is no sustained polemic against Torah observance, and no specific Jewish adversaries are in view; even the earlier persecution involving imprisonment and confiscation of possessions (10.34) is unlikely to have been Jewish, especially if in Rome.[3]

[3] Nor indeed does the evident fulfilment and supersession of the Old Covenant in the New make Jewish heritage and Christian faith 'mutually exclusive' in the writer's view, any more than a building is mutually exclusive of its own blueprint (8.5). Similarly, the call to join Jesus 'outside the camp' (13.13) here concerns acceptance of the all-sufficiency of Christ's sacrifice outside and in place of the Jerusalem cult, rather than Christian Jews renouncing a wholly non-Christian entity called 'Judaism'. Despite obvious differences, both the Dead Sea Scrolls and the early chapters of Acts suggest that criticism of temple and City could entail much more nuanced implications, *pace* Walker 1994.

Instead, the immediate danger here is a lapse from faith, a lack of trust in the sufficiency of Christ's atonement, and a return to the unbelieving world like that of Israel in the wilderness (2.1; 3.12; 4.11; 6.4–6; 10.35, 38–39; 12.15). That danger, of course, could be equally acute whether the readers are Jewish Christians or Gentile Christians attracted by the more palpable claims of Jewish cult and identity. On balance, the language of Hebrews will make sense to those who see themselves as part of Israel and understand its history to be their own (cf. e.g. 1.1; 3.7ff; 11.1ff), whether their ethnic origin is Jewish or Gentile.

(c) *Specific or General?* If we cannot be sure that the recipients are themselves Jewish Christians, a related question arises with increased urgency: does Hebrews address a specific congregation at all, or does this pastoral 'word of exhortation' (13.22) have in view a general situation which is typical for the sub-apostolic period? Perhaps not unlike Ephesians, there is little if anything in Hebrews 1.1–13.21 which its writer would not arguably have wanted *all* Christians of his time to take to heart: the problems addressed seem characteristic of the second and third generation.

The writer certainly looks back to the time of apostolic proclamation as foundational, and recalls the first fervour of his readers' faithfulness to Christ (6.10; 10.32–34). Now, however, their faith has become tired and listless (5.11; 6.12), their eschatological hope and perseverance have become worn out and are giving way to doubts about God's promise (10.23, 35–36); some at least are in danger of abandoning the mutual encouragement of the Church (10.24–25) and even of discarding their faith and confidence altogether (10.35–39). The author's response to this problem involves no new doctrine, but instead recalls his readers to life-giving faith and hope in the Christ who is greater than the angels and whose atonement is better than the old covenant's sacrifices. His fundamental hermeneutical principle, in other words, is to find the solution to the readers' present predicament in a reapplication and interpretation of the apostolic tradition – an approach which similarly characterizes other early Christian writings.

Several aspects of the argument do, of course, lend this writer's work a more distinctive flavour. They include his cultic stress on the 'once and for all' of Christ's sacrifice (7.27; 9.12; 10.10), the superiority of Christ to Moses (3.2–6) and the angels (1.4ff) and his relative de-emphasis on an immanent parousia (but see 9.28; 10.25, 37) in favour of a hope for the heavenly 'better country' (11.13–16) into whose presence believers in Christ have now come (12.18–24). What is more, occasional appeals to the readers' own Christian experience (e.g. 5.11–12; 6.9–10), including a period of persecution and imprisonment (10.32–34; 13.2–3; NB not martyrdom: 12.4), suggest that the author's relationship with his readers is perhaps not merely abstract and perfunctory – even if we cannot say more than that. If Hebrews is in any sense a circular, it is perhaps best seen as addressed to the churches within the region of the author's own ministry and influence.

At the end of the day, it may be that our text is best understood as *both* widely inclusive *and* highly specific in application. The only really concrete and specific reference to the readers occurs in 13.22–25, which some scholars have regarded as a covering letter appended when the document was sent to a particular church. Here, then, we learn that the text is sent as a 'word of exhortation' (13.22); it is addressed to a group of people instructed to 'greet your leaders and all the saints' – perhaps implying that they constitute only one part of the church in their locality. They know and are concerned about the fate of Paul's one-time assistant Timothy, until recently imprisoned elsewhere (13.23: Ephesus?), and about Italian acquaintances. The most plausible scenario may be that the readers are one of several house churches in Rome.[4]

B. THE PEOPLE OF CHRIST

Bearing in mind this knotty and somewhat inconclusive debate about the intended readership of Hebrews, we turn now to the issue which more properly concerns us here: its author's vision for the Church. We will begin with some general remarks on the Church in Hebrews, followed by a brief description of seven ways in which the writer wishes the Church to mature and develop.

1. General

(a) *Lack of Ecclesiology* 'Hebrews', writes Lindars 1991:127 in something of an understatement, 'does not have a developed theology of the church'. Indeed one could argue that Hebrews, perhaps along with the Gospel and Letters of John, is notable among the books of the NT for its relative lack of explicit interest in this topic. It is perhaps symptomatic that the customary Christian technical term ἐκκλησία ('church') is used only in a quotation from Ps 22.23 (2.12) and in relation to the *heavenly* assembly (12.23). The homily's most characteristic term for 'church', if it has one at all, is οἶκος, 'house' (3.1–6; 10.21; cf. 1 Tim. 3.15 and John 14.2f; one passing reference to Christ's 'flock' is also found: 13.20).

Similarly, the very difficulty of identifying the letter's origin and addressees could be regarded as indicating a relatively underdeveloped practical doctrine of the Church: by comparison with most Pauline letters, which tend to be so situation-specific as to make them virtual case studies in applied ecclesiology, Hebrews in much of its doctrinal and even

---

[4] A connection with Rome may also be confirmed by certain parallels with the high priestly theology of *1 Clem.* 36.

paraenetic material seems to remain curiously at arm's length from its readers. While we hear about 'leaders' (13.7, 17, 24), and 'meetings' (10.25: NB ἐπισυναγωγή), Hebrews gives no indication as to who the former are and what the latter do. (This is a feature which is not explained simply by the assumption that Hebrews confines itself to addressing a small sub-group of a particular church, *pace* Rissi 1987:117.)

Several scholars, moreover, have concluded on the basis of 13.9 and the general silence on the matter that the author actively disapproves of the Eucharist (e.g. recently Roloff 1993:286; cf. the survey in Weiss 1991:726–29; contrast Swetnam 1989). Be that as it may, a de-emphasis on priest-hood and liturgy may well be in keeping with the writer's wider theological purpose of highlighting the sufficiency of the New Covenant priesthood and sacrifice of Christ as fulfilling and superseding the Old. There is therefore leadership in the Church, but no priesthood other than Christ's. Similarly, the sacrifices of praise and thanksgiving are offered by all Christians (13.15), just as the task of 'overseeing' (ἐπισκοποῦντες 12.15) is entrusted to all; and all ought, at least in principle, to be teachers (5.12; cf. 8.11–12).

(*b*) *The Church Constituted by Christ*   Certain contours of a people of Christ do nevertheless emerge, if perhaps often indirectly. By humbling himself lower than the angels and dying on behalf of human beings, Jesus, the pre-existent Son of God, came in solidarity with God's many 'sons' (2.6–10; cf. 12.5–8),[5] freed us (2.15) and constituted a new community of 'brothers and sisters' (2.11–12), who by faith become his 'partners' (μέτοχοι, 3.14 – a term which in this sense is distinctive to Hebrews; cf. 1.9; 3.1; 6.4; 12.8 and see Nardoni 1991). By 'passing through the heavens' (4.14) and ascending to the heavenly Holy of Holies, Jesus opened up for his people 'a new and living way through the curtain' (10.20). He has thus become not only their access to God but also the 'pioneer and perfecter' of their salvation and of faith (2.10; 12.2), and the source of Christian social identity and cohesion (cf. also 2.17–18).

In him, Christians now speak and live as one people: Christ is *our* High Priest, *our* Lord, the apostle and High Priest of *our* confession (3.1; 7.14, 26; 8.1). They are thus united as a people around their representative High Priest, in a sense related to that found in ancient Jewish views of the high priesthood (e.g. 2 Macc 15.26; cf. Horbury 1983:44f, 64f).

At the same time, Hebrews closely integrates the Church's 'horizontal' expectation of the coming resurrection and parousia (6.2; 9.28; 10.25, 37; 11.35) into the 'vertical' orientation towards the reality of the assembly in heaven (e.g. 12.18–25; 13.14; cf. Col 3.2–3; Eph 2.6). The goal of Christian

---

[5] NB the logic of this passage is completely missed in the NRSV, which for the sake of 'inclusive language' loses the christological reading of Ps 8.

hope here lies beyond space, time and history. Intriguingly, it is on the whole the Church which moves towards that heavenly reality, rather than vice versa (but note 9.28): we find here no eschatological descent of the heavenly Jerusalem (cf. Rev 21.2), perhaps because it would distract from the great soteriological emphasis on the incarnation and the ascension of Christ.

(c) *The Church as the One People of God* With regard to the identity and membership of this people of Christ, no social distinctions are drawn: all believers in Christ are equally part of the Church.

In spite of the 'new vs. old' rhetoric there is certainly no animosity against Jews, and no sense that the Jews as such have been rejected. Hebrews makes no attempt to contrast the *people* of the new covenant with that of the old: there is only one people of God called to faith, only one 'house of God' (3.5–6). Along with indications that author and readers do not observe the food laws (13.9, if that is what is meant) and are not plagued by disputes about circumcision (3.7–4.11 remains less clear about Sabbath observance), the vexing 'ethnic issue' of other early Christian writings is never addressed here, if it exists at all. However, this does not mean that the notion of Israel is for him no longer of any interest (so Chilton and Neusner 1995:183). Instead, the identity of the OT people of God has simply been mapped onto the people of Christ, in complete continuity. In this respect, it is worth noting that just as the wilderness generation perished and lost its chance to enter its Sabbath rest (3.17), so even the people of Christ may imperil their salvation by falling away and abandoning faith (3.12–13; 4.1, 11; cf. 6.4–6). It is, of course, true that the Christian cult is superior to the priestly temple cult (13.10 and *passim*), and that Christ's lordship over God's house is greater than Moses's servant status in that same house (3.5–6). But while the resulting tension between the old and new dispensations clearly marks the experience of the people of God, there is no doubt that it is one people.

Similarly, this people of God is not obviously polarized in terms of social, economic or power relationships. There are no signs of internal tension between men and women or masters and slaves, for instance. And while there are people referred to as 'leaders' (13.7, 17, 24), their identity is never specially highlighted and no clear functions or titles of such leadership are defined. Once again, the unity and identity of this people of God is essential.

C. SEVEN HIGHLIGHTS OF A VISION FOR THE CHURCH

In view of this author's rather 'low-key' interest in ecclesiology, what, if anything, can we say about his vision for the Church? What is it that

Hebrews wants the Christian Church to be and to do? Seven themes may be highlighted here, for the sake of convenience rather than of completeness. Of these, the first five are straightforward principles, while the last two are best understood in dialectical form as characterized by a desire to hold together different priorities in tension.

1. A Christian Church

Perhaps the most general and all-inclusive theme of the writer's vision for the Church is that it should be what it has been made and called to be: resolutely and confidently Christian, as the people of God. This is the theme which re-appears over and over in regard to each aspect of the writer's argument, and it is here that he sees the fundamental solution to the Church's crisis of confidence and faith. Instead of merely doctoring the symptoms or trumpeting a hollow rhetoric of discipline and endurance, the author summons his readers to a deeper understanding and appropriation of the same gospel in which they first believed. Nor is his primary aim to remedy some particular doctrinal or moral aberration.

Beginning from 1.1, he sets out to enliven the Church's faith on a firm foundation, rehearsing the basic content of that message about God's decisive and surpassing Word in Jesus Christ. His deliberate purpose is to exhort the Church to be unhesitatingly what it has been called to be: none other than the people of God, the inheritors through Christ of the 'better hope' (7.19) and the 'better country' (11.16; 12.18–24) that was promised to believers of old. They are at once pilgrims to that better country and already present citizens of it (McKelvey 1969:151–54). To be resolutely Christian, however, the Church must at the same time also follow Jesus in leaving behind other loyalties, foregoing the familiarity of the sacrificial cult to join him who was put to death outside the gate of Jerusalem, like the animals whose blood was brought as a sin offering on the Day of Atonement (Lev 16.27). This is part of what it means to belong to the 'city to come' (13.11–14).

For the writer to the Hebrews, perhaps the most important challenge to the Church, in a sense encompassing all the others, is whether it will accept in the gospel of Jesus Christ his gift and calling to be itself, to be the Lord's people.

2. A Pilgrim People

Despite the writer's limited interest in the doctrine of the Church, it remains true that his vision for the people of God is in fact profoundly corporate and ecclesial in nature. His emphasis on a confidently *Christian* Church is not contained in the mere desire for *esprit de corps*, but bears fruit also in a mutuality of relationships that characterizes the community as a whole. True, the answer to the present crisis of faith lies for him not in an increased emphasis on better 'fellowship', but rather in a renewed affirmation and lively engagement with the fundamental message of grace in the gospel (1.1ff). Nevertheless, and despite what has rightly been seen as a deliberately 'Word-centred' approach (cf. below), his conception of how people actually arrive at this deeper experience and assurance of grace is in fact profoundly Church-shaped – not least, perhaps, because of his uniquely *covenantal* understanding of the Christian message (διαθήκη is used seventeen times, more than in all the other NT books put together). Believing and belonging are inseparably interdependent.

The members of God's people are to strengthen one another against being hardened by the 'deceitfulness of sin' (3.13), and to spur each other on to good works and to faithful attendance at church meetings for mutual encouragement in the face of the eschaton (10.24–25). The Church follows Christ the forerunner into the eschatological Sabbath rest with all its members, and it is a corporate task to see that no one should fail to enter it or to obtain the grace of God, that one person's bitterness, immorality or godlessness should pollute the many (4.1; 12.15–16; cf. Deut 29.17). Indeed the author's stress on the concern of the whole community for each of its members emerges in the repeated exhortation 'lest anybody' (μὴ . . . τις) should fail to be included in the final salvation (3.13, 4.1, 11; 12.15–16). Some are indeed in serious danger of falling away, not least because they have ceased to attend the meetings for mutual encouragement (10.25–31).

Although this theme pervades a number of key passages in Hebrews, it comes to the fore especially in the important motif of the Church conceived in analogy to the 'wandering people of God' in the desert (3.7–4.11). This theme, which is here developed on the basis of Ps 95, rarely comes to explicit expression elsewhere in the NT (but cf. 1 Peter; also 1 Cor 10). During four weeks in 1938 while awaiting trial in a Nazi jail, Ernst Käsemann produced a path-breaking study on this theme (ET 1984; cf. März 1993:173). His exegetical observations about the true Church as the typologically interpreted 'wandering people of God' have been widely accepted as accurate (Buchanan's literal, Zionist interpretation has found few followers). Käsemann's proposal of a Gnostic background, by contrast, has received only minority support; more seriously for our purposes, a number of scholars have criticized him for overrating the communal dimension of this image of the wandering people of God (e.g. Lindars 1991:126; Roloff 1993:285–86; cf. below).

The Church discovers the encouragement and exhortation of the OT Scriptures as pointing through Christ to its own experience: 'the good news came to us just as to them' (4.2; cf. similarly 1 Cor 10; Rom 15.4ff). Like the wilderness generation, the Church is invited to enter the eschatological Sabbath rest promised by God; whereas they did not reach it due to unbelief (3.11, 18), believing Christians are now urged to enter it without fail (4.1–11). In keeping with this reading of Ps 95, the present is also a corporate challenge: 'Today' becomes the time of critical decision, for the Church to move forward in faith and enter that eschatological rest whose promise to this day is still unfulfilled – possibly even awaiting imminent consummation at the end of 'forty years' (so e.g. Walker 1994:62–65 on 3.9, 17; 8.13; 10.25, 37; 12.27).

The author's somewhat understated, but unambiguously corporate vision of the Church comes to expression in a number of perhaps unexpected ways. These include, for instance, the writer's own carefully crafted argumentation, which is now widely recognized to manifest some of the NT's most accomplished stylistic and rhetorical erudition (cf. e.g. the survey in Koester 1994:125–28). Not only are many of his central exhortations set inclusively in the first person plural, but by opening with a rehearsal of the common ground of Christian doctrine (ch. 1–2), the author structures his overall argument in such a way as to enrol his readers' goodwill and consent from the start. This is characteristic of a document which develops its 'word of exhortation' from a basis of consensus rather than of authoritarian command or confrontation.

The thesis of a vision of corporate solidarity in Hebrews is, to be sure, not without its problems. It suffers on the one hand from the homily's generally underdeveloped ecclesiology, which we noted earlier. Even when Hebrews is taken on its own terms, however, one comes away with the impression that corporate and individual responsibilities have been left in an awkward and unresolved tension. The Church's communal entrance into the Sabbath rest, sustaining the weak and faint-hearted along the way, is seemingly compromised by a strongly individual view of sanctification. This comes to the fore particularly in the author's dramatic threefold denial of a second repentance after falling away from an initial state of grace (6.4–6; 10.26–31; 12.16–17), which in this form is without parallel in the NT. (*Hermas, Vis.* 2.2.5 allows one further repentance after baptism; but Hebrews is, of course, concerned with apostasy rather than with post-baptismal sin – 10.26 should be read with 10.29.) On the one hand, the author's stance is perhaps best seen against the general background of his desire to reinvigorate the listless and flagging faith of his readers: at a time of fading vision and commitment, the writer's stark warning lends to his exhortation a theological *gravitas* likely to instil in his readers a heightened sense of the importance of remaining faithful here and now as God is faithful to them (a point which arises quite naturally from the 'Today' of Ps 95 expounded in 3.7–4.11; cf. 10.23).

Unlike Paul, however, the writer to the Hebrews makes no attempt to relate this serious warning against individual apostasy to an overall view of the Church – be it in terms of sustaining the weak, rebuking and restoring the errant (e.g. 1 Thess 5.14), or on the other hand in terms of preserving the purity of a sanctified Church (as in 1 Cor 5.6–13).

Exclusion here seems rather more individually conceived: it is not excommunication so much as effective *self*-exclusion with fateful consequences (but note the divine reference implied in the passive of Esau's rejection in 12.17, and possibly in the impersonal πάλιν ἀνακαινίζειν ['restore again'] in 6.6). It may still be preferable on balance to understand these passages in light of the Jewish traditions of exclusion from the covenant (on which see Horbury 1985); the impossibility of repentance for apostates is, moreover, repeatedly discussed in rabbinic literature (e.g. Mishnah, *Aboth* 5.18; *y. Ḥag.* 2.1, 77b57–62 (Elisha b. Abuya); cf. further Attridge 1989:168). Rhetorically, too, it seems that the author's positive paraenetical intent does not in fact regard apostasy among his readers as an acute danger, but rather as something which in the light of 6.4–5 would be inconceivable (e.g. Lane 1991:145; Weiss 1991:347–51). Despite his warning he is 'confident of better things' as far as they are concerned (6.9). It remains the case, however, that an explicitly ecclesiological or covenantal reflection on this matter is lacking in Hebrews.

Such difficulties notwithstanding, the leading images of the writer's description of the Christian life are clearly corporate and covenantal. God's speech is to 'us', and 'we' have access to the Sabbath rest, the throne of grace and the heavenly Mount Zion. The writer's vision of the Church is of the pilgrim people of God, whose constitution and vocation make them more than a casual collection of individuals. They are bound together by the common ground of their identity, in the Christ who freed them from bondage, made them his 'brethren' (2.11–15) and built them into God's 'house' (3.3, 6). As such, they also find their common aim in journeying together to the better country, the heavenly assembly of Mount Zion. As we shall see below (para. 7), it is only there that one finds a vision of the true Church at home, in the perfect communion of saints. (Contrary to its use in some modern theology, this motif of pilgrimage in Hebrews is neither a self-contained abstraction nor directed towards a this-worldly 'temple' or 'city', 'land' or 'kingdom'; instead, it aims explicitly at a transcendent and eternal fulfilment in the presence of God [6.9; 9.24; 11.16; 12.22–24, 28]. Cf. Williams 1995; also Hofius 1970; Isaacs 1992.)

3. Christ-Centred

If the courage to be Christian is the writer's overall concern for the Church, that vision is at the same time set in vigorously christological terms. What it means to be saved, what it means to live as a Christian, and what it means to be the Church – all this finds its unmistakable focus in Jesus. He is the 'pioneer of our salvation' (2.10; 12.2), the High Priest like us who entered the holy of Holies and sat down at the right hand of God (4.14; 8.1), the guarantor of the better covenant based on better promises (7.22; 8.6). It is his ministry, and his alone, which provides for his people a redemption that is eternal: a 'new and living way' of dealing with sin ἐφάπαξ ('once and for all': 7.27; 9.12–14; 10.20), and a way of 'making holy' that is equally ἐφάπαξ (10.10). In the Church's present crisis of faith, Jesus as the great shepherd of his sheep (13.20) constitutes the assured 'anchor of the soul', the link with both the origin of the gospel in the past and the coming consummation in the future: he is 'the same yesterday and today and for ever' (13.12; cf. 6.19–20). The writer's vision, then, is that the Church should grasp this reality of being rooted in Christ, and in this as in every sense to look to him as the pioneer and perfecter of its faith and salvation. Given his representative role as 'our' High Priest, the appeal to Christ's example does carry clearly ecclesiological implications (4.14–5.10; 12.2; and cf. para. 2 above on passages like 10.24f).

At the same time, however, there are a number of unexpected and striking lacunae in the writer's Christ-centred vision for the Church. A number of scholars have pointed out that there is here no trace of the sort of Christ mysticism which one finds in Paul or in the Fourth Gospel: we hear nothing, for instance, of being 'in Christ' or 'with Christ', and no description of the Church as the 'body of Christ'.

Of particular interest in this respect is the seeming lack of interest or even (as some have argued) antipathy for the notion of a presence of Christ in the Eucharist. Several allusions may imply a familiarity with certain eucharistic traditions (6.4–5; cf. 9.20 with 1 Cor 10.16; 10.29 with 1 Cor 11.27; 13.9–10), but scholars are deeply divided on this issue and the evidence is by no means straightforward. The stress in Hebrews lies in any case on the Word rather than the sacrament (note also 1.2; 2.3; 4.2, 12f), and the focus of attention is clearly the heavenly Christ himself.

Matters are similar in relation to the Holy Spirit. On the one hand, the Christian experience means to be made 'partakers of the Holy Spirit' (6.4; cf. 2.4; 10.29). At the same time, however, it remains wholly unclear whether and if so how far the writer views the Spirit in anything like Pauline or Lucan terms as the empowering presence of the heavenly Christ (e.g. Rom 8.9–10), or Christians as 'baptized by one Spirit into one body' (1 Cor 12.13).

All in all, then, the vision for the Church in Hebrews is intensely christological, but that affirmation is quite specifically defined. The Christology is narrowly focused on the writer's overall purpose, that is, above all on soteriology (the sufficiency and superiority of Christ's Melchizedekian high priesthood) and on ethics (his example as the pioneer and perfecter of faith). Other elements, it seems, are less important for the Church in Hebrews.

4. Rooted in the Word of God

Even a superficial reading suffices to see that Hebrews is deeply conversant in the OT Scriptures, and this subject alone has been the subject of several monographs. More particularly for our purposes, the writer regards Scripture as an essential source of encouragement and reproof for the Church. It is woven into every argument and presupposed at every turn. Indeed, given the widely recognized rhetorical skill of this writer, it is highly significant that he begins his argument about the superiority of Christ with an extended appeal to Scripture (ch. 1). A Church whose understanding of itself or the Gospel had become detached from Scripture would be a Church detached from the Holy Spirit, who functions as the voice of Scripture speaking eschatologically to Christians (e.g. 3.7; 9.8; 10.15). Using a metaphor also found in the Talmud and Midrashim (*b.Ber.* 5a; cf. Str.-B. 3:687–88), the Word of God in the warning from Scripture is 'living and active, sharper than any two-edged sword, piercing to the division of soul and spirit, of joints and marrow, and discerning the thoughts and intentions of the heart' (4.12). Despite all the rhetoric of 'New' vs. 'Old' Covenant, Hebrews like the rest of the NT unhesitatingly affirms the Hebrew Scriptures as telling 'our' story, and as the sure prophetic witness to the Word of God.

At the same time, the Word of God is not simply identified with Scripture. It is a dynamic and transcendent power which comes to expression above all in the apostolic preaching. God creates and upholds the universe by his Word (1.3; 11.3), and his Word was spoken and taught to the readers when they heard the Christian message (5.12; 6.5; 13.7). The programmatic affirmation that 'God spoke' in the prophets and in Christ (1.1–2) is developed through the whole of Hebrews to the culminating warning not to 'disregard the one who is speaking' (12.25; cf. Lane 1991:1; Hegermann 1988:16–19). As in Scripture so in the Christian message, it is the Holy Spirit himself who is active through the Word of God (2.4; 1.1).

The author's vision, then, is almost exclusively in terms of a Church of the Word, as we already surmised above (cf. also Roloff 1993:282). One could argue that his theology is somewhat arid in this respect, given his failure to develop the complementary themes of Christ's presence through the Spirit or in the sacraments. And yet we are probably well advised not to extrapolate overmuch from the silences conditioned by the writer's central aim. In extolling the superiority of Christ's once-for-all redemption over the Old Covenant's sacrificial ritual it is after all hardly surprising that he should concentrate on the sufficiency of the *word* of Christ's achievement rather than, say, on a re-enacted liturgical drama.

All the while, of course, the writer's message shows the Word of God itself to bear a rich fountain of grace and living hope, an 'anchor for the soul' in Christ as our pioneer (6.17–20). Given the readers' crisis of confidence in the gospel and loss of ecclesial nerve, it may also be significant that it is the Word of God which links the creational, prophetic and incarnate revelation of the past with the readers' present experience and with the 'powers of the age to come' (6.5).

Three further characteristics of the vision for the Church in Hebrews can be discussed rather more briefly; they concern the Church's holiness and its perspective on time and eternity.

5. Holy

In view of the explicit identification of Hebrews as a 'word of exhortation' (13.22), it is not surprising to find a good dose of ethical appeal alongside the writer's doctrinal concerns (e.g. 2.1–4; 3.7–4.11; 4.14–16; 5.11–6.20; 10.19–39; 12.1–13). The logical link between doctrine and moral exhortation is clearly one of the major emphases of Hebrews, and one which relates intimately to its author's pastoral vision for the Church (cf. Weiss 1991:95; Schmidt 1992; Matera 1994). At a time of waning faith and confidence, it is appropriate to exhort Christians to 'pay greater attention' to the Christian message, strengthen their drooping hands and weak knees, 'hold fast' to their confession and 'make every effort' to enter the Sabbath rest of God (2.1; 12.12; 4.14, 11).

In keeping with the discussion of the work of Christ on the basis of the OT sacrificial cult, key terms in this respect are those of 'holiness' and 'sanctification', understood here in moral and spiritual terms as that which is in keeping with the presence and character of God. Similarly, just as 'purification' here pertains to Christ's act of atonement from sins (1.3; 9.14; 10.22), so 'defilement' is explicitly transferred from a concern with ritual purity of the 'flesh' to the greater purity of 'conscience' in the Spirit (9.13–14). Through his sacrifice, the eternal and holy High Priest has 'sanctified' Christians once and for all (2.11; 9.12–13; 10.10, 14, 29; 13.12). At the same time, however, sanctification is also a goal of the Christian life: believers are exhorted to endure trials as God's way of preparing them to share in his holiness (12.10), and they are to pursue that holiness actively (12.14). Similarly, Christians must still avoid defilement, which is contracted above all through bitterness (12.15) or sexual immorality (13.4).

While the pursuit of holiness is in 12.14 closely linked with the 'horizontal' concern to pursue 'peace with everyone', concrete moral instruction is not really encountered before chapter 13. There, the writer begins with an exhortation to continue mutual love (φιλαδελφία, 13.1), a quality which, it seems, his readers have long manifested in their service of the saints out of love for God (ἀγάπη, 6.10). In addition, we find instructions to show hospitality, visit (Christian?) prisoners, guard the purity of marriage and abstain from the love of money (vv. 2–5). In place of the sacrifice of animals, those who have joined Jesus outside the 'camp' must now offer the sacrifices of praise, good works and sharing of who they are and what they have (αἴνεσις, εὐποιΐα, κοινωνία: 13.15–16). Finally, we also find a conventional and in some ways Pauline-sounding appeal to 'obey your leaders' (13.17; cf. e.g. 1 Thess 5.12–13) and to pray for the author (13.18). All this seems a perfectly appropriate application of the writer's vision for holiness to the practical realm of Christian life together, in keeping with similar instructions in other early Christian writings.

At the same time, it is noteworthy that unlike the authors of some other parts of the NT this writer does not seem interested in developing a specifically Christian ethic, or in commending distinctively ecclesial forms of Christian life. There is, as Roloff 1993:286 puts it, little if anything that goes beyond the general virtues of life in community. The readers have an impressive track record of steadfastness in persecution and of service to the saints (6.10; 10.32–34; 13.2–3). Other than a general commendation of the imitation of Christ's endurance in the face of abuse (12.2–3; 13.13), however, we hear little that is ethically distinctive to Christianity: no reference to love as the sum of the commandments, no appeal to Christ's example for a disposition of humility or forgiveness (despite Heb 4.15; 5.2, 5, 8; contrast e.g. Rom 15.6; 2 Cor 8.9; Phil 2.5–11), no reminder of the moral teaching of Jesus.

Once again, however, the writer's rhetorical situation may to some extent account for this lacuna. His primary concern is to stress the effectiveness and surpassing heavenly reality of Christ's sacrificial atonement and to reinvigorate his readers' faith on that basis. While he warns against apostasy, there is little evidence that his readers are confused or unsure about substantive practical questions of morality: the problem is not knowing what to do but doing what they know they should do (cf. Matera 1994:169, citing A. Verhey). Indeed he acknowledges the continuing diligence and service to the saints which most of them still manifest despite the current crisis of assurance (6.9–12).

In that regard, then, the writer's prescription against the Church's slackness and failure of faith involves a renewal of unfailing assurance about the gospel of Jesus Christ, whose work and example in turn empowers Christian pursuit of his holiness and endurance with the certain hope of entering the Sabbath rest and the heavenly city.

6. Progressive and Conservative

Two sets of complementary priorities for the Church's view of time and eternity conclude our survey. The first heading somewhat provocatively juxtaposes two kinds of verbs employed in the writer's paraenesis. One stresses endurance, 'holding fast' and 'maintaining' Christian faith and confidence, showing diligence and taking care not to 'drift away' from it or be 'carried away' by false teachings, not to 'leave behind' church attendance or 'abandon' their hope (2.1; 3.6, 14; 4.14; 6.11–12; 10.23, 25, 35; 12.2–3; 13.9). The other group of verbs exhorts or describes how to 'go to Jesus outside the camp', to 'set out' and 'look forward' like Abraham, to 'lay aside' all that hinders and 'run the race', to 'go on' and 'approach' the throne of grace or 'arrive' at the heavenly Mount Zion, to 'seize' the hope set before them, to 'reach' and 'enter' the Sabbath rest and the shrine behind the curtain, to 'pursue' peace and holiness, even to engage in mutual 'provocation' (παροξυσμός) to love and good works (4.1, 6, 11; 6.1, 18–19; 10.22; 11.8, 10; 12.1, 14; 13.13).

These two kinds of exhortation concern two fundamental and complementary dispositions of the Christian life, attested throughout the NT: one which affirms, nourishes, protects and conserves what has been received, and another which looks to the future, abandons all that hinders and presses forward to the hope set before us. In contemporary Christian rhetoric these two movements are frequently viewed as mutually incompatible polarities. In the NT, however, and in the vision of Hebrews in particular, they clearly stand in a vital symbiotic relationship, each helpless and useless without the other. In addition to their evident theological interdependence in this letter, the writer uses both principles quite unself-consciously side by side (e.g. 6.11–12; 10.22–24; 12.1–2) or even urges both attitudes in regard to the same object of 'hope' (6.11, 18–19; 10.23). The Church cannot be faithful to the pioneer of salvation if it does not 'hold fast' the confession of hope in God's unchanging promise *and at the same time* reach out to 'seize' that same hope which 'enters' the inner shrine of God's presence.

7. Militant and Triumphant

Even the casual reader cannot fail to notice in Hebrews a grand cosmic integration of earthly and heavenly reality, and of time and eternity. While even the Old Covenant ritual already operated entirely on the basis of copies of true originals in heaven (8.5, citing Exod 25.40), the New Covenant has dispensed with the copies altogether and exists in the presence of the transcendent reality constituted 'once for all' by its superior High Priest. Similarly, we noted above (para. B. 1. c) that anticipation of the parousia and day of judgement seem to be virtually subsumed under the present reality of the heavenly Jerusalem. Somewhat as in apocalyptic literature, we find here a co-existence of both anticipation and participation; God's purposes are both eagerly awaited in history and already accessible to the believer in heaven.

This motif is also of profound significance for the writer's ecclesial vision. While a future eschatology is still evident and entrance into the 'better country' is still merely imminent, the writer is at the same time happy to speak of the Christian hope as 'entering' the heavenly rest (present tense, e.g. 4.3; 6.19) with Christ who has already 'entered' (6.20; 9.12, 24). More clearly still, Christians have already 'arrived' (προσεληλύθατε 12.18, 22) at the heavenly Mount Zion, which represents the writer's most comprehensive picture both of the present heavenly worship and of the future events of judgement and resurrection: 'the assembly of the firstborn who are enrolled in heaven, and to God the judge of all, and to the spirits of the righteous made perfect' (12.23).

Thus, all that the Church is called to be is already fully present in the heavenly reality to which Christians have come by virtue of faith in Christ. From that perspective, the ostensibly deficient ecclesiology of Hebrews turns out on closer inspection to offer perhaps the NT's richest, most majestic panorama of the transcendent eschatological reality that is the Communion of Saints, the eternal fellowship of pilgrims past and present.

It is this perspective which must be seen to balance both the writer's ardent concern for the Church's pursuit of holiness and his solemn warnings against apostasy. Neither is intended to take away from a covenantal vision of the universal people of God; on the contrary, both must be understood as driven by the writer's overwhelming desire to see the Church reach the heavenly city intact and holy, with all its members, in its faithful profession of the better hope.

CONCLUSION

It remains to sum up briefly. We saw that the writer to the Hebrews does not have a particularly systematic or developed ecclesiology. Nevertheless, he understands the Church to be constituted by Christ as the one people of God, at one with the faithful of the Old Testament. His vision for the Church is that it should be a confidently Christian pilgrim community, centred on the high priestly person and work of Christ for its experience of salvation, and rooted in the Word of God in Scripture and the gospel. This doctrinally based vision for renewed confidence at a time of declining faith is matched by a concern for the Church's holiness, both as a gift achieved in Christ and as a goal to be implemented. As a pilgrim people on its way to its true home in the promised 'better country', the Church must engage with this Christian hope in a way that is at once conservative in its reception and affirmation, and yet courageous and forward-looking in approaching and entering the Sabbath rest that God has prepared.

BIBLIOGRAPHY

Attridge, H. W. 1989. *The Epistle to the Hebrews*. Hermeneia. Philadelphia: Fortress.

Attridge, H. W. 1992. 'Hebrews'. *ABD* 3:97–104.

Buchanan, G. W. 1972. *To the Hebrews*. AB 36. Garden City: Double-day.

Chilton, B. and Neusner, J. 1995. *Judaism in the New Testament: Practices and Beliefs*. London/New York: Routledge.

Feld, H. 1985. *Der Hebräerbrief*. Darmstadt: Wissenschaftliche Buchgesellschaft.

Frey, J. 1996. 'Die alte und die neue διαθήκη nach dem Hebräerbrief'. In F. Avemarie & H. Lichtenberger (eds.), *Bund und Tora: Zur theologischen Begriffsgeschichte in alttestamentlicher, frühjüdischer und urchristlicher Tradition*. WUNT 92. Tübingen: Mohr (Siebeck). 263–310.

Hegermann, H. 1988. *Der Brief an die Hebräer*. THKNT 16. Berlin: Evangelische Verlagsanstalt.

Hofius, O. 1970. *Katapausis: Die Vorstellung vom endzeitlichen Ruheort im Hebräerbrief*. WUNT 11. Tübingen: Mohr (Siebeck).

Horbury, W. 1983. 'The Aaronic Priesthood in the Epistle to the Hebrews'. *JSNT* 19:43–71.

Horbury, W. 1985. 'Extirpation and Excommunication'. *VT* 35:13–38.

Hurst, L. D. 1990. *The Epistle to the Hebrews: Its Background of Thought*. SNTSMS 65. Cambridge: Cambridge University Press.

Isaacs, M. E. 1992. *Sacred Space: An Approach to the Theology of the Epistle to the Hebrews*. JSNTSup 73. Sheffield: JSOT.

Käsemann, E. 1984. *The Wandering People of God*. Tr. R. A. Harrisville and I. L. Sandberg. Minneapolis: Augsburg.

Koester, C. R. 1994. 'The Epistle to the Hebrews in Recent Study'. *CRBS* 2:123–45.

Lane, W. L. 1991. *Hebrews*. WBC 47. 2 vols. Waco: Word.

Lindars, B. 1991. *The Theology of the Letter to the Hebrews*. Cambridge: Cambridge University Press.

März, C.-P. 1993. 'Ein "Außenseiter" im Neuen Testament'. *BiKi* 48:173–79.

Matera, F. J. 1994. 'Moral Exhortation: The Relation between Moral Exhortation and Doctrinal Exposition in the Letter to the Hebrews'. *TJT* 10:169–82.

McCullough, J. C. 1994. 'Hebrews in Recent Scholarship'. *IBS* 16:66–86, 108–20.

McKelvey, R. J. 1969. *The New Temple: The Church in the New Testament*. Oxford: Oxford University Press.

Nardoni, E. 1991. 'Partakers in Christ (Hebrews 3.14)'. *NTS* 37:456–72.

Rissi, M. 1987. *Die Theologie des Hebräerbriefs.* WUNT 41. Tübingen: Mohr (Siebeck).

Roloff, J. 1993. *Die Kirche im Neuen Testament.* Göttingen: Vandenhoeck & Ruprecht.

Schmidt, T. E. 1992. 'Moral Lethargy and the Epistle to the Hebrews'. *WTJ* 54:167–73.

Schweizer, E. 1961. *Church Order in the New Testament.* Tr. Frank Clarke. London: SCM Press.

Söding, T. 1993. 'Gemeinde auf dem Weg: Christsein nach dem Hebräerbrief'. *BiKi* 48:180–87.

Swetnam, J. 1989. 'Christology and the Eucharist in the Epistle to the Hebrews'. *Bib* 70:74–95.

Vanhoye, A. 1985. 'Hebräerbrief.' *TRE* 14:494–505.

Walker, P. 1994. 'Jerusalem in Hebrews 13:9–14 and the Dating of the Epistle'. *TynB* 45:39–71.

Weiss, H.-F. 1991. *Der Brief an die Hebräer.* KEKNT 13. Göttingen: Vandenhoeck & Ruprecht.

Williams, S. N. 1995. 'The Pilgrim People of God: Some General Observations'. *IBS* 17:129–37.

II

James, 1 Peter, Jude and 2 Peter

RICHARD BAUCKHAM

THE so-called 'catholic' letters of the NT (from which I here exclude the Johannine letters, the subject of another chapter) are surely, along with the book of Revelation, the most neglected voices among the canonical contributors to a biblical vision of the Church. For ordinary readers they seem to be tucked away in what seems virtually an appendix of minor letters, negligible by comparison with the great Pauline letters which precede them, though it is worth remarking that this impression is a result of the Western ordering of the canon. In the canonical order which, following patristic tradition, is found in Eastern Orthodox Bibles, the 'catholic' letters follow Acts and precede the Pauline letters, since they are the letters of those who were apostles before Paul. A quite different impression of canonical importance is given. But, of course, for many theologians and scholars, the traditional authorship of the 'catholic' letters has long ceased to give them importance, while some of these letters – James, 2 Peter, Jude – have been probably more subjected to theological criticism and downright denigration than any other part of the canon. However, a wide range of recent scholarship on these letters has been contributing in a variety of ways to dispelling the clouds of misrepresentation and ignorant neglect with which the older scholarly tradition obscured them. In the process the individual distinctiveness of these works, each a quite different voice from the many parts of the early Christian movement which were neither Pauline nor Johannine, is emerging. Since nothing more than convention justifies their treatment together in a single chapter, no attempt will be made here to synthesize their individual voices. Each will be heard for its own sake. (An exception will be made in the case of 2 Peter and Jude, which in many respects are much more diverse than scholarly tradition has allowed, but which do converge in their vision of the Church.)

JAMES

Responsible interpretation of the letter of James must take seriously the superscription (1.1), which identifies its author and addressees. In the light of recent scholarship (e.g. Johnson 1995), there are no longer any cogent reasons for thinking that the name James is used pseudonymously or that 'the twelve tribes in the diaspora' are to be understood metaphorically. The letter is a circular letter from James, the Lord's brother, leader of the Jerusalem church, to Jews throughout the diaspora. James writes in the well-established Jewish tradition of letters from the authorities at the centre of the Jewish world, Jerusalem, to the communities in the diaspora. The reference to all twelve tribes is not purely ideal, but indicates that the letter is intended for the whole diaspora, including not only the western but also the eastern diaspora, where descendants of the exiles of the northern tribes still, in this period, formed communities known and in communication with the rest of the Jewish world.

All that the superscription leaves unsaid about the epistolary situation is that the addressees are evidently not all diaspora Jews without distinction, but specifically those who belonged to the early Christian movement. This is clear from the facts that James writes explicitly as a leader of this movement (1.1) and that his letter is not designed to convert readers to faith in Jesus as the Messiah but takes for granted that its readers share this faith (2.1). From a practical point of view, the superscription does not need to specify that its addressees are Christians, because such a letter would be delivered to groups of Christian Jews by messengers who themselves belonged to the movement. But the fact that the super-scription differs in this respect from all other superscriptions to NT letters (which all indicate in some way that their addressees are Christians) is probably indicative of the way James views the early Christian movement. He does not see it as a specific sect distinguished from other Jews, but as the nucleus of the messianic renewal of the people of Israel which was under way and which would come to include all Israel. Those Jews who acknowledge Jesus to be the Messiah are the twelve tribes of Israel, not in an exclusive sense so as to deny other Israelites this title, but with a kind of representative inclusiveness. What James addresses in practice to those Jews who already confess the Messiah Jesus, he addresses in principle to all Israel. The description of the addressees as 'the twelve tribes in the diaspora', as well as referring to their actual tribal membership and geographical situation, would probably also evoke the lively first-century Jewish hope of the return of the exiles of all twelve tribes to the land of Israel. It incorporates the addressees in the messianic programme of redemption which Jesus had initiated by appointing twelve apostles.

That Gentiles could become members of the people of Israel, as Rahab (2.25) did, was, of course, wholly uncontroversial. But the possibility, raised by the Pauline mission, that Gentiles who believed in Jesus could belong to the eschatological people of God as Gentiles, without becoming Jews, does not impinge on James's concerns in the letter. He discusses the issue of faith and works (2.14–26) not at all in the way that it features in the Pauline letters, where it is always a matter of the relationship of Jewish and Gentile Christians. In James the issue has nothing to do with qualifications for belonging to the people of God, and nothing to do with the distinctives of Jewish identity, such as circumcision, which concerned both Paul and his opponents because of their implications for the status of Gentile Christians. James addresses, not a polemical issue, as Paul does in Galatians, but the practical failure of people who pride themselves on their monotheistic belief (cf. 2.19) to express their faith in works of love. The fact that this section of James (2.14–26), which at first glance appears to relate closely to Pauline discussions, is in fact entirely oblivious of the issues raised by Paul's Gentile mission, shows how completely the letter assumes the Jewish Jesus movement as its context, and probably indicates that it dates from a period before the status of Gentile converts had become a controversial issue. James's vision for the Church certainly does not exclude Gentiles, but, like Jesus' own mission, it is still focused on the messianic renewal of Israel as the necessary first stage in the messianic redemption of the world.

The messianic renewal of Israel certainly has the messianic redemption of the world as its goal. This is clear from 1.18, where those Israelites who have received new birth as children of God, thus constituting the renewed Israel, are called 'a kind of first fruits of his creatures'. They are the first sheaf of the eschatological harvest, offered to God in thankful assurance of the full harvest to come. The new birth of messianic Jews, the renewal of Israel, is the representative beginning of God's new creation of all things. Thus James addresses the twelve tribes, but he does so with the consciousness he shares with all early Christians that God's purpose now being fulfilled through Jesus the Messiah has a universal goal.

Since the Church, for James, is the messianically renewed Israel, his vision for the Church is of a community which fully expresses in its life the values expressed by God in his law. There are two broad angles from which we can explore this vision. One is James's characteristic concern for wholeness, while the other is his characteristically sharp dualism. While these two forms of thought have a surface-structure which appears to be contradictory, since formally one requires of James's readers 'not only this, but also that', whereas the other requires their allegiance 'only to this, not to that', in reality as we shall see the two forms of thought complement each other and cohere in the paraenetic goal at which they aim. Together they structure a vision of a community which wholeheartedly embraces and fully practises the values of God's kingdom, and which thereby distinguishes itself radically from the dominant values of the world.

The first of the many aphorisms in which James encapsulates his teaching (1.3–4) introduces the theme of wholeness or integrity which pervades the letter. Of the two synonyms used here, 'complete' (τέλειος) and 'whole' (ὁλόκληρος), paired for emphasis, the first, with its cognates, forms a word-group which is a favourite of James and is one (but only one) of the ways in which the theme of completeness or integrity recurs through the letter (cf. 1.17, 25; 2.8, 22; 3.2). In contrast with double-mindedness (1.8; 4.8), it indicates wholehearted and single-minded loyalty to God and God's values. Therefore it requires that Christians should not only hear but also act (1.22–25), not only say but also do (2.16), not only believe but also *complete* their faith with works (2.14–26, esp. 22). It requires that they should not pick and choose which commandments to keep, but *complete* (fulfil) the *whole* of God's *complete* law (2.8–12; cf. 1.25). It requires that they should not curse people with one side of the mouth while blessing God with the other (3.9–10). In these kinds of ways wholeness is equivalent to consistency of living out the values expressed in God's law in the whole of life. Such consistent living manifests the divine gifts, which are always *complete* (1.17), in the sense of wholly and unequivocally good, and the wisdom from above, whose *seven* characteristic qualities are indicative of completeness (3.17).

Wholeness, with its roots in the undivided devotion and loyalty of the heart to God, is a matter of the integrity of the individual, involving the whole person (3.2). But it is also applicable to the community. Loyalty to God and to each other should unite individuals in a community characterized by peaceable, gentle, considerate, caring and forgiving relationships (2.13; 3.13, 17; 4.11–12; 5.16, 19). James connects the conflict within an individual, which impairs integrity of the person (4.1), and the conflict which tears the community apart (4.1) and against which he especially warns (3.16; 4.1–2, 11; 5.9). Competitive ambition (3.14) threatens the wholeness of the community, just as peacemaking (3.18) promotes it.

While James's emphasis on wholeness aims to unite (both . . . and), his dualism promotes a certain sort of division (either . . . or). It insists on a distinction in reality which requires of Christians a choice. Either they can be friends with God (4.4), like Abraham (2.23), or they can be friends with 'the world' (4.4), but the choice must be made. The distinction cannot be fudged. The compromise ('both . . . and') which the 'double-minded' (4.8) attempt, dividing their loyalties between God and the world, is in reality not possible. In this sharp contrast the dualism is fundamentally one of value-systems. One lives either by God's values or by that dominant value-system which James calls 'the world' (1.27; 2.5; 4.4). 'Friendship' (4.4) has connotations of loyalty and sharing of values. Hence friendship with both God and the world, indicating opposed systems of values to live by, is impossible. In the same context (4.4) James uses the image of marriage and adultery in the manner of the OT prophets: God's people who compromise with worldly values are adulterous women, attempting the impossible task of combining marriage to God their husband, who requires exclusive loyalty, and liaison with another partner, the world. This dualism between God and the world appears also in 1.27, where religion that is undefiled in the eyes of God involves keeping oneself unstained by the world. The latter phrase does not imply avoiding contact with outsiders, but refusing to comply with that approach to life which is inconsistent with God's values. That the issue is primarily one of values is very clear in another manifestation of James's dualism: the contrast between two kinds of wisdom, one of which is 'earthly' (i.e. of earthly origin rather than coming from heaven), 'natural' (i.e. purely human rather inspired by the divine spirit) and 'demonic' (i.e. associated with the evil spirits who inhabit this earthly realm), while the other is 'from above' (i.e. from God; cf. 1.17). The former is characterized by competitive self-seeking (3.14), the latter by the love which respects and seeks the good of others (3.17).

The motif of wholeness and the dualistic motif cohere and reinforce each other, because the former involves wholehearted devotion to God and single-minded loyalty to God's values. The double-minded lack wholeness, because in relation to God they are half-hearted (e.g. in desiring the wisdom God gives [1.6–8], since they also indulge self-seeking and competitive desires [4.1–3]), and because their loyalties are divided and conflict. Wholeness is manifested in a life-style and a community at odds with dominant values in society. This situation is intelligible in the overall context of messianic redemption, in which the Church is the representative first fruits of the whole creation, itself as yet unredeemed (1.18). As the messianically renewed Israel, James's readers are called to live a counter-cultural life for the sake of the universal coming of God's kingdom. The eschatological expectation in James functions to validate the values by which the readers are called to live as those of the kingdom of God which is going to prevail universally (2.5, 13; 3.18; 4.10).

It is important to notice that the dualism involved in this vision is evidently not designed to draw a sociological boundary between insiders and outsiders in order to reinforce the Christian community's sense of identity. None of the passages cited so far refer to outsiders at all. There are no references in these passages to the readers' non-Christian neighbours or to the social institutions of the wider society. By contrast, as we shall see, with 1 Peter, there is no discussion of how the readers should relate to non-Christian neighbours, household structures or political authorities. The concern is not with sociological boundaries but with values. In particular, the readers are to see that the competitive self-seeking characteristic of the dominant system of values is inconsistent with the values of God's kingdom. It is not for the sake of distinguishing themselves from outsiders that the double-minded should purify their hearts (4.8), but in order that they should be 'complete', wholehearted in their loyalty to God, living out God's values consistently.

However, this serves to highlight the issue of the rich in James, a theme which has not yet been mentioned. The one passage which seems to be clearly a reference to non-Christians refers to wealthy people who are the oppressors of Christians (2.6–7). Since James is a circular letter, this must be regarded, not as reflecting some specific social context, but as a situation which James regards as typical, likely to apply to many of his readers in the communities of the Jewish diaspora. Rich people can be regarded as typically the oppressors of Christians. This lends plausibility to the view that the rich to whom James refers elsewhere in the letter (1.10–11; 3.13–5.6) are also treated as outside rather than inside the Christian community, especially as the wealthy landowners addressed in 5.1–6 are condemned precisely for oppression of the poor. The second-person address, both to the businessmen (4.13–16) and to the landowners (5.1–6) need not mean that these categories of people are expected to read the letter or to hear it read, but is sufficiently explained as rhetorical. If we have to decide whether the rich are envisaged as within or outside the Christian community, then the evidence seems to indicate the latter. Yet the ambiguity of the texts can be understood if, once again, we recognize that the issue is fundamentally one of values. The acquisitive, self-confident, self-seeking values of the rich, which make them heartless oppressors of others, are what James sees as inconsistent with the values of God's kingdom. Consequently, the rich person who enters the Christian synagogue (2.2) need not be an interested outsider paying a visit. Even if he professes Christian faith, James objects to the honour shown to him at the expense of the poor (2.2–4), because this is the reverse of God's values (2.5), and, whether he is a Christian or not, the rich man's values associate him with the typical rich who oppress Christians (2.6–7). The fact that James's readers typically experience the rich as oppressors (2.6–7) serves to demonstrate to them that they belong on God's side of this conflict of values and to show them how inconsistent it would be for them to show deference to the rich.

If James, then, excludes the rich from his vision of the Church, in the sense that the values of the rich are opposed to those of God's kingdom, in what sense does he identify the Church with the poor? It is important to realize that the majority of James's readers are not poor, any more than they are rich. Addressing his readers, his brothers and sisters, as 'you', James refers to the poor in the third person (2.1–5), not because he expects none of his readers to be poor, but because he expects most not to be poor. This is because ancient society was not divided into rich and poor. Both rich and poor were small minorities, at the top and bottom of the social scale, while the vast majority of the people were not regarded and did not regard themselves as poor. Whether they had only enough to live on or a little more than enough, they had reasonable security of life. The poor were not those who lived modestly but with reasonable security, but those who lived from hand to mouth, like the day labourers (5.4) who earned each day enough for the next day's needs but were employed only a day at a time with no security, or like the widow and the orphan (1.27), with no means of providing for themselves. The poor were either the wholly destitute, or those whose means of support were so uncertain they constantly risked destitution. Most of James's readers are not in this position, and he does not require them to be, though he does expect them to share what little they have with the really poor who have nothing (2.15–16). Yet the poor are those God has chosen 'to be heirs of the kingdom he has promised to those who love him' (2.5). The poor are the paradigm heirs of the kingdom.

While James's vision of the Church does not exclude those who are neither rich nor poor, it does require of all a kind of identification with the poor as paradigm heirs of the kingdom. This appears in his language of 'lowliness' (ταπεινόω and cognates: 1.9–10; 4.6, 10), together with that of 'boasting' (καυχάομαι and cognates: 1.9–10; 3.14; 4.16). This is language of social status. The poor are those who have no social status, who cannot put themselves above anyone else, who cannot take advantage of others, who find their status solely in God's evaluation of them. Others can find salvation only in renunciation of status and social advantage, together with the arrogance before others and before God which status promotes. All must make themselves lowly before the Lord (4.10), which means to put themselves on the same level as the poor, so that none may set themselves above others or take advantage of others.

In summary, James's vision of the Church is of (1) the messianically renewed Israel as the harbinger of the messianic redemption of the world; (2) a community living out God's values with wholehearted commitment and consistency; (3) a community which rejects the values of the rich, renounces social status and advantage, and lives in identification with the poor who are the paradigm members of God's people.

1 PETER

1 Peter addresses churches scattered across a wide area of Asia Minor. It shares a number of themes with James, but most striking is the fact that both are addressed to 'the diaspora'. In this resemblance, however, hides a very great difference. James addresses the Jews of the diaspora. Though he addresses them with a view to the messianic renewal and eschatological destiny of the people of God, their identity as Israel in the diaspora is the identity they have always had, the way they have always defined and understood themselves. Though presupposed, it plays hardly any further part in the explicit argument of the letter. In 1 Peter, on the other hand, the addressees are not Jews, their identity as the people of God in diaspora is a new identity they have been given, and much of 1 Peter is devoted to

expounding this identity and its implications for the way its readers live and relate to their social context. Whereas the diaspora in James is a presupposed fact of Jewish life, though not without theological meaning, in 1 Peter the diaspora is a potent theological interpretation of the facts of Gentile Christian existence.

1 Peter clearly addresses its readers as converts from pagan society (1.14, 18, 21; 4.2–4). It is inconceivable that this writer, who (whether he was Peter or writing on Peter's behalf) was himself evidently a member of a circle of Jewish Christian leaders (5.12–13), did not envisage any Jewish Christians among his readers. But it must be indicative of the rapid spread of Christianity in the area addressed (cf. Pliny, *Ep.* 10.96) that he imagines his audience as predominantly of Gentile origin. The whole question of relations between Jewish and Gentile Christians is as absent from 1 Peter as it is from James. 1 Peter never mentions Jews, Christian or non-Christian, but on the other hand the term 'the Gentiles' is used to refer to non-Christian outsiders (2.12). This is a vision of the Church in which the Jewish people of God have simply dropped out of the picture altogether, but in which the new people of God are distinguished from 'the Gentiles' in terms borrowed from those in which diaspora Jews identified themselves. The readers' pagan neighbours no longer confuse them with Jews but call them 'Christians' (4.16; in the NT the term occurs only here and in Acts 11.26; 16.18; but cf. again Pliny, *Ep.* 10.96), yet 1 Peter addresses them as 'elect exiles of the diaspora' (1.1). This is the controlling image which overarches everything else 1 Peter has to say about its readers' identity and situation.

However, this image and the range of other images which follow in its wake through the letter should not be seen as a transference of Jewish identity to the Church, nor even as simply the application of descriptions of OT Israel to the Church. Though some kind of continuity with the people of God of the first covenant is presumed (cf. 3.6), it is certainly not the emphasis, and the new identity which these pagan converts to Christianity are given is not focused on such continuity. The identity is that of the people of God who were once not a people but have now been constituted God's people (2.10) by the event of the eschatological Exodus (1.18–19). The Church is the eschatological people of God which the prophets foresaw (1.10–12). Its titles and descriptions are drawn from the prophetic accounts of this eschatological people of God. Its identity lies, not primarily in its continuity with the people of the first covenant, but in its own election, calling, constitution, destiny and prospective inheritance (e.g. 1.1–9; 2.9–10) as the eschatological people of God. This emphasis should not be construed as anti-Jewish, but as designed to meet the needs of self-identification among Christians whom neither the synagogue nor their pagan neighbours identify as Jews. Their relationship to Israel is not as such the issue. What is at stake is their own identity, as the people of God living among 'the Gentiles', an identity which, as converts from paganism, they have yet to make fully their own.

The language of diaspora and exile (1.1, 17; 2.11–12; 5.13) belongs to a complex of images of the eschatological people of God which we can conveniently enter by way of the key passage for defining this people of God: 2.9–10. This is the second part of the exegetical section (2.4–10) which plays a key role in the structure and theology of the letter. The section is designed to relate Jesus Christ as the elect one to his Church as the elect people. The introduction states the theme (2.4–5), which is then developed by three scriptural texts about Christ as the elect stone (2.6–8) and three scriptural texts about the Church as the elect people (2.9–10). Parts of Isa 43.20–21 ('my chosen race . . . to proclaim my mighty acts') and Exod 19.5–6 ('a people for my possession . . . a royal priesthood and a holy nation') are conflated and expanded in verse 9, and Hos 2.23 (cf. 1.6, 9; 2.1) is paraphrased in verse 10.

That Isa 43.20–21 is here the leading text is important. The Deutero-Isaianic prophecies of redemption are fundamental to 1 Peter, as to many early Christian writings (cf. 1.18 [Isa 52.3]; 1.24–25 [Isa 40.6–8]; 2.22 [Isa 53.9], 23 [Isa 53.7], 24 [Isa 53.4–5, 12], 25 [Isa 53.6; 40.11]). They depict the eschatological redemption as a new Exodus, accomplished by the Servant, whose suffering as a sacrificial lamb 1 Peter understands as the sacrifice of the Passover Lamb of the new Exodus (1.19; cf. Isa 53.7; Exod 12.5). Isa 43.20–21 depicts the people of God being led through the wilderness (Isa 43.19–20) in the new Exodus from Babylon (Isa 43.14; cf. 1 Pet 5.13). The text from Hosea is connected because it too, depicts an event in the wilderness like that when Israel came out of Egypt (Hos 2.15), and because the opening verse of the passage (Hos 2.14) has a close verbal connexion with Isa 40.2. This enables 1 Peter to understand the new Exodus as the event when God made those who had previously not been a people his own elect people (Hos 2.23; 1 Pet 2.10).

1 Peter's image of 'new birth' (1.3, 23), effected by God's word which accomplishes the new Exodus (1 Pet 1.24–25; Isa 40.7–8), is probably also to be connected with the prophecy of Hosea. This new birth makes those who previously were not God's people 'children of the living God' (Hos 1.10). Exod 19.5–6 is brought into connection with these passages because it describes the constitution of Israel as God's elect people in the wilderness after the first Exodus: typologically the terms apply to the people of the new Exodus (cf. also 1 Pet 1.2 with Exod 24.6–8).

This depiction of the Church as the people God has created for himself by the new Exodus which Jesus Christ, the Suffering Servant and the Passover Lamb accomplished, seems at first sight difficult to reconcile with the language of diaspora and exile (1.1, 17; 2.11–12; 5.13). The texts quoted locate the people of God in the wilderness after they have left Egypt or Babylon, but, in describing the readers as 'exiles of the diaspora'

(1.1) and 'aliens and exiles' (2.11), living 'in the time of your exile' (1.17), 1 Peter seems to locate its readers still in Egypt or Babylon, not yet led out by God in the new Exodus (cf. Isa 52.4; Gen 15.13; 47.4; Deut 23.7). The reason for this is that 1 Peter understands the new Exodus not as a geographical movement out of the pagan society in which its readers live, but as a redemption from 'the futile ways inherited from your ancestors' (1 Pet 1.18). They have received mercy and become God's people (2.10) so that they 'may proclaim the mighty acts of him who called you out of darkness into his marvellous light' (2.9). This they do by continuing to live 'among the Gentiles' (2.12) as 'aliens and exiles' (2.11), witnessing by their holy life as the people of God to God's 'mighty acts' – God's great act of eschatological redemption so that the Gentiles may 'glorify God' (2.12). 1 Peter thus takes up the Deutero-Isaianic theme of the people of God as his witnesses to the nations. The new Exodus, like the old, is designed to demonstrate God's deity to the nations (Exod 15.11–16; Isa 52.10). This it does as the people of God created by it live as God's people among the nations.

In this way diaspora and exile are given a positive meaning and purpose. But they are, of course, temporary. The eschatological redemption cannot leave the people of God in Babylon for ever. The time of their exile (1.17) lasts until they come into their inheritance (1.4), which is no longer understood as the geographical land of Israel, but as a salvation kept ready in heaven until it will be revealed in the last time (1.4–5). Part of the new identity the readers are given as the eschatological people of God is a homeland from which they should think of themselves as presently exiled. Like diaspora Jews, they live among the Gentiles as aliens and exiles. But whereas for diaspora Jews the homeland was a geographical centre to which they expected to be restored in the eschatological future, for the readers of 1 Peter it is a purely heavenly inheritance to be revealed in the eschatological future. The definition of the readers as the people of God of the new Exodus, still living as exiles among the Gentiles, therefore places them not geographically in relation to a centre, as the Jewish understanding of the diaspora did, but temporally between, on the one hand, their election and calling, their ransoming and sprinkling by the blood of Christ, their new birth as the children of God, their receiving of mercy and being made God's people, and, on the other hand, their entering into their inheritance in glory when Jesus Christ is revealed. It is in this period that they must live as God's holy people among the Gentiles.

As well as being the eschatological people of God, they also form the new temple and its priesthood (2.5). For diaspora Jews the Jerusalem temple was the central focus of identity, where their relationship with God as his people was enacted and guaranteed in the daily sacrifices. Once again, 1 Peter's readers are not given a geographical focus of identity. They themselves form the house of God (2.5; also 4.17, where the allusion to Ezek 9.4 shows that the reference is not to 'the household of God', but to 'the house of God', the temple) where God is present and they serve him in his presence. Since the description in 2.5 anticipates 2.9–10, the 'spiritual sacrifices' are best understood as the whole way of life which, as God's holy people, they are called to lead, and by which they proclaim his mighty acts to the Gentiles.

The development of the image of the new people of God therefore has a strong orientation towards this people's relationship to outsiders. These are not mentioned until 2.12, from which point on the readers' relationships with the structures of the society in which they live and with their pagan neighbours dominate the letter. The exegetical section (2.4–10) forms a transition. Before it the emphasis is on the election of the Church, its origin in redemption and new birth, its hope and destiny, and its calling, in the meantime, in the time of its exile (1.17), to be the holy people of the holy God (1.15–16). The exegetical section introduces the further thought that this calling to holiness is a mission to proclaim God's mighty acts, a thought which is then immediately taken up in 2.11–12, where for the first time exile is seen in relation to those among whom they are exiles, 'the Gentiles'.

'Aliens and exiles' (2.11) certainly does not describe, as J. H. Elliott argued in his pioneering sociological study of 1 Peter (1981), the actual social status of the readers *before* their conversion to Christ. The whole complex of imagery to which the phrase belongs requires that it describe the readers *as the eschatological people of God*. But this does not mean that its significance is purely religious, in the sense of unrelated to a social situation. It corresponds to the social alienation and hostility which the readers have suffered as a result of their conversion. In this society in which they were once fully at home (4.4–5) they are no longer at home, since their way of life no longer resembles their neighbours' (1.14; 4.4). They experience a variety of forms of discrimination and accusation from their pagan neighbours who now treat them with the hostility and suspicion which difference so often attracts (2.12; 3.14, 16; 4.12, 14, 16). What the image of exiles in the diaspora does is to put such experiences of social alienation in an interpretative context of religious meaning. Such experiences belong to the calling of God's elect people, while they live among the Gentiles, awaiting their inheritance. They even serve a positive purpose of testing (1.6–7; 4.12), a notion which is once again rooted in the prophetic accounts of the eschatological people of God (Isa 48.10; Zech 13.9: note this latter text's close link with Hos 2.23). The new identity the readers are given as exiles of the diaspora is one which interprets their experience of social alienation and hostility, and enables them to understand it in the context of an identity which transcends it.

From this perspective of the meaning of the diaspora identity of the Church, we can approach the question of differentiation or acculturation, which has occasioned some recent discussion in study of 1 Peter. Is 1 Peter's strategy to resist the danger of its readers' assimilation to pagan society by giving them a cohesive identity sharply distinguished from society around them? Or is the strategy to reduce friction and hostility by accepting the social structures and the values which support them? On the one side, there is 1 Peter's strong emphasis on a distinctive way of life, contrasted with the way the readers had lived before conversion (note the favourite word ἀναστροφή, of which 1 Peter has half the NT occurrences: 1.15, 18; 2.12; 3.1, 2, 16). On the other side, there is the acceptance of secular authorities both of the state and of the household (2.13–3.7). But we should also notice another feature of the letter which seems to point in two directions. On the one hand, there is recognition, even expectation, that the distinctive way of life the readers are called to live provokes hostility from pagan neighbours (4.3–4), and that, even if false and malicious accusations can be avoided, there will be abuse and suffering even for good conduct (3.16). On the other hand, there is the hope that good conduct will win the approval of pagans, even leading to their conversion (2.12; 3.1). This latter duality is probably only an apparent paradox. It was specifically because of their withdrawal from ordinary social life, which they saw as immoral and idolatrous, that Christians were regarded as antisocial (4.3–4), and therefore suspected of worse crimes. But this does not mean that there could not be significant overlap of moral values in other respects, such that Christians' lives could be admired and thereby mitigate the stigma of being antisocial. This conclusion gives some help towards the resolution of the issue of differentiation or acculturation. A distinctive way of life need not entail total rejection of every aspect of the social context.

Further help, however, comes from recalling the missionary thrust of the calling to be the holy people in diaspora. In the first place, holiness is required simply because they are God's people (1.15–16). It is certainly not that a distinctive way of life is urged *in order to* consolidate identity. It is rather that the identity of being God's people necessarily entails holiness. But holiness *in the diaspora situation* is also a calling to witness to the holy and redemptive God. This witness is not served by assimilation. But it is served by accepting the structures of society as the place in which to live the distinctive Christian way. These exiles in a society not their own are in no position to change the structures in which they are predominantly the subordinates: slaves of non-Christian masters (2.18–21; note that there are no instructions to Christian masters of slaves, as there are in Ephesians and Colossians) and wives of non-Christian husbands (3.1–6; whereas the husbands addressed in 3.7 have believing wives). In these situations, the scarcely tolerable insubordination simply of being Christians itself makes a tacit but vast difference to the acceptance of the structures of authority, while the distinctively Christ-like and Sarah-like practice of submission gives it a Christian character. 1 Peter's social strategy, therefore, is neither to buttress sectarian identity for its own sake nor to promote assimilation for the sake of avoiding hostility. It is to urge the living of a distinctively Christ-like way within the given structures of society. It is the strategy for those called to be the holy people of God as aliens and exiles among the Gentiles.

In summary, 1 Peter's vision of the Church is of (1) a community of people who have been given a new identity as God's elect and holy people, destined for an eternal inheritance; (2) God's people living until the parousia as 'exiles' in the midst of the pagan society from which they have converted; (3) God's elect and holy people called to be, in this situation, a light to the Gentiles, witnessing to God's act of redemption in Christ by living a distinctively Christ-like way of life in the midst of the structures of pagan society.

JUDE AND 2 PETER

Though they are very different in other respects, in delineating their visions of the Church it will be useful to consider these two letters together. Both address situations in which false teaching is promoting moral carelessness or even deliberate flouting of accepted Christian standards of behaviour. Therefore the particular concern for the Church which both express is that the Church will lose its very identity as God's people if it lacks moral seriousness in seeking to live out God's righteous-ness in its life. Jude encapsulates in four instructions what his readers can do to work out the moral implications of the gospel in their life as a community (20–21), and trusts God's power to preserve them from moral disaster and to bring them, sanctified, into his presence (24–25). The eschatological emphasis (Jude 21, 24) is stronger in 2 Peter, because the false teachers in this case combined their ethical libertinism with eschatological scepticism. 2 Peter sees that without the expectation of the triumph of God's righteousness, concern for righteousness now lacks adequate theological motivation. 2 Peter's vision of the Church is therefore of a community which lives from the grace and the knowledge of Jesus Christ given in Christian conversion (1.3; 3.18), developing from this God-given source the ethical virtues which are summed up in Christian love (1.5–7), and which lives towards the new creation, a world in which righteousness will be at home and only those can live who are at home with righteousness (3.12–14). In both letters the vision of the Church is of the community defined by its alignment with God's cosmic purpose of righteousness. The brevity and rather specific aims of these letters do not allow the kind of comprehensive vision of the Church which both James and 1 Peter, in their different ways, provide. What they do contribute to the total canonical kaleidoscope of ecclesial visions is an intense concern for the moral integrity of the Church, a limited but entirely essential contribution.

BIBLIOGRAPHY

Balch, D. L. 1981. *Let Wives Be Submissive: The Domestic Code in 1 Peter.* SBLMS 26; Chico, California: Scholars Press.

Chester, A. and R. P. Martin. 1994. *The Theology of the Letters of James, Peter, and Jude.* Cambridge: Cambridge University Press.

Chin, M. 1991. 'A Heavenly Home for the Homeless: Aliens and Strangers in 1 Peter.' *TynB* 42:96–112.

Elliott, J. H. 1966. *The Elect and the Holy: An Exegetical Examination of 1 Peter 2:4–10 and the Phrase* βασίλειον ἱεράτευμα. NovTSup 12. Leiden: Brill.

Elliott, J. H. 1981. *A Home for the Homeless: A Sociological Exegesis of 1 Peter, Its Situation and Strategy.* London: SCM Press.

Elliott, J. H. 1992. 'The Epistle of James in Rhetorical and Social Scientific Perspective: Holiness-Wholeness and Patterns of Replication'. *BTB* 23:71–81.

Johnson, L. T. 1985. 'Friendship with the World/Friendship with God: A Study of Discipleship in James'. In F. Segovia (ed.), *Discipleship in the New Testament.* Philadelphia: Fortress Press. 166–83.

Johnson, L. T. 1995. 'The Social World of James: Literary Analysis and Historical Reconstruction'. In L. M. White and O. L. Yarbrough (eds.), *The Social World of the First Christians* (W. A. Meeks FS). Minneapolis: Fortress Press. 178–97.

Martin, T. W. 1992. *Metaphor and Composition in 1 Peter.* SBLDS 131; Atlanta, Georgia: Scholars Press.

Maynard-Reid, P. U. 1987. *Poverty and Wealth in James.* Maryknoll, New York: Orbis.

Talbert, C. H. (ed.). 1986. *Perspectives on First Peter.* Macon, Georgia: Mercer University Press.

Wengst, K. 1988. *Humility: Solidarity of the Humiliated.* Tr. J. Bowden; London: SCM Press.

Wolf, M. 1994. 'Soft Difference: Theological Reflections on the Relation Between Church and Culture in 1 Peter'. *Ex Auditu* 10:15–30.

The Hearing Formula and the Visions of John in Revelation

G. K. Beale

THE role of the seven letters of Rev 2–3 in relation to the entire book has been debated.[1] Some have thought that the primary purpose of the letters is to describe the condition of the first-century churches, and by implication, the pre-eschatological condition of the Church throughout the ages until the beginning of the final tribulation, directly preceding Christ's final coming. Others have thought that the primary purpose of the letters is to express the major themes of the following visionary portion of the book (Rev 4–21). Both of these interpretations exhibit an 'already and not yet' end-time perspective.[2] This essay sets out to argue the plausibility of the second view, and to propose in particular that the letters, especially their repeated conclusions, anticipate the symbolic visions and even explain the theological purpose of the symbolic communication of the book.

1. INTRODUCTION TO THE LETTERS

(a) *The Relation of the Letters to the Rest of the Book*[3] Phrases and concepts from the letters are related to the introductory vision of chapter 1, to the visions of chapters 4–20 and to the concluding scene of the new creation in 21.8–22.5 (see Beale 1997:Introduction). The express development of the Son of Man vision (1.9–20) throughout the letters makes more viable the proposal that the letters function in the same manner in relation to the remainder of the book. Such a proposal best

---

[1] I am happy to be able to contribute an article in honour of John Sweet. He has given wise and invaluable guidance to me, not only in my doctoral work, but also in my research on John's Apocalypse during the past decade.

[2] For a fuller discussion of both views and their respective supporters, see the introductory section ('The Structure and Plan of John's Apocalypse') of G. K. Beale 1997 and *passim*.

[3] For discussions of the historical background of the letters in their Asia Minor context, see Ramsay 1904 (and sources cited therein); Beale, 1997:*in loc.*

explains the presence of phrases and concepts from the letters in the following visionary portion. The Son of Man vision is primarily developed in the introductions of the letters (as well as in the body of some of the letters and in subsequent parts of the book). The concluding promises of salvific reward in the letters overtly anticipate the end of the book and the final paradisial vision (cf. ch. 19–22; Sweet 1979:77; Minear 1969:61; see below). Even the deceptive threats to the churches are echoed again in the concluding description of the character of those who posed the threat and will consequently experience the 'second death' (see 21.8). This observation points still further to the plausibility that the body of the letters is integrally related to the body of the book. This accords with the fact that John places the visions within the framework of the traditional Christian letter form with an extended introduction (ch. 1–3), concluding admonitions (22.6ff) and benediction (22.20–21; so Schüssler Fiorenza 1973:575).

One of the main features of the typically Pauline epistolary pattern is that the themes of the introductions are developed throughout the body of the letter (cf. P. T. O'Brien 1977). This feature is also true of the Apocalypse to some degree. It is clear that the introductions of the seven letters and the introductory Son of Man vision pertain to the same general time period and mutually interpret one another, as primarily do also the conclusions of the seven messages and the book's final vision of bliss. This points to the likelihood that the same relationship exists between the body of the letters and the visionary body of the book. It is in this sense that we can call the letters the literary microcosm of the entire book's macrocosmic structure.

An important issue for brief consideration is whether or not the symbols which appear in the letters should be interpreted primarily by the context of the chapter 1 vision or mainly by the historical context of the letters themselves. In particular, should the various descriptions of Christ in chapters 1–3 be interpreted by the historical situation in which these images have their origin or from the OT literary context from which they also come? There is probably a reciprocal interpretative relationship between the chapter 1 vision and the letters. Therefore, the historical background of the churches and the OT literary background mutually interpret one another.

(b) The Literary Structure of the Letters and the Function of the Hearing Formula Therein   Although 1.9–20 is best considered a call narrative and, therefore, a separate introductory unit, it should also be viewed as part of the larger literary segment of 1.9–3.22. This is clear from the fact that the command to write in 1.11 and 1.19 is repeated at the beginning of each of the letters, as is also a description from some facet of

the Son of Man vision, which is usually developed later in the body of each letter.[4]

There have been different proposals for the structure which is common to all seven letters (see Aune 1983:275–78; *idem*. 1990). Generally speaking, each letter typically can be divided into seven parts, although there is sometimes slight alteration: (1) command to write to an angel of a church; (2) a self-description by Christ from chapter 1 introduced by the introductory formula 'these things' (τάδε λέγει); (3) a commendation of a church's good works (lacking in the letter to Laodicea); (4) an accusation because of some sin; (5) an exhortation to repent with a warning of judgement or an encouragement; element (4) and the second part of (5) are lacking in the letters of Smyrna and Philadelphia, since they are seen as faithful; elements (3) to (5) could be viewed as one section introduced by οἶδα ('I know') followed by commendations or accusations with corresponding encouragements or exhortations to repent to avoid judgement; (6) exhortation to discern the truth of the preceding message ('he who has an ear . . .'); (7) a promise to the conquerors.

Each message can also be divided into four broad sections: (1) commission formula with christological descriptions; (2) an 'I know' section (typically containing elements of praise, exhortation and accusation, perhaps including calls for repentance, threats of judgement and promises); (3) exhortation to discern; (4) exhortation to conquer (so Aune 1983:275–78 and the book's appendix).

The logical flow of thought in each letter generally conforms to the following pattern: (1) Christ presents himself with certain attributes (particularly suitable to the situation of each church, faith in which provides the basis for overcoming the specific problem faced); (2) the situation and the particular problem are reviewed (introduced by 'I know'); (3) on the basis of the situation and the problem, Christ issues either an encouragement to persevere in the face of conflict (for faithful churches) or to repent, in order to avoid judgement (for unfaithful churches); (4) then both the prior situation and problem together, especially with the corresponding encouragements to persevere or exhortations to repent, form the ground for Christ issuing a call for the churches to respond by heeding ('hearing') either the preceding encouragement or exhortation; (5) on the basis of a positive response (= 'hearing' followed by 'overcoming'), Christ promises the inheritance of eternal life with him, which uniquely corresponds to Christ's attributes or to the churches' situation (the hearing formula still functions as a ground clause, together with overcoming, even when placed after the promise in the last four letters).

---

[4] For the relation of the christological introductions to the body of the letters cf. B. Gerhardsson 1977.

In view of the similar logical development and theme of all of the letters, the general main point of chapters 2–3 can be formulated in the following manner: *Christ encourages the churches to witness, warns them about compromise, and exhorts them to 'hear' and to overcome compromise in order to inherit the promise of eternal life with him.*

Therefore, the logical flow of each letter climaxes with the promise of inheriting eternal life with Christ, which is the main point of each letter. The body of each letter provides the basis upon which the Spirit calls the churches to respond by 'hearing', which should inextricably result in overcoming, the consequence of which is inheriting the respective promises.

The concluding 'hearing' exhortations are not merely addressed to each particular church but 'to (all) the churches'. Although each letter is addressed to the particular situation of a church, it is relevant for the needs of all 'seven' of the churches, and probably, by implication, for the universal Church or Church 'at large' (see 1.4 for this figurative significance of 'seven').

Three general divisions can be discerned among the seven churches. The first and last are in danger of losing their very identity as a Christian church. Therefore, they are exhorted to repent in order to prevent their judgement and to inherit the promises which genuine faith deserves. The churches addressed in the three central letters have, to varying degrees, some who have remained faithful and others who are compromising with pagan culture. Among these, Pergamum is in the best condition and Sardis is in the worst. These churches are exhorted to purge the elements of compromise from their midst in order to avert judgement on the compromisers (and probably also themselves) and to inherit the promises due those who overcome compromise. The second and sixth letters are written to churches which have proved themselves faithful and loyal to Christ's 'name' even in the face of persecution from both Jews and pagans. Even though they are 'poor' and 'have little power', they are encouraged to continue persevering as the 'true Israel', since more trials will confront them. They are to endure with the hope that they will inherit the promises of eternal salvation (both will receive a 'crown').

In this light, the condition of the churches is presented in the literary form of a chiasm: a b c c c b' a'. The significance of this is that the Christian Church *as a whole* is perceived as being in poor condition, since not only are the healthy churches in a minority but the literary pattern points to this emphasis because the churches in the worst condition form the literary boundaries of the letters and the churches with serious problems form the very core of the presentation. This is highlighted by recognizing that at the centre of the middle letter stands a general statement that 'all the churches will know' that Christ is the omniscient judge of his unfaithful followers (2.23). The reference in 2.23 is conspicuous because the only other collective reference to the churches occurs at the conclusion of each letter.

All of the letters deal generally with the issue of witnessing for Christ in the midst of a pagan culture. The churches with problems are all exhorted to strengthen their witness in various ways and the two churches without problems are encouraged to continue to persevere in the faithful witness which they had been maintaining. Consequently, the hearing formula functions to exhort Christians to witness despite the temptations to compromise. Therefore, the hearing formula is a key to understanding the major theme of the letters, and, as we will see, is crucial for understanding the theme of the entire book.

(c) *The Literary Genre of Revelation 2–3 and the Function of the Hearing Formula*   The seven letters do not technically correspond to the typical epistolary form and, therefore, are better referred to as 'prophetic messages'.[5] There has also been a recent attempt at a rhetorical analysis of chapters 2–3 (see Kirby 1988).

W. H. Shea (1983) has proposed that five essential segments are observable, which thematically reflect the fivefold ANE-OT covenant form imposed upon Israel by Yahweh in Exod 21ff and throughout Deuteronomy: (1) preamble (the words of Christ ['these things says'] + his descriptive titles from ch. 1); (2) prologue ('I know your works . . .', which include the two sections labelled above as commendation and accusation); (3) stipulations (expressions built around variants of 'therefore . . . repent', along with other hortatory words); (4) witness to the covenant ('hear what the Spirit says to the churches'); (5) concluding blessings and curses ('to him who overcomes I will give . . .').

Shea's proposal is overstated, since a verse-by-verse study exposes a number of exceptions to the overall pattern (so Aune 1990:182). Nevertheless, a qualified version of Shea's view is plausible. Although he does not attempt to fit into his scheme the initial command to write, the addition of such a command is natural since it occurs in contexts where Yahweh is addressing his covenant to Israel through his covenant messengers (whether Moses or the later prophets; see on 1.11). Furthermore, the blessings and cursings are separated in the letters, the latter typically occurring as a conclusion of the 'stipulations' section. Because each of these sections begins with a set formula, they are best seen as the five literary divisions of each letter, although certainly the initial formulaic command to write must be included as a sixth element in the pattern.

That the proposed covenantal scheme forms at least part of the general background is supported by several factors. *First*, the fivefold covenant pattern has also been observed to be influential for the book as a whole

[5] See Hahn 1971; Hartman 1980; Müller 1975:47–100; Aune 1983:274–79, who also provides a summary and evaluation of Hahn's and Müller's discussions; Muse 1986.

(see Strand 1983); of particular note in this respect is the conclusion of the book in 22.7b, 18–19, part of which alludes to Deut 4.2, and 22.16–20, where an angel, the Spirit, the Church and Jesus are formally termed 'witnesses'. *Second*, the high degree to which allusion is made elsewhere in the book to OT phrases and themes permits the plausibility of the employment of such a major theme as this. *Third*, the covenant theme is a particularly appropriate one, since Jesus is now viewed with attributes of Yahweh who is addressing the churches, which are now also seen as the continuation of true Israel. For example, Jesus introduces himself (τάδε λέγει) with a stock formula from the prophets of the OT which was used to introduce the prophetic sayings of the Lord to Israel: τάδε λέγει κύριος ('these things says the Lord'; the OT formula occurs 190x in Ezekiel and Jeremiah, and 44x in the Minor Prophets). The recapitulation of the covenant formula is suitable because a new covenant community has now been inaugurated to be the continuation of the true people of God. If the Church is faithful, it will inherit the covenantal blessings of the new creation originally promised to Israel (e.g. see Isa 40–60). But unfaithfulness will bring the curse of being excluded from the blessings.

D. Aune (1990) has thoroughly discussed the multiple genre of the seven letters. In particular, he has argued that the literary genre of chapters 2–3 is 'that of the *royal* or *imperial edict*, while the *mode* is that of the prophetic form of speech called the *parenetic salvation-judgement oracle*' (1990:183 and *passim*). If the background of the pagan royal edict genre is in mind, then Christ would be presenting himself as a king addressing his subjects. Furthermore, he would be portraying himself as the true sovereign in contrast to the pseudo-kingship of the Roman Emperor (1990:199, 204). This perspective need not exclude the covenantal form discussed above, since the covenantal background would enhance the OT prophetic speech form, which itself was a development of the covenantal cursings and blessings of Exodus and Deuteronomy.

In the light of the above analysis, the hearing formula functions as the Spirit's witness to Christ's (the King's) new covenant ('hear what the Spirit says to the churches') to exhort true Israel to faithfulness to her acknowledged Lord.

2. The Formula 'the One Having Ears Let Him Hear' in the Letters and Its Interpretative and Theological Significance for the Apocalypse as a Whole

(a) *The Background of the Hearing Formula* This formula has its background in the Synoptics and the OT, where in both cases it occurs in connection with symbolic or parabolic revelation. In the OT it refers to the effect which the symbolic revelation of the prophets had on the Israelites. The primary function of the prophets Isaiah, Jeremiah and Ezekiel was to warn Israel of its impending doom and divine judgement. They delivered their warnings initially in a rational and sermonic way, exhorting the audience about their sin and reminding them about their past history in which God had judged their fathers because of the same kind of selfish disobedience. But these prophetic messengers had little success because of Israel's idolatrous allegiances, spiritual lethargy and stiff-necked attitude against changing the ways to which they had grown accustomed. They had become spiritually hardened to rational, historical and homiletical warnings.

As a consequence, the prophets began to take up different forms of warning. They started to employ symbolic action and parable in order to get attention (Jeffrey 1977 first attracted my attention to this transition in the prophets). But such a change in warning form is effective only with those who already have spiritual insight. Symbolic parables cause those who 'have ears to hear and hear not' to misunderstand further. The literary form of symbolic parable (e.g. *mashal*) 'appears whenever ordinary warnings are no longer heeded (cf. Matt 13.10)' (so Jeffrey) and no warning will ever be heeded by hardened people who are intent on continuing in disobedience. This is the point of Isa 6.9–10, where the prophet is commissioned to tell Israel to '*keep on listening* but do not perceive . . . render the hearts of this people insensitive, *their ears dull* . . . lest they . . . *hear with their ears* . . . and repent and be healed'.

Isaiah's preaching is intended as a judgement to blind and deafen the majority in Israel and to have a positive effect only on the remnant (cf. ch. 7ff; for sources discussing aspects of the exegetical and theological problems in Isa 6.9–10, see Beale 1991). Isaiah's message in chapters 1–5 is predominantly a non-parabolic warning of judgement and promise of blessing conditioned on repentance. Then the parabolic message comes in 7.3 and 8.1–4, which has already been anticipated by the vineyard parable in 5.1–7. The parabolic aspect of the prophet's message is then closely linked to the hardening commission of Isa 6.9–10 and, therefore, may be considered one of the means by which the people are to be blinded and deafened (which is viewed as beginning fulfilment, e.g. in Isa 42.20 ['your ears are open but none hears'] and 43.8).

Yet the parables are also intended to have a jolting effect on the remnant who have become complacent among the compromising majority. Israel did not want to hear the truth, and when it was presented straightforwardly to convict them of sin, they would not accept the fact of their sin. The parables, however, functioned to awake those among the true, righteous remnant from their sinful anaesthesia. The same pattern found in Isaiah is apparent in Ezekiel, where the Isaianic hearing language occurs in Ezek 3.27 (ὁ ἀκούων ἀκουέτω: 'he who hears, let him hear'), followed directly by the prophet's first parable, and in 12.2 (ὦτα ἔχουσιν τοῦ ἀκούειν, καὶ οὐκ ἀκούουσιν: 'they have ears to hear, but they do not hear'), followed immediately in verses 3–16 by the prophet's first parabolic act before onlooking Israel (for similar wording to Ezekiel's hearing formulae cf. Jer 5.21; 17.23). Ezekiel's usage is a development of that already found in Isaiah.

The shock effect of the parables on the believing yet sinfully complacent remnant is a phenomenon observable also in the case of Nathan's parable addressed to David, after he had sinned by committing adultery with Bathsheba and killing her husband, Uriah. David was not ready to hear an outright, direct accusation. He had become spiritually anaesthetized to his spiritual and moral decline. Therefore, Nathan the prophet uses the approach of symbolic language (cf. 2 Sam 12.1–9, 13–15). The symbolic story catches David off guard. It causes him to focus objectively on the meaning of the story because he does not think it is related to him personally. Only after he had fully understood the pictorial story and felt its emotive impact, does Nathan then apply it to David. And then David is pierced to the heart and is able to accept the accusation of his sin and repent.

Against this background, Jesus' use of the hearing formula is not novel but in line with the OT prophetic pattern. In the majority of synoptic uses, the phrase 'the one having ears, let him hear' (cf. Matt 13.9–17, 43, and the almost identical form in Mark 4.9, 23; Luke 8.8) is a direct development of Isa 6.9–10 and has the dual function of signifying that revelation in parables is intended to enlighten the genuine remnant but blind those who, though they confess outwardly to be part of the covenant community, are really unbelievers (Matt 7.15–23); cf. Matt 13.9–16 and the use in conjunction with a parable in Luke 14.35 (see also Matt 11.15 in connection with Isaianic prophecy; for uses in the Apocrypha in connection with parables see Aune 1990:194).

Isa 6.9–10 is probably reflected in the repeated call to 'hear' in John's letters. However, that the Matt 13 background also lies behind the hearing formula in the letters of Revelation is apparent from the fact that the same wording is found in both the Matthean and the Johannine formulae. An additional connection is observable from the following parallels: (1) that μυστήριον ('the mystery') in both Matt 13 and Rev 1–3 occurs after an initial parabolic portrayal and before the formal interpretation of that portrayal to indicate that the hidden meaning of the preceding parable will be unveiled (cf. Matt 13.11 and Rev 1.19–3.22); (2) both uses of μυστήριον are linked to an interpretation of the OT (respectively, of Isa 6 in Matthew and of several OT allusions, including some from Isa 44–49, in Rev 1.12–18); (3) indeed, μυστήριον itself in

Matt 13.11 and Rev 1.19 is a conscious allusion to Dan 2.28–29, 45, where the word occurs in reference to the prophetic vision concerning the establishment of the end-time kingdom of God, a topic also of primary concern to these two NT texts (Matt 13.11, 19ff; Rev 1.6, 9);[6] strikingly, both Matthew and Revelation employ μυστήριον, not only to refer to the hidden meaning of pictorial language but also to connote that the prophesied messianic kingdom has begun fulfilment in an unexpected, even ironic manner.[7]

There is consensus that the repeated hearing formula in Rev 2–3 is an allusion to the synoptic formula, though commentators appear to assume the validity of this rather than providing the analysis of parallels cited above. Some interpreters contend that the contextual use of the phrase in the synoptics has been lost sight of and that the use of the formula has lost the idea of hardening or blinding which it had in the synoptics (e.g. see Enroth 1990). In addition, however, to the above-noted affinities to Matt 13, the repetition of the hearing formula at the same concluding point in each of the letters suggests further that the phrase is not a mere early Christian stock-in-trade reflection of the Gospel expression, but is utilized quite consciously, so that awareness of its synoptic context is, at least, plausible (so Vos 1965). Therefore, as in Isa 6 and the synoptics, the formula refers to the fact that Christ's message will enlighten some but blind others.

Ezek 3.27 is also probably in the background, since its wording is not only most similar to the saying in both Matthew and Revelation, but only in Ezek 3.22–27 is this formula said to be the very words of the Spirit and of Yahweh, as well as of the human prophet, as in the Revelation formulae (where John writes, and yet what he writes is also presented as the words of Christ *and* the Spirit). The emphasis of the formula in the Ezekiel context is upon Israel's refusal to listen, and consequent judgement, though the notion of a righteous remnant responding to the hearing exhortation is included in the context (cf. 3.17–21; 9.4–8; 14.12–23).

Now, however, the formula of Revelation is addressed to the Church, which is the continuation of the true covenant community from the OT. But like Israel, the Church has also become compromising and spiritually lethargic and has entertained idolatrous allegiances, so that the parabolic method of revelation is instituted. The parables throughout the book not only have a judicial effect on the unbelieving but are meant also to shock believers caught up in the Church's compromising complacency by revealing to them the horrific, beastly nature of the idolatrous institutions with which they are beginning to associate. As in Isaiah, Ezekiel and

---

[6] For argument concerning the allusion to Dan 2 in Matt 13, cf. Ladd 1974:225; and on that in Rev 1, see Beale 1992.

[7] Cf. Matt 13.19–23, and the analysis of Ladd 1974:218–42, as well as Rev 1.9 and the analysis of Beale 1984:176–77.

Jeremiah, John is addressing a covenant community, the majority of which is unfaithful and compromising in one way or another.

It is true that the hearing formula is stated more positively ('he who *has* an ear let him hear') in Revelation than in Isa 6 ('make heavy their ears . . . lest . . . they hear with their ears'). Nevertheless, the positive formulation occurs also in Ezek 3 and Matt 13 with awareness still, as in Isaiah, that the majority would not respond positively, but only the authentic remnant would be able to 'hear'.[8] Whether or not John's warning was met with the same negative response by the majority is not known. Nevertheless, since he stands squarely in the prophetic tradition of Isaiah, Ezekiel and Jesus in his use of the parables, we should not be overly optimistic about thinking that there was an overwhelmingly positive response (likewise, 2 Tim 1.15 pessimistically narrates that 'You are aware of the fact that all who are in Asia turned away from me [Paul]'). Just as the parables signalled imminent judgement for the majority of Israel in the past, so likewise the heavenly parables of John probably functioned for the majority of the Church and the world. In this respect, it is likely that John held a 'remnant' concept as did the OT prophets and Jesus. The hearing formula was one of the means by which he called out the remnant from among the compromising churches.

(*b*) *An Example of the 'Shock-Effect' Function of the Apocalyptic Parables*   An example of the jarring role of the heavenly parables for the readership occurs in Rev 2 and 17. In Rev 2 Christ addresses a sinful situation in which the Christians have become spiritually anaesthetized. The Christians in Thyatira may have thought it was wrong for 'Jezebel' to teach a more lax morality and that it was religiously allowable to worship idols together with Jesus (Rev 2.19–20). The idols she was teaching about were economic idols, as Baal was for the Israelites. Israel did not deny Yahweh but worshipped Baal for prosperity of the economy. 'Jezebel' was teaching something similar, though in an updated Christian guise.

The Thyatiran Christians, however, 'tolerated' her teaching. Though they may have disagreed with her views, the church officials did not think her ideas destructive enough to disallow her from teaching any more within the church.

John wants to shock the sluggish Christians so that they will discern the gravity of the situation. Therefore, in Rev 17 John paints Jezebel in

[8] Ezek 3.27b was changed from an expression of non-repentance ('and he who refuses, let him refuse') into a positive statement of repentance by the Targumist, who apparently could not resist altering such a negative exhortation: 'let him who will refrain, let him refrain *from sinning*'. This conforms also to a general tendency in the early versions of Isa 6.9–10, as well as to post-biblical Judaism's interpretation of the same Isaiah text, to soften the original Hebrew text by shifting the ultimate cause for the condition of hardening away from God to Israel (so Evans 1989:164, and *passim*); some rabbis even understood Isa 6.9–10 to imply forgiveness (Evans 1989:145).

her 'true colours'. For example, the phrase 'they will eat her flesh' (τὰς σάρκας αὐτῆς φάγονται) in Rev 17.16 is reminiscent of Jezebel's destiny in 2(4) Kings 9.36: 'they ... will eat the flesh of Jezebel' (καταφάγονται ... τὰς σάρκας 'Ιεζάβελ)'. Jezebel's destruction likewise happened according to the 'word of the Lord' (4 Kings 9.36), as is true of Babylon in Rev 17.17.[9]

The link between Babylon and Jezebel in Rev 2 suggests that Jezebel more precisely represents the apostate sector of the church through which the religious-economic system of the ungodly Graeco-Roman (= Babylonian) society makes its incursions into the Church and establishes a fifth columnist movement. Therefore, the point in Rev 2.19–20ff is this: as long as the church of Thyatira allows 'Jezebel' to teach such things within the confines of the church, the church itself is beginning to have spiritual intercourse with the Devil's whore and with the devilish beast himself, upon whose back she rides in chapter 17. She is the opposite of the pure woman of Rev 12.1–2 who symbolizes the true people of God. John is saying to the Christians in Thyatira: 'Oh, you want to tolerate this teaching which you do not think is too bad – well, if you do, you are dealing with the Devil himself, and you will be destroyed.' What they thought was insignificant compromise and sin, was really a crack in their spiritual dikes which could have let through a flood of spiritual evil, overwhelming them (cf. Rev 12.15).

The hearing formula occurs outside of the letters only in Rev 13.9, where it has a function similar to that of Babylon/Jezebel in Rev 17: to shock the Christian readers into the reality that compromise with the ungodly state and economic system (= the beast) is equal to idolatry and to following the satanic dragon himself (cf. Rev 12.3 and 13.1–18).

John uses metaphorical language because it communicates on both a cognitive and an emotive level which has more potential to jar people so that they can re-focus on the cognitive and perceive better the reality of their dangerous situation. In addition to knowing that there was signifi-cant suffering in Nazi concentration camps, if Christians in Germany could have seen pictures of what was really occurring, they might have been moved to react against this reality more than they did. It is one thing to hear abstract explanations about the devastation resulting from the atomic bombs dropped on Japan in World War II, but quite another to see actual pictures of this devastation. Pictorial representation makes a greater impact than mere abstract communication, and this is one of the reasons that it is used in the Apocalypse.

[9] Mauro (1925:490), Chilton (1987:439), and Ruiz (1989:367) see a connection between the 4 Kings text and Rev 17.16. See Beale 1997 in discussion of Rev 17, where eleven additional parallels are drawn between the Harlot Babylon and Jezebel in 1 and 2 Kings.

3. CONCLUSION: THE HEARING FORMULA AND THE SIGNIFICANCE OF ITS OLD TESTAMENT AND GOSPEL BACKGROUND FOR THE THEOLOGY OF THE APOCALYPSE

The preceding analysis suggests that the symbolic visions of chapters 4–21 are parabolic portrayals of the more abstract, propositionally expressed exhortations, warnings and promises of the letters, so that the latter interpret the former and vice versa. This thesis finds corroboration in the visions of trumpets and bowls being modelled, not coincidentally, on the Exodus plague signs, which functioned originally to harden Pharaoh and the Egyptians but to convey revelation and salvation to Israel. This model is now applied to the Church and the world, which dovetails with our suggested use of Christ's parabolic 'hearing' formula. Therefore, there is a theological reason for the presence of so much symbolic communication in Revelation.

Recalling that the hearing formula is rooted ultimately in Isa 6.9–10 helps explain why it is used in a context of compromise with idols. Just as idols have eyes but cannot see and ears but cannot hear, so Isa 6.9–10 describes apostate Israelites likewise to indicate figuratively that what they had revered, they had come to resemble spiritually (so also Pss 115.4–8; 135.15–18). They had become as spiritually lifeless as their idols. In fact, the overwhelming OT use of the basic phraseology 'having ears but not hearing' refers to unrepentant members of the covenant community who had become as spiritually lifeless as the idols which they had insisted on continuing to worship (for the full exegetical argument for this in Isa 6 and elsewhere in the OT, see Beale 1991; cf. Evans 1989:17–80).

Though the seven churches have not yet capitulated to the idols of the culture, some are in the process of doing so, while others are facing the temptation. Therefore, the hearing formula is suitably addressed to the churches in the midst of this idolatrous atmosphere in order to warn them not to become identified with the idols and the mores of the surrounding idolatrous culture. In this light, 'hearing' refers figuratively to perceiving truth and desiring to respond in obedience to it (cf. Rev 1.3; 22.17; Ezek 44.5 and *Sifre Deuteronomy*, Piska 335).

In conclusion, the repeated hearing formulae underscore the Spirit's exhortation that the churches be loyal to their sovereign Lord despite temptations to compromise by participating in idolatry and despite threats of persecution. And this is the major theme of the letters as a whole, as well as of the entire book. The readers are to express their loyalty by means of being faithful witnesses to Christ, which necessitates no compromise with idolatry. John's strategy to move the readers to this ethical-theological goal is to address them through the medium of prophetic parabolic communication. Such a medium had already been used by the OT prophets and by Jesus to move the remnant in Israel away from its idolatry and self-serving economic sin, which may suggest that John also held a remnant theology. And, just as parables signalled imminent judgement for the majority of Israel in the past, so likewise the apocalyptic parables of Revelation function for the majority of the Church and the world. Nevertheless, the hearing formula is an exhortation conveying both notions of salvation and judgement. Consequently, the formula indicates that a significant purpose of the letters is to anticipate the symbolic communication of chapters 4–21.

BIBLIOGRAPHY

Aune, D. E. 1983. *Prophecy in Early Christianity and in the Ancient Mediterranean World.* Grand Rapids: Eerdmans.

Aune, D. E. 1990. 'The Form and Function of the Proclamations to the Seven Churches (Revelation 22–3)'. *NTS* 36:182–204.

Beale, G. K. 1984. *The Use of Daniel in Jewish Apocalyptic Literature and in the Revelation of St. John.* Lanham: University Press of America.

Beale, G. K. 1991. 'Isaiah VI 9–13: A Retributive Taunt Against Idolatry'. *VT* 41:257–78.

Beale, G. K. 1992. 'The Interpretative Problem of Rev 1.19'. *NovT* 34: 360–87.

Beale, G. K. 1997 (forthcoming). *The Book of Revelation.* New International Greek Testament Commentary Series. Grand Rapids: Eerdmans/Carlisle: Paternoster.

Chilton, D. C. 1987. *The Days of Vengeance.* Fort Worth, Texas: Dominion Press.

Enroth, A.-M. 1990. 'The Hearing Formula in the Book of Revelation'. *NTS* 36:598–608.

Evans, C. A. 1989. *To See and Not Perceive: Isaiah 6.9–10 in Early Jewish and Christian Interpretation.* JSOTSup 64. Sheffield: JSOT Press.

Gerhardsson, B. 1977. 'Die christologischen Aussagen in den Sendschreiben der Offenbarung'. In A. Fuchs (ed.), *Theologie aus dem Norden.* SNTU, Serie A, Band 2. Linz, Austria: Plöchl, Freistadt. 142–66.

Hahn, F. 1971. 'Die Sendschreiben der Johannesapokalypse: Ein Beitrag zur Bestimmung prophetischer Redeformen'. In G. Jeremias, H.-K. Kuhn and H. Stegemann (eds.), *Tradition und Glaube.* Göttingen: Vandenhoeck & Ruprecht. 357–94.

Hartman, L. 1980. 'Form and Message: A Preliminary Discussion of "Partial Texts" in Rev 1–3 and 22.6ff'. In J. Lambrecht (ed.), *L'Apocalypse johannique et l'Apocalyptique dans le Nouveau Testament.* BETL 53. Gembloux: Duculot/Leuven: University Press. 129–49.

Hemer, C. J. 1986. *The Letters to the Seven Churches of Asia in Their Local Setting.* JSNTSup 11. Sheffield: JSOT Press.

Jeffrey, D. L. 1977. 'Literature In An Apocalyptic Age: Closure and Consolation'. Unpublished paper.

Kirby, J. T. 1988. 'The Rhetorical Situations of Revelation'. *NTS* 34:197–207.

Ladd, G. E. 1974. *The Presence of the Future.* Grand Rapids: Eerdmans.

Mauro, P. 1925. *The Patmos Visions: A Study of the Apocalypse.* Boston: Hamilton.

Minear, P. S. 1969. *I Saw a New Earth: An Introduction to the Visions of the Apocalypse.* Washington: Corpus Books.

Müller, U. B. 1975. *Prophetie und Predigt im Neuen Testament.* Studien zum Neuen Testament 10. Gütersloh: G. Mohn.

Muse, R. L. 1986. 'Revelation 2–3: A Critical Analysis of Seven Prophetic Messages'. *JETS* 29:147–61.

O'Brien, P. T. 1977. *Introductory Thanksgivings in the Letters of Paul.* NovTSup 49. Leiden: Brill.

Ramsay, W. M. 1904. *The Letters to the Seven Churches of Asia and Their Place in the Plan of the Apocalypse.* London: Hodder & Stoughton.

Ruiz, J.-P. 1989. *Ezekiel in the Apocalypse: The Transformation of Prophetic Language in Revelation 16,17–19,10.* European University Studies. Series XXIII, Vol. 376. Frankfurt am Main, Bern, New York, Paris: Peter Lang.

Schüssler Fiorenza, E. 1973. 'Apocalyptic and Gnosis in the Book of Revelation'. *JBL* 92:565–81.

Shea, W. H. 1983. 'The Covenantal Form of the Letters to the Seven Churches'. *AUSS* 21:71–84.

Strand, K. A. 1983. 'A Further Note on the Covenantal Form in the Book of Revelation'. *AUSS* 21:251–64.

Sweet, J. P. M. 1979. *Revelation.* London: SCM Press.

Thompson, S. 1985. *The Apocalypse and Semitic Syntax.* SNTSMS 52. Cambridge: Cambridge University Press.

Vos, L. A. 1965. *The Synoptic Traditions in the Apocalypse.* Kampen: J. H. Kok.

13

The Lamb and the Beast, the Sheep and the Goats: 'The Mystery of Salvation' in Revelation

Christopher Rowland

THE study of academic theology started for me in John Sweet's study thirty years ago. There was no theological fellow at my college, and so John was asked to look after the one new student embarking on the Theological Tripos. He duly did that and then taught me NT for the rest of my undergraduate career. I owe to him not only academic but also personal debts. The overawed and fearful Yorkshire state school boy coming to Cambridge, uncertain about whether he could keep up with the work, uncertain even about what theology might imply for faith and life, found in John, from such a different background, a friendly and supportive supervisor. I learnt to study the NT but more importantly I learnt *how* to study it – imbibing, in that way which only example can offer, a culture of prayerful and careful study, Christian living, and the recognition that the Apocalypse must be at the heart of any NT theology (Sweet 1979:51).

A perennial question for Christians is how they deal with that strong exclusive strand within their tradition, largely (though not entirely) due to the eschatological inheritance in which Jesus was the goal of the promises, not a stage in their fulfilment. The humanitarian instincts of Christians rightly shy away from consigning the majority of humanity to perdition, and a variety of more inclusive ways have been explored. The apocalyptic tradition, to which John Sweet has contributed so greatly by his writing, teaching and advice, deserves to be considered, though, as we shall see, a surprisingly more inclusive aspect emerges in the midst of its grim depiction of human delusion. In this essay I want to explore how the book of Revelation prompts readers to a searching examination of assumptions concerning the identity of 'insiders' and 'outsiders' in the divine economy and compare it with the judgement scene in Matt 25.31ff.

Revelation, paradoxically one of the most 'veiled' texts of all in the Bible, makes great demands of those who read or hear it.[1] We are tempted to 'translate' its imagery into a more accessible mode of discourse. John, as recipient of a book from Jesus Christ, has left us an apocalypse or a prophecy – not a narrative or an epistle – a text requiring of its readers particular interpretative skills (imagination and emotion, for example) to help cast light on its images. Biblical exegetes long to be able to tie up loose ends. But often the texts and the resources available for interpretation deny them the ability to achieve that purpose. They are compelled, therefore, to use analogy (parallels from within and beyond the text studied). The use of analogy infrequently provides the satisfaction of interpretative certainty as it involves an appeal to the imagination rather than the presenting of a definitive logical case; 'it persuades rather than coerces'.[2] Like this method, the medium of apocalyptic may startle and disorientate, before possibly (though not inevitably) pointing to a fresh view of reality by its extraordinary imagery and impertinent verbal juxtapositions. However difficult it may be for us, we must learn to exercise those faculties which are needed to engage with such a medium. Unlike the philosophical essay which demands its readers' intellectual submission by the force of argument, Revelation's word pictures seek to address and involve readers and relocate them in the divine economy. In some respects its function is illuminated by the opening chapters of 1 Corinthians, where Paul renounces plausible words of wisdom (2.4) in favour of 'God's wisdom, secret and hidden' . . . 'revealed to us through the Spirit' . . . (which) 'we speak . . . in words not taught by human wisdom but taught by the Spirit' (1 Cor 2.7, 10, 13). Apocalypse does not consist of 'propositional, logical, (or) factual language' but persuades by means of 'the evocative . . . power of its symbolic language compelling imaginative participation' (Schüssler Fiorenza 1991:31). Commentators on it also need to respond in order to be sensitive to its medium, as they seek to explore its distinctive wisdom.

In Revelation's imagery there are allusive hints of the way for those who wish to participate in the new age: not worshipping the beast. Rev 13 offers a terrible vision of the whole world seemingly following after in amazement (v. 4) and worshipping the dragon. In other words, amazement at the beast leads to worship of the dragon (perhaps unknowingly). People engage in activity which should be reserved for God. John is given strict instructions to worship God alone (22.9; cf. 19.10). The amazed question 'who is like the beast?' (reminiscent of similar sentiments expressed of God in Exod 15.11) is followed by 'who can make war on it?'

[1] Cf. J. Derrida, 'Of an Apocalyptic Tone Recently Adopted in Philosophy' in *The Oxford Literary Review* 6 (1984) 3–37.
[2] D. Nicholls, *Deity and Domination* (London: Routledge, 1989) 5.

In other words, amazement is linked to a sense of awe at its military power. The apparent universality of worship offered to the beast is qualified, however, by the reference to the Lamb's book of life. Those who are not written in the Lamb's book of life will worship the beast. Until the books are opened (20.12) and judgement takes place, the identity of the names contained in it is unknown, and the threat remains that one's name might be removed. Inclusion in the book of life means not worshipping the beast.

In Rev 13.11ff John sees another beast but this time arising from the land. The similarities of its character with the Lamb are explicit, but the fact that it speaks as the dragon (v. 12) suggests that this beast acts as an agent of the first beast and exercises its authority as a kind of grand vizier in its presence (cf. 13.14). The whole earth and its inhabitants worship the first beast. John speaks not only of the human populace but also of the cosmos as if the created world as a whole is under the thrall of the beast and is affected by it (cf. 11.18; 13.3; 17.5; 19.2). The second beast works miracles (16.14; cf. Matt 24.4f, 11, 24; cf. 2 Thess 2.9). The second beast is a deceiver, like Satan (cf. 20.3). Signs deceive in order to persuade the earth's inhabitants to make an image for the beast which will be the object of worship, something that is to be resisted (14.9, 11; 15.2; 16.2; 19.20; 20.4).

The point at issue in Rev 13 is not just about worshipping the beast and the dragon which stands behind the beast. The false marvels and bewitching words which come from the image presage a threat of death for those who do not worship the image of the beast (13.14; cf. Dan 3.5f) which is all-encompassing and covers all strata of society (cf. 6.15; 19.5, 18; 20.12). The act of worship is not a private matter, for those who worship will be marked with a mark on their right hand and on their foreheads (cf. 14.9, 11; 16.2; 19.20; 20.4), contrasting with those who stand with the Lamb who are marked with the name of the Lamb and of God (14.1; cf. 22.4). It is something which is imposed on the worshippers of the beast (v. 16). There are public, social and economic consequences, therefore: exclusion from regular social intercourse. Without the name of the beast or the number of its name it becomes impossible to buy or sell. Those 'bought' with the blood of the Lamb (5.9; cf. 14.3) must behave differently, however (cf. Mark 10.42f).

There is, inevitably and, perhaps, understandably, pressure to conform (13.14). Those who refuse to do so are offered reassurance that being marked with the Lamb is a sign of righteousness even if it means social ostracism (13.16). In the present age those marked with the beast *apparently* have freedom to go about their activities, whereas those who refuse to be so marked and side with God and the Lamb are persecuted, and their deaths are greeted with glee by the inhabitants of the earth (11.10). In reality it is those who maintain their integrity, even at the price of their lives, who will be vindicated, whereas those who have the mark of the beast 'drink the wine of God's anger' (14.10). Those who persevere (whether they be inside or outside the churches) see that the might of state power is itself extraordinarily fragile, and its affluence, so attractive and alluring, is destined for destruction – destroyed by precisely that power which has maintained it (as we shall see when we look at 17.16).

As the Beast has some of the characteristics of the Lamb (13.3, 14), one has to be watchful to avoid religion becoming a means of supporting or colluding with that which is opposed to the divine justice. The bewitching effects of a prevailing set of ideas to form outlooks cannot be underestimated. This is the function of ideology.[3] It makes one think that the ideas which are widely held are 'obvious', 'common-sense' and 'normal', when in fact they often cover up the powerful vested interests of a small group which has and wants to retain power. In John's vision the task of the second beast from the land is to persuade ordinary people that what they see in the first beast is normal and admirable, so that any deviation or counter-attraction is regarded as strange, antisocial and to be repudiated. John's vision helps to unmask these processes and is a pointed reminder that what everybody does need not be right or be copied (13.3, 8).

As with chapter 7 where the sealing is contrasted with the judgement on an unjust world, so chapter 14 offers the contrast to the previous chapter. Those who conform to the ways of the beast may achieve a temporary respite and prosperity but ultimately that cannot continue. John's vision offers hope to those who stand firm (14.1, 12). The stress on integrity and truthfulness (14.5) contrasts with the duplicity and deceit manifest in the previous chapter where what is false (13.14) leads astray and is met by the self-serving response of the world's inhabitants. Those who have compromised are urged to realize the error of their ways as the truth is revealed (14.6). In rather brutal fashion the vision brings home the ultimate character of apparently harmless actions. The odd bit of compromise in the old order is nothing less than being marked by the beast (14.9). For John all action, however small, is ultimately significant and of infinite value in the divine economy.

The significance of human behaviour is expressed in chapter 15. When the people of Israel reached the other side of the Red Sea they sang a song of deliverance (Exod 15). That is echoed in Rev 15. 'Those who had been victorious over the beast' (15.2) is a metaphor of non-conformity and refusal to accept its dominion and way of life.[4] That action becomes equivalent to the redemptive crossing of that threatening sea to God's

[3] T. Eagleton, *Ideology: An Introduction* (London: Verso, 1991).
[4] On the importance of worship as a counter-cultural act, see Kreider 1995.

side. The problem of the apparently 'innocent' act of not conforming is well illustrated by this dialogue from the *Martyrdom of Polycarp*:

> Polycarp was brought before the governor . . . who tried to persuade him to recant. 'Have some respect for your years', he said . . . 'Swear an oath "By the Luck of Caesar" – Own yourself in the wrong and say, "Down with the infidels"'. Polycarp's brow darkened as he threw a look round the turbulent crowd of heathens in the circus; and then, indicating with a sweep of his hand, he said with a growl and a glance to heaven, 'Down with the infidels'. (Extracts from *Martyrdom of Polycarp* 10 and 12.)

The apparently neutral, secular action is an event of supreme importance in the eyes of God, on a par with that fundamental redemptive moment in Israel's history. The redemptive moment means siding with the Lamb at the moment of testimony and standing firm in one's convictions and commitment to the horizon of hope symbolized by the Lamb who bears the marks of slaughter.

At the time when John was writing Rome had inspired his views, but because of the description of the city as Babylon the image can be of universal application,[5] a symbol of military power, exile and, for those who witness to the ways of the Lamb, oppression. Babylon was the place of exile and alienation (Ps 137 and 1 Pet 5.13). Yet it is a place where the person with the eye of vision can see the glory of God as Ezekiel did (Ezek 1), in whose footsteps John follows, as is evident throughout the book. John writes and readers read in the midst of the dominion of the beast and Babylon's luxurious consumption. However strong the desire of the saints to 'come out from the midst of Babylon' (18.4), the Apocalypse is addressed to people who breathe Babylon's ethos whether they like it or not, and who need a vision of how to live under her imperium though not to be part of it. There is no escape from exile this side of the millennium, except, that is, in the difference of perspective this vision of a common life based on different values offers.

In the end, the kings of the earth weep and wail over Babylon (18.9ff) as they are the ones who have committed fornication with her. Babylon has been the means of their own enrichment and they lament from afar on account of fear (cf. 11.11) just as the sailors did over the fall of Tyre (Ezek 27.30ff).[6] The merchants also weep and lament, 'since no one buys their cargo any more'. Babylon had been at the hub of trade and the merchants had depended upon her. Those who refused to worship the beast had been excluded from buying and selling (13.17). The merchants did not suffer this ostracism but colluded with Babylon (they committed 'fornication') as they made their wealth (v. 15).

---

[5] See the approach of Minear 1968 and Wengst 1987.
[6] Kraybill 1996; Bauckham 1992; and Garnsey, Hopkins and Whittaker 1983.

There is a list of the commodities found in Babylon, culminating with the brief but dismal reference to 'human lives' (18.11; cf. Ezek 27.13). Slaves are just bodies, more commodities to add to the long list. But the Apocalypse cannot allow that to pass without glossing the word: they are 'human lives'.

The reference to souls at the end of verse 13 prompts a short refrain on Babylon's loss: 'the fruit for which her soul longed' (v. 14). The word ἐπιθυμία is used here, with its echo of Exod 20.17 and the fruit in the garden in Gen 3.6. Babylon's soul is taken up with 'dainties and splendour' reminiscent of the attachment to affluence and property of the 'antichrists' opposed in 1 John 2.16. In that epistle the way of God based in love of the 'brethren' is contrasted with the way of Cain, who hated, oppressed and killed.[7]

The wealth of Babylon comes at the expense of millions (particularly 18.13). The description of Babylon (together with the account of its wealth) owes much to Ezek 27–28 and Jer 51. The goods are in large part luxuries, hardly the basic necessities which formed the subsistence of most people in John's (or in our) day (Rev 18.11ff; cf. Ezek 27.12ff). Luxury goods here gravitate to the centre to supply an insatiable need. This has the effect of making the rest of the world peripheral. Those on the periphery become merely means of supplying the needs of others (O'Donovan 1986b:85). In the extravagant search of the few for luxury of life and wealth there lies a hidden cost to human lives and societies.

Such sentiments are rudely interrupted, however, when there is a different kind of cry, one of rejoicing in verse 20 echoing the joy of heaven at Satan's ejection in 12.12. Apostles, as well as saints and prophets, are commanded to rejoice, because God has given judgement in favour of them rather than of Babylon who has been drunk with the blood of the saints (17.6). The tone of sadness is resumed in verse 22, this time in the words of the mighty angel, and concerns the end of Babylon's music. Babylon as a place of art, music, craft and trade is ended and the round of marriage and light which characterizes the life of a city living normally is rudely interrupted (cf. Matt 24.38). Her merchants were 'the magnates of the earth' (cf. 6.15). The readers receive a rude shock if they think that there is a neutral character to all the activity of trade, commerce and socializing. It is sorcery, which will be excluded from the new Jerusalem (21.8; 22.15) and of which humanity has refused to repent (see Esler 1994:131–46). God's witness against sorcery is closely linked with the oppression of the hired labourer, the widow, the orphan and the stranger in Mal 3.5, when the refining fire of judgement comes. The lament for her culture and sophistication and wealth cannot pass without the reminder that in her the blood of the prophets was to be found (6.10; 16.6; 17.6;

[7] In Josephus *Ant.* 1.60 Cain's sin is the enclosure of land and acquisitiveness.

18.24; cf. Matt 23.35ff), together with that of all those slaughtered on the earth. Babylon is a place of vicious violence towards humans, as well as enabling a few kings and magnates to grow rich.

A feature of chapters 18–19 is the welter of different voices which confront the reader oscillating between triumph at Babylon's fall and a searing lament at the end of her culture. The perspective of the beneficiaries of Babylon's wealth is included. There is sadness expressed at the passing of the splendour of Babylon, though none from the heavenly voices. The perspective of those who have profited from Babylon's greatness includes all of us who have become prosperous. The lament looks at the event from the perspective of the merchants and reminds those of us reading this text in the rich world that there is another world whose impoverishment is the price to be paid for our ease and wealth. As Allan Boesak has put it, it is 'the viewpoint which is so typically the one of those who do not know what it is like to stand at the bottom of the list' (1987:121f). These verses make explicit that Revelation is full of competing voices, symbolic systems and world-views. We are called to John's visionary voice, compared with which any claim to vision (such as that of Jezebel, Balaam, or the false prophet) is to be rejected. Voices even within John's own church which commend the eating of idol meat and com-promise with the social mores have their echoes in the merchants and mighty who lament Babylon's fall. It is a persisting voice in all of us which is never resolved at the end of the book. The 'unclean' still lurks at the gates of the city.[8]

This vision invites us to consider carefully the history of wealth and to assess the extent to which the trading which forms a part of the business of international 'order' is neutral in its inspiration and effects. Trade as much as violence and conquest can defile communities which become dominated by the benefits that it brings and the priorities it demands. Babylon with whom the kings and mighty have committed fornication demonstrates the lengths that are gone to in order to achieve wealth, status and power. This comes about through trade, which is fornication, 'a cultural promiscuity by which one power exploits and drains the resources from many others'.[9]

There is no view here of economic and political activity as autonomous enterprises devoid of any theological meaning. Acts of trade and commerce are shown to be shot through with human interest (so also 13.14ff). The supposition that politics and economics are impossible to interpret in the light of the gospel, have laws of their own and should be left to experts, is not encouraged by Revelation. However uncomfortable and however out of their depth they might feel, Christians are obliged to

[8] Schüssler Fiorenza 1991:132ff and Long 1996.
[9] O'Donovan 1986b:85, and his suggestive comments well summarizing the challenge of apocalyptic in 1986a:100ff.

read and understand the nature of what confronts them through the lens of the story of Christ which casts its shadow over every human trans-action. No activity can be regarded as morally neutral and beyond the critique and need for redemption of the Lamb who was slain. In the mundane situations of life there is present a challenge, threat and opportunity of the hidden life of God, a mix of the mundane and the heavenly. Neither membership of the Christian church nor credal assent is the criterion for faithfulness to God but resistance to Babylon.

Matt 25.31ff is another text for those who want to find 'elements which can be read in an inclusivist way in terms of the meaning of ultimate salvation'.[10] In other words, service of the hungry, thirsty, naked and imprisoned is the criterion for a place among the sheep or the goats, not membership of the Church. That the weight of exegetical opinion, however, has favoured the exclusive interpretation in which the 'brethren' of the Son of Man are identified either with disciples or Christian missionaries, needs to be recognized (see Rowland 1995). Francis Watson (1993) has challenged conventional wisdom which doubts whether this famous text can be appropriately used to justify an option for the poor and outcast, by pointing to features in the text which deconstruct the neat assumption that this passage serves a threatened Church needing assurance of vindication and retribution of its enemies.

If we stay with the text of Matthew's Gospel as we have it rather than the 'hidden' story of the community, which is the product of decades of patient historical reconstruction,[11] a neat identification of 'the least of these my brethren' with Christian disciples becomes less clear. The letter of the text does not *demand* the 'exclusive' interpretation as the only possible reading, particularly when we read the Last Judgement in the context of the narrative as a whole. Rather, the Gospel leaves readers uncertain whether they can have assurance that they will be among the 'sheep' rather than the 'goats' (Davies 1993:127). Indeed, there is surprise at the identity of the children of God when the Last Assize takes place (25.37, 45; cf. Rom 8.21). While it is not possible to demonstrate that Matthew's Gospel is more inclusive in its attitude to the weak and outcasts than much mainstream exegesis has allowed, the text of Matthew, like Revelation, does not allow the reader to be complacent in the face of judgement.

In Matt 25.31ff there is a subtle relationship between the eschatological judge and his hidden presence in the least of his 'brethren' in the midst of the present age: final judgement indeed is now being gestated in the womb

---

[10] The Doctrine Commission of the Church of England 1996:168.

[11] Some forms of historical criticism which rely on the reconstruction of another story 'behind' the literal sense of the text (authorial intention, community struggles, historical Jesus, etc.) have an uncanny resemblance to ancient allegorical exegesis. The major difference, of course, is the referent of the hidden story; see Barr 1989.

of history. All of life is an issue for the religious person, from eating to buying, words and deeds as well as what is narrowly regarded as worship. There is no area of existence which is neutral and unaffected by religious significance. Christianity inherited from Judaism a concern in this area. To use contemporary religious terminology, 'spirituality' is not a matter of private cultic devotion unconnected with the demands of ordinary life. It preserves an indissoluble link between the public and the private, the spiritual and political which has become such a central feature of catholic Christianity.

Texts like Matt 25 and Revelation do not so much offer a precise description of what is to come as a means of gaining a different perspective on the world, which challenges neat assumptions about priorities, inclusiveness and values in society. They are most disturbing for any ecclesiology. As the letters to the seven churches indicate, who is 'in' and who is 'out' is not at all clear. Those who are most confident (the Laodiceans) turn out to be the least fit for inclusion. Confessing the name and being part of an ecclesial community is not what counts; it is whether one has worshipped the beast and drunk deep of the fornication of Babylon. What we find in these texts leads us to question whether the Doctrine Commission of the Church of England has got it quite right when its authors write, 'this openness to the affirmation of the righteousness of some outside the believing community does not normally extend to an affirmation of their religious quest'. There is an unacceptable divorce between righteousness and religious quest as if the religion and the acts of mercy, etc. might in some way be divorced. Paul obviously thought that idolaters would find it enormously difficult to do God's will but in principle it was not impossible. The habit of *doing* righteousness was (and is) a religious obligation and must not be separated from it. Relationship with God through Jesus Christ must not be interpreted solely or even primarily in terms of ecclesiastical, liturgical or spiritual acts and words – the religious narrowly defined. Matthew and Revelation suggest that to be in Jesus Christ means to follow in his footsteps, engaging in acts of mercy to the outcast and in humility sharing the lot of those who like the Son of Man have nowhere to lay their head (Matt 8.20). Confession and membership of a specific religious group is less important than non-conformity with the mores of the beast and Babylon. Of course, that detachment from 'false consciousness' is assisted by the illumination which the perspective of explicit identity with the Lamb who is slain can offer, though it does not guarantee it. There remains the possibility that resistance to the beast and Babylon can be discerned by all those who instinctively do what is required of them by God (cf. Rom 2.13f).

Neither text allows that certainty or assurance of status or destiny. These texts, by virtue of their character and form, with all the vicissitudes and suggestiveness of narrative and symbol, do not allow readers to rest confident that they can be assured of ultimate vindication. There is an ambiguity in the refusal to allow that complacency in the face of judgement. The mix of parable, symbol and narrative functions like metaphor which should stop attentive readers in their tracks by the disturbing juxtaposition and get them to think about the world from another perspective, another set of experiences:

> Through being intractably uninterpretable metaphor demands, in terms of conventional modes of discourse, alternative methods of interpretation ... Through metaphor the speaker may attempt to represent the nature of her being ... outside the rationalising and normalising tropes and figures of conventional language ... The interpreter ... must attempt to identify with the speaker.[12]

Of course, we can ignore a text like Revelation and the experience of its author, or we can get used to it by familiarity with its contents or domestication of its concerns within a wider doctrinal framework, just as we become immune to the provocative and disturbing effect of metaphor, so that it becomes dead and lifeless in the midst of the familiarity of our discourse. John Sweet has reminded us of the need to take seriously the contribution of apocalyptic epistemology and the humility needed by all of us who have been formed by Western rationalism in approaching the interpretation of apocalyptic texts (Sweet 1996:165). Where an attempt is made to challenge convention, metaphor offers the attempt to exploit the crevice which opens up as language fails to do justice to the complexity of experience and the poet and visionary resorts to the disturbing, unconventional and bizarre to open our eyes to the reality of God and the world – 'to open the Eternal Worlds, to open the immortal Eyes of Man into the Worlds of Thought, into Eternity ever expanding in the Bosom of God, the human Imagination' (William Blake, *Jerusalem* 5.18). Once those 'Eternal Worlds' are opened up, however, there are disconcerting things to learn about 'the mystery of salvation', namely a different 'Vision of the Church', and the identity of children of God.

BIBLIOGRAPHY

Barr, J. 1989. 'The Literal, the Allegorical, and Modern Biblical Scholarship'. *JSOT* 44:3–17.
Bauckham, R. 1992. 'The Economic Critique of Rome in Revelation 18'. In *The Climax of Prophecy*. Edinburgh: T. & T. Clark. 338–83.

---

[12] I am grateful to C. M. F. Rowland for permission to quote from his unpublished essay, 'Are there things that can only be said metaphorically?'; see also Wolterstorff 1996:193ff.

Boesak, A. 1987. *Comfort and Protest*. Edinburgh: St Andrew Press.

Davies, M. 1993. *Matthew*. Sheffield: JSOT Press.

The Doctrine Commission of the Church of England. 1996. *The Mystery of Salvation*. London.

Esler, P. F. 1994. *The First Christians in Their Social Worlds*. London: Routledge.

Fox, R. Lane. 1987. *Pagans and Christians*. Harmondsworth: Viking.

Garnsey, P., K. Hopkins and C. Whittaker. 1983. *Trade in the Ancient Economy*. London: Chatto & Windus: Hogarth Press.

Kraybill, N. 1996. *Imperial Cult and Commerce in John's Apocalypse*. Sheffield: JSOT Press.

Kreider, A. 1995. *Worship and Evangelism in Pre-Christendom*. Nottingham: Grove Books.

Long, T. M. S. 1996. *Narrator Audiences and Messages: A South African Reader Response Study of Narrative Relationships in the Book of Revelation*. Diss. University of Natal.

Minear, P. 1968. *And I Saw a New Earth*. Washington, DC: Corpus Books.

O'Donovan, O. 1986a. 'Humanity's Last Flight from God'. In D. Mills-Powell, *Decide for Peace: Evangelicals and the Bomb*. Basingstoke: Marshall Pickering. 100–107.

O'Donovan, O. 1986b. 'The Political Thought of the Book of Revelation'. *TynB* 37:61–94.

Rowland, C. 1995. 'The Gospel, the Poor and the Churches'. In M. Davies, P. Davies and D. Carroll (eds.), *The Bible in Ethics*. Sheffield: Sheffield Academic Press.

Rowland, C. M. F. 1996. 'Are there things that can only be said metaphorically?' Unpublished essay.

Schüssler Fiorenza, E. 1991. *Revelation: Vision of a Just World*. Philadelphia: Fortress Press. Rev. edn. Edinburgh: T. & T. Clark, 1993.

Sweet, J. 1979. *Revelation*. London: SCM Press.

Sweet, J. 1996. 'Revelation'. In J. Barclay and J. Sweet (eds.), *Early Christian Thought in its Jewish Context*. Cambridge: Cambridge University Press. 160–173.

Watson, F. 1993. 'Liberating the Reader'. In F. Watson (ed.), *The Open Text: New Directions for Biblical Studies?* London: SCM Press. 57–84.

Wengst, K. 1987. *Pax Romana and the Peace of Jesus Christ*. London: SCM Press.

Wolterstorff, N. 1996. *Divine Discourse*. Cambridge: Cambridge University Press.

14

The Vision of the Church in the Apostolic Fathers

JAMES CARLETON PAGET

AN INTRODUCTION TO THE APOSTOLIC FATHERS

THE term 'Apostolic Fathers' is traditionally used in scholarly circles to describe a collection of non-canonical Christian works written between approximately 90 and 160 CE. According to the great J. B. Lightfoot (1890[vol. 1]:3), whose solemn portrait hangs in the room in the Cambridge Divinity School where, both as an undergraduate and a graduate, I learnt so much from the honorand of this volume, it is ultimately J. B. Cotelier whom we have to thank for the term. In 1672 the Frenchman published an edition of Barnabas, Clement, the Ignatian epistles and Polycarp. In the title of the edition, Cotelier describes the authors under discussion as 'those who flourished in the times of the apostles'. It was Thomas Ittig, writing twenty-seven years later, who, in his own edition of these writings, gave expression to the implications of this description by calling their authors 'apostolici patres'.

Whichever texts we decide should be designated a part of a collection called the Apostolic Fathers (Lightfoot/Holmes 1989:3 n. 5), few would accept that the authors of these works flourished in the time claimed by Cotelier (indeed many of them refer back to the time of the apostles; see *1 Clem.* 5.2; 42.1; Ignatius, *Eph.* 11.2; 12.2; *Hermas, Sim.* 9.15.4; 16.5; 25.2), or that they possess, at least in most cases, any direct relationship to those traditionally designated apostles. Moreover, few would regard them as a coherent collection representing a particular school of Christian thought – they are far too heterogeneous a group of writings for that to be the case. What binds them together, as implied above, is the accident of history (most of them appear in a collection which was first created in the seventeenth century), and the fact that they are *early* Christian writings which, for whatever reason, did not find their way into the canon of the NT, and which were principally preserved by those we might now term 'orthodox'.

Indeed their importance lies in the fact that they are early, and that they shed some light upon a very significant period of church history, which is otherwise only sparsely documented, namely the period which runs approximately from the writing of the last book of the NT to the beginning of Justin Martyr's literary career (approximately 160 CE). Importance should also be attached to the fact that they are addressed to communities located in a variety of parts of the Roman Empire.[1]

These writings are in the main very specific responses to the situations of those they are addressing. These situations differ from each other. So, for instance, *1 Clement* is written to a community which has recently experienced a schism of some kind; the Ignatian epistles are in the main hortatory works addressed to a bishop and to a variety of churches in which the threat of schism seems ever-present;[2] *Barnabas* is a response to a community which feels itself attracted to Judaism; *Didache* is also written to a community which lives in close proximity to Jews, and is a compilation from several sources in which a variety of traditional material, relating to ethics and church order, is brought together for the edification of its addressees; and *Hermas*, again a composite work, seems to have been written for a community at odds with itself over the question of post-baptismal sin. Reconstruction of the social make-up of the audiences addressed is almost impossible. Some might want to emphasize the varied social constituency implied by these texts (see, for instance, the concern with rich and poor in *Hermas*), but this is, more often than not, guess-work.

As 'situational' texts, some of these writings possess a strongly ecclesial dimension. This does not mean that they contain systematic discussions of the nature and character of the Christian Church, but rather that they are, to varying degrees, based upon each writer's assumptions about that subject. The Apostolic Fathers (from now on, AF) wrote during a period when the Church was subject to both internal (schism of various kinds) and external pressures (both from Jews and pagans). In the face of these, they attempt, some more consciously than others, to give voice to what they understand are the essential characteristics or defining marks of Christian life (though among the AF, Ignatius alone uses the noun 'Christianity' and, with the exception of *Did.* 12.4, the adjective

---

[1] *Hermas* was written in Rome; *Barnabas* was probably written in Egypt; the Ignatian epistles in Asia Minor, though Ignatius was bishop of the Syrian city of Antioch and he addresses one of his letters to Rome; *Didache* is thought to have been written in Syria; *1 Clement* was written in Rome and addressed to the Christians of Corinth; *2 Clement* might have been written in either Syria or Egypt; Polycarp addresses the Philippian Christians, though he was bishop of Smyrna.
[2] For the thesis that the real context against which to understand the Ignatian correspondence is the situation which pertained in Antioch, the church of which Ignatius was bishop, see Schoedel 1985:10–11.

'Christian'). It is the aim of this essay to show what, in their different ways, the AF understood these different characteristics to have been.

I have decided to set out the essay according to themes and not individual authors, partly because such an approach seems better suited to addressing the subject-matter of this volume in the space available. In proceeding in such a way, an attempt will be made to avoid producing the type of scholarly 'blancmange' which loses sight of the particular perspectives of various writers. Under the title 'AF' I have included the letters of Ignatius, Polycarp *ad Phil., 1* and *2 Clement,* the *Didache,* the *Epistle of Barnabas,* the *Shepherd of Hermas,* and the *Martyrdom of Polycarp.* This corresponds to the collection of Kirsopp Lake in his Loeb edition (first published in 1913) minus the *Epistle to Diognetus,* which I would wish to include amongst the writings of the Apologists.

I. UNITY

Fear of the forces of fragmentation looms large in the AF. Clement of Rome and Ignatius of Antioch, who address communities where schism or the threat of schism are a reality, are blunt in their condemnation of division and those who cause it. Clement speaks of 'abominable and unholy sedition, alien and foreign to the elect of God' (1.1; see also 3.1; 14.1; 46.5). Ignatius is, in his own words, a man set on unity (*Magn.* 8.1), and sees the role of a bishop as best expressed in a concern for unity, for, in words addressed to Polycarp, he states that 'there is nothing better' *(Polyc.* 2.1).[3] He frequently urges his addressees to flee divisions (*Eph.* 7; *Magn.* 8; 11), and refers to those who would deny the reality of Christ's incarnation (and in so doing cause division) as 'wild beasts in human form' (*Smyrn.* 4.1), or 'wicked offshoots who bear a deadly fruit' (*Trall.* 11.1).[4] For both these writers, perhaps echoing the language of Hellenistic political rhetoric,[5] it is the pursuit of 'peace and concord' (εἰρήνη and ὁμόνοια), the fruit of unity, which is central to the expression of Christian identity (*1 Clem.* 60.4; 62.5; Ignatius, *Eph.* 4.1, 2; 13.1; *Magn.* 6.1; 15.1; *Trall.* 12.2; *Phld.* inscr.; 11.2), and which reflects the divine calling of the Church.

---

[3] In the AF words for unity (ἕνωσις [ἑνόω] ἑνότης) only occur in Ignatius' letters, and usually refer to unity within the churches. For a general discussion, see Tugwell 1989:111f.

[4] Schoedel (1980:31) argues that Ignatius drew the boundaries within the Church more sharply than did those he was addressing. See Trevett 1992:147f, for a not dissimilar conclusion.

[5] On this see Schoedel 1980:51. *1 Clement* also makes considerable use of terminology with a political application. See in particular στάσις and the verb στασιάζω to refer to the strife within the community (H. Kraft 1963:404) and πολιτεία and πολιτεύομαι to refer to the Church as in some sense a body of citizens (H. Kraft 1963:367).

This concern for the unity of the Church, for the avoidance of division, is evidenced elsewhere in the AF (see *inter alia Did.* 4.3; 14; 15.3; *Barn.* 4.8; 19.12a; *Hermas, Vis.* 3.5 and 3.9), and gives voice to the essentially communal character of their vision of the Church (in both *1 Clement* and Ignatius, those who would oppose unity are portrayed as morally reprobate). In all this the idea is conveyed of churches as closely knit groups, in which regular communal gatherings, whether at the eucharist or otherwise, are often seen as one of the most effective ways of promoting unity.[6]

Unity here pertains to relations between, as well as within, local churches. The writings of the AF give us evidence of a growing conception of the Church as a universal body, in which a concern for churches other than one's own is in evidence. In this respect one might take note of the fact that Clement is writing as a representative or leader of the Christian community at Rome to the Christian community at Corinth, and of the evidence for communication between the churches of Syria and Asia Minor manifested in Ignatius's correspondence (Trevett 1992:154–55). Interestingly, in what some hold to be eucharistic prayers (Niederwimmer 1989:173–209), the writer of the *Didache* expresses the hope, perceived in eschatological terms, and paralleled in Jewish thought about the ingathering of the twelve tribes at the end-time (Isa 11.12; Jer 39.37; Wisd 2.10; *Eighteen Benedictions* no. 10), that 'as this broken bread was scattered upon the mountains, so let the church be gathered together from the ends of the earth into thy kingdom' *(Did.* 9.4; see also 10.5).

2. Governance

For Ignatius of Antioch and Clement of Rome, the maintenance of ecclesiastical unity is understood in terms of submission to an established hierarchy.

Ignatius, who of all the AF has the most developed understanding of church order, sees the idea of the Church or ἐκκλησία as defined principally by the presence of the threefold order of bishops, presbyters and deacons. 'Without these', he states, 'the name of "church" is not given' (*Trall.* 3.1), and their presence together reflects the heavenly order (*Trall.* 3.1; see also *Eph.* 4.2). Taking precedence is the bishop who stands in a line of authority proceeding from Christ (*Eph.* 3.2), and who, as a source of authority, appears at times to be interchangeable with God (*Magn.* 3.1; see also *Eph.* 5.3 and *Smyrn.* 9.1). Without his consent, the community

---

[6] Ignatius' statement that when the community is gathered together, 'the powers of Satan are destroyed, and his mischief is brought to nothing' (*Eph.* 13.1), gives a sense of the importance that some attributed to communal gatherings.

cannot act (*Trall.* 7.1, *Smyrn.* 9.1; his presence is necessary at many signifi-cant communal events, including eucharists [*Eph.* 5.2] and marriages [*Polyc.* 5.2]), a sentiment which takes on another dimension in Ignatius' view that the relationship between the bishop and his community should reflect that which exists between Christ and God (*Magn.* 7).[7]

For Clement of Rome the established hierarchy to which Christians should submit does not consist in a threefold order, but rather in a presbyterate,[8] whose existence is justified by reference to an argument from apostolic succession (42.4), and from OT priestly practice (43). The call to submit to the presbyterate (57.1; see also 47.6) forms part of a wider argument, which sees church order as intimately linked to a form of stratification in which each member of the Church, like each member of the army (37.1), the Jewish priesthood (43), the household (1.3f), and indeed the Empire at large (61), is aware of his rank and position.

We should note, however, that Ignatius and Clement do not have an exclusively disciplinarian perception of Christian leadership, even if in Ignatius's case this is more to the fore than in Clement's. When Ignatius sets out the duties of a bishop in his letter to Polycarp, these consist in a form of service in which the problems and concerns of the community are borne by its leader (*Polyc.* 1.2); and in this context there is some truth in Schoedel's observation that 'the threefold ministry promoted by Ignatius is more remarkable for its sense of solidarity with the community than for its emergence as a distinct segment of the group' (Schoedel 1980:55). Furthermore, Ignatius is keen to emphasize that office should not allow individuals to exalt themselves (*Smyrn.* 6.1), and this, amongst other things, may lie somewhere in the background of his commendation of the silence of the bishop (*Eph.* 5.3–6.1; Tugwell 1989:118). When Ignatius calls for bishops to live according to the pattern or 'typos' of God (*Trall.* 3.1 and *Magn.* 6.1, though for the textual difficulties connected with this reference, see Schoedel 1985:112), this is a pattern marked by suffering and service. Equally, while it is quite true that in *1 Clement* vertical perceptions of inter-communal relations predominate (that is, a view of inter-communal relations determined by subordination to a hierarchy), they exist in a dialectical relationship with horizontal ones (that is, a view of inter-communal relations based upon a sense of equality

---

[7] For a discussion of the way in which Ignatius' understanding of the relationship between bishop and community reflects the Johannine understanding of the relationship between Jesus and the Father, see Grant 1964:168.

[8] It is true that at *1 Clem.* 42.4 Clement refers to the appointment by the apostles of bishops and deacons. But the same apostles then provide for the succession of individuals called presbyters (44.3, 5), and their office is referred to as 'overseeing' or 'episcopate' (44.1, 4). This would seem to imply that in *1 Clement* those called 'presbyters' are the equivalent of bishops, though not bishops as understood by Ignatius.

between members of the community [see Bowe 1988:104–05]). So, for instance, in chapter 37, after Clement has endorsed the military (and vertically-oriented) model of communal life, he goes on to endorse the more horizontally oriented model of the body, which itself is complemented by the content of chapter 38.[9] Moreover, when recommending that those who have disturbed the community should go into voluntary exile (54), Clement cites a number of examples of kings who have acted in a selfless way for the sake of the community (55); and he certainly allows for the possibility that bad presbyters might exist (44.3, 4, 6), and that their dismissal in particular contexts might be justified. While the attitudes of self-sacrifice and humility are characteristics that the schismatics should show in submitting to the presbyters (2.1), these characteristics should also be present amongst those who lead the community.

Elsewhere in the AF, where we are in a position to make a judgement, we find the endorsement of different models of governance, where the vertical dimension appears to play a less significant role. The *Didache* shows a reliance on a form of charismatic leadership where the principal players seem to be apostles (not to be confused with the historical apostles), prophets, and teachers (*Did.* 11), though there is an indication in chapter 15 that the community is moving to a model based upon bishops and deacons.[10] What is particularly striking about the *Didache* is the extent to which the writer goes to warn the community against the misuse of office by those who hold it, and the way in which the community is portrayed as exercising considerable authority over its ministers (see *Did.* 6.1; 11.1–2; 12.1, and in particular 15.1, where the writer asks his addressees not to despise the bishops and deacons). This evident suspicion of office holders recurs in *Hermas* (see *Sim.* 9.27.2, where grasping deacons are condemned),[11] and in *Barnabas,* where the author expresses the fear that his addressees' perception of him as a teacher might adversely affect their reception of him and his letter (1.8; 4.9).

[9] Bowe (1988:144) notes how ch. 37–38 and 46–50, both of which endorse horizontal understandings of communal relations, surround, and therefore, balance those chapters which call for submission to the presbyters.

[10] See Grant 1964:160f. Streeter (1929:151f) argued that there was an evolutionary continuity between *Didache*'s view of order and that adopted by Ignatius. For Streeter the order implied in the *Didache* could have hardened into a threefold ministry, and in this respect Ignatius was simply a prophet turned bishop.

[11] It is difficult to establish precisely what offices existed in the Roman church of Hermas, not least because the document appears to be composite. At *Vis.* 2.4.3 elders are mentioned, and at *Vis.* 3.5.1 we hear of apostles, bishops, deacons and teachers (where apostles and teachers appear to belong to the Church's past). Bishops are mentioned again as providing hospitality to widows and orphans (*Sim.* 9.27.2). On all this, see Brox 1991:533f.

3. COMMUNITY AND ETHICS

We have already touched briefly on the concept of communal life which pervades some of the AF. Many of the images used by these writers to express their understanding of the community emphasize a sense of the corporate nature of Christian life: brotherhood, flock, army, temple, body, the elect, tower. These images form part of a wider picture in which Christians are bound to a life of mutual support, in part necessitated by the difficult circumstances in which they live. As the writer of *2 Clement* remarks: 'For if we have commandments to do this also, to tear men away from idols and to instruct them, how much more is it our duty to save from perishing a soul that already knows God? Let us then help one another and bring back those that are weak in goodness . . .' (17.12); and in his letter to bishop Polycarp, at a point where he appears to be addressing the community and not just the bishop, Ignatius states that Christians should 'labour together, struggle together, rise up together as God's stewards and assessors and servants' (*Polyc.* 6.1).

This sense of the mutuality of Christian life is seen by some to be particularly manifested in the gift of love (*1 Clem.* 49; *2 Clem.* 4.3; 9.6; Ignatius, *Magn.* 6.2; Polycarp, *ad Phil.* 1). Christians form a society marked by righteous deeds, and not simply by righteous words (*2 Clem.* 4.2; Ignatius, *Eph.* 14.1). Of particular importance here are acts of charity, such as help for the widow and orphan (*1 Clem.* 8.4; *Hermas, Vis.* 2.4.3; 5.3.7), and more particularly for the poor (*1 Clem.* 38.2; *2 Clem.* 16.4; *Polyc.* 10.2, *Did.* 4.8). In this latter manifestation of Christian charity, attention should be drawn to Hermas's parable of the vine and the elm (*Sim.* 2). In the parable Hermas sees a vine, which is supported by an elm. The shepherd explains to him that the vine bears fruit, and the elm is sterile. But without the elm the vine would not be able to bear much fruit. So it is with the rich and the poor within the community. 'But when the rich man rests upon the poor, and gives him what he needs, he believes that what he does to the poor man can find a reward with God, because the poor is rich in intercession and confession, and his intercession has great power with God. The rich man, therefore, helps the poor man in all things without doubting.' (*Sim.* 2.5; see Osiek 1983:78–90). Here a type of reciprocity exists between the generous rich and the needy poor.[12]

The concerns with practical charity outlined above, and indeed the general importance attributed in the AF to ethics, both of a communal and a personal kind (one thinks in particular here of sexual ethics), have

---

[12] Note how some of the material in *Hermas* on riches and poverty is close to passages in the Epistle of James (1.9–11; 5.1–5), a document which in all probability Hermas knew.

their root in the Judaism from which Christianity emerged. Few would now deny that, for instance, the Two Ways, important to both *Didache* (1–5) and *Barnabas* (18–20, and elsewhere), and to a lesser extent, *Hermas*, have their origins in Jewish paraenesis (Niederwimmer 1989:48f; R. A. Kraft 1965:134f). The Two Ways is itself the result of reflection upon the Hebrew Scriptures, and the significance of these texts for Christian ethics in this period cannot be disputed. Aside from the Two Ways, particular attention in this context might be paid to *1 Clement*'s frequent usage of scriptural paradigms for the promotion of particular forms of behaviour, or *Barnabas*'s ethically-oriented allegorical interpretation of scripture. When the latter urged his reader to see how well Moses legislated (*Barn.* 10.11), he was being quite serious. Paradoxically perhaps, it was precisely the author of *Barnabas* and indeed to a lesser extent, the author of *Didache* (8.1f), who sought to denigrate Jewish understanding of scripture, and implicitly to assert the quite distinctive character of Christian ethical standards,[13] though we should note that in *Hermas*, a document which is similarly influenced by Jewish parenesis, there is no evidence of such anti-Judaism.[14]

The quest for a distinctive Christian ethic emerges in those writings of the AF which show a concern with reflection upon the example of Christ himself. In this context we might point to Clement's emphasis on the humility of Christ in his attempts to combat those in Corinth who have acted in a haughty way by overthrowing some of the presbyters. 'For Christ is of those who are humble-minded, not of those who exalt themselves over their flock' (*1 Clem.* 16.1), he states before going on to cite Isa 53.1–12 as proof, not of the salvific effect of Christ's death, but rather of his self-humbling, concluding the section with the words: 'You see, beloved, what is the example which is given to us; for if the Lord was thus humble-minded, what shall we do, who through him have come under the yoke of his grace?' (*1 Clem.* 16.17). The implication of this section of *1 Clement* is that Christ's passion and death are the ultimate reference

---

[13] Some might contend that the extent to which the writer of *Barnabas*, and in particular the *Didache*, are quite *consciously* seeking to present an ethic which is distinct from that of the Jews is by no means clear. The *Didache* simply calls its addressees to fast on a different day to the Jews and to pray in a different way to them. The differentiation called for is not specifically ethical. Similarly, *Barnabas* distinguishes Christian understanding of the scriptures (not Christian behaviour) from that of the Jews. But in this latter case the understanding of the scriptures which *Barnabas* advocates is ethical, and so implicitly he could be seen to be distinguishing Christians from Jews with reference to their behaviour. On this see in particular *Barn.* 10.12 and the assertion that Christians have a righteous understanding of the commandments and announce them as the Lord wished.

[14] It is striking that such a strongly Jewish document as *Hermas* (see Brox 1991), written in Rome when Jews were clearly a presence in the city, should contain no reference to Jews at all.

points for an understanding of the nature of Christian self-sacrifice (see also *Barn.* 7.11). This seems to be reflected in a more dramatic way in the letters of Ignatius, where together with the incarnation, Jesus' suffering and death play a vital role in the expression of this singular writer's understanding of the Christian life. Here, as Rowan Williams has put it, martyrdom appears as 'the culmination of a far more prosaic process of un-selfing' (Williams 1991:14f), and the climax of our attaining to God, which began in the incarnation. Against this backcloth, the grounds for Ignatius' vehement opposition to the docetists become clearer (see *Eph.* 7; 16; *Trall.* 6; 9; 11; *Phld.* 2–3; *Smyrn.* 4–5). By denying the reality of Christ's incarnation and suffering, not only do these individuals deny the legitimacy of Ignatius' own martyrdom *(Smyrn.* 4; 5.1–2; *Trall.* 10), but they deny the legitimacy of the life of selfless service, of which martyrdom is the ultimate expression, and which emerges from a belief in the real nature of God's incarnation and suffering in his son. They are merely living a phantasmal and unreal existence *(Smyrn.* 2), and their separation from the community, their unwillingness to celebrate the eucharist, leads inevitably to a lack of concern for communal love *(Smyrn.* 6).

4. CHRISTIAN SOCIETY AND THE WORLD

For many of the AF the world is a place in which Christians feel as though they are resident aliens (*Hermas, Sim.* 1.1; see also *Ep. Diog.* 5). In part this is a feeling inspired by the hostility which Christians have experienced at the hands of non-Christians.[15] This sense of a 'hostile world' is maintained, indirectly at least, by a veneration of the martyrs (*1 Clem.* 5 and 6; *Hermas, Vis.* 3.2.1, 3.5.2), and the frequent calls found in the AF to endure (see Polycarp, *ad Phil.* 8.2).

But Christians do not feel alienated from the world simply by dint of the world's negative reaction to them. It is, according to some of the AF, necessary for their own moral well-being that they distance themselves from the world around, for the values of the world are not the values of the Church. The writer of *2 Clement,* who begs those he is addressing to go forth from this world (5.1), does so because he is conscious of the evils from which Christians have been saved: 'We were maimed in our understanding, worshipping stone, and wood, and gold, and our whole life was nothing more than death . . . but we have received our sight, and by his will we have cast off the cloud which covered us' (*2 Clem.* 1.6; 17.3; see also *Barn.* 16.7). A fear of too much involvement in pagan society,

---

[15] For references to persecution see *1 Clem.* 1.1; *2 Clem.* 17.7; *Hermas, Vis.* 4; *Martyrdom of Polycarp* 2.1. See also Ignatius's statement at *Rom.* 3.3 that Christianity is a work of greatness whenever it is hated by the world.

particularly in relation to daily affairs, is a central concern of *Hermas*. Hermas himself is initially condemned for too much of an attachment to daily affairs (*Vis.* 1.3; *Sim.* 4), especially a concern with money; and some of those excluded from membership of the tower, which in Hermas' vision stands for the Church, are precisely those who have become too concerned with the acquiring of wealth (*Vis.* 3.6.5; see also *Sim.* 8.8.1; 9.20.2). In the first Similitude a potential dichotomy is set up between wealth and membership of the Christian Church. 'What then are you going to do, seeing that you have a law in your own city? Will you because of your fields and other possessions altogether deny your law, and walk in the law of this city?' (*Sim.* 1.1.5; see also *Sim.* 8.9.1). Similar sentiments in which Christian life and the life associated with the world appear as polarities, though here not related specifically to the question of the accrual of wealth, are found in Ignatius' letters. So, for instance, he notes that there are two coinages, one of this world and one of God (*Magn.* 5.1), and demands that those he is addressing cannot speak of Jesus Christ and at the same time desire the world (*Rom.* 6.1; see also *Rom.* 7.1f). A feeling of hostility towards the world is also conveyed by the apocalyptic world-view of some of the AF, in particular *Hermas* and *Barnabas*. One can see how such attitudes could lead some to believe that Christians were people who entertained a hatred of the human race (*odium generis humani*; cf. Tacitus *Annals* 15.44).

It would, however, be wrong to deduce from the above that the AF adopted to a man what we might term 'counter-cultural' ideologies, that their various visions of the Church involved the adoption of 'world-views' of a revolutionary kind. The picture is perhaps more complex than that. If, for instance, we examine *Hermas,* we find that the author's attitude to wealth is tempered by a certain realism. In many respects the aim of the writer is not to excoriate wealth in itself (wealth is a gift from God – *Vis.* 3.9.2; *Mand.* 2.4), but rather to highlight the way in which too great a concern with money leaves Christians half-hearted in their commitment to the faith. For Hermas wealth is desirable insofar as it benefits those most at need in the community (*Sim.* 1.9).[16] It should also be noted that several of the AF appear to adopt social ethics of a relatively conservative kind, in which marriage and the structures of the οἶκος or household,[17] including the ownership of slaves, receive approval (note, *inter alia, 1 Clem.* 1.3f; Ignatius, *Polyc.* 4.2; 5.2; Polycarp, *ad Phil.* 4.2); and where, in spite of the experience of persecution, at least one writer seems to endorse the political structures of the Roman Empire

---

[16] On this complex question see Osiek 1983 and Brox 1991:517–20.

[17] An exception to this observation might be the *Didache*. Tugwell (1989:8) notes that the omission in the Two Ways section of any reference to the commandment to love mother and father, notable in a text which is so obviously based upon the Ten Commandments, indicates the fact that for this writer family ties are subordinate to ties to the Christian community.

itself (*1 Clem.* 61). Ascetic behaviour of various kinds is very rarely endorsed.[18]

Finally, while none of the AF can be referred to as proselytic or notably outward-looking in orientation, a concern for the uninitiated does manifest itself in some of their writings. The writer of *2 Clement* (13.1f) and others (Ignatius, *Trall.* 8.2; Polycarp, *ad Phil.* 10.3), quoting or alluding to Isa 52.5, note, with some regret, the adverse effect that negative Christian behaviour has on pagan onlookers (see 1 Cor 14.23–24); at *Eph.* 10.2 Ignatius calls the Ephesians to pray unceasingly for those outside the Church in the hope that they might repent and find God. He continues: 'Be yourselves gentle in answer to their wrath; be humble minded in answer to their proud speaking; offer prayer for their blasphemy . . . be gentle for their cruelty, and do not seek to retaliate. Let us be proved their brothers, and let us be imitators of the Lord . . .'. For Ignatius the fact of the incarnation of God in Christ obliges Christians to interact with the alien world, just as Christ did. And just as Christ's interaction with the world involved suffering, so will Christians' interaction with the world involve the same thing. But this is no reason to abrogate one's responsibility towards that world.

5. THE PERFECT SOCIETY

We have seen that for many of the AF, Christians see an important part of their distinctive identity as bound up with their moral conduct. The Christian community is different not simply because Christians find themselves in a unique relationship with God as a result of their baptism, but also because the society of which they are members has a distinctive ethic. The ethical texture of so much in the AF gives voice to this conviction. And yet the AF give us evidence of the fact that Christians are constantly falling short of this ideal. Can we see in the AF a tension between the vision that they have of the Church, and the reality that is the Church? And is there any attempt to resolve that tension?

In many of the AF the question of the disjunction between ecclesial vision and ecclesial reality is noted implicitly or explicitly, but does not in fact loom large as a topic for agonized reflection. Ignatius, for instance, seems to hold the communities he addresses, in terms of their ethics at least, to be perfect manifestations of Christian life. This much seems clear from the inscriptions of many of the letters. But Ignatius is keen to draw

---

[18] See, for instance, Ignatius' rebuke of those who boast of their sexual continence (*Polyc.* 5.2), and the possibility that parts of *Hermas* are directed against those who would wish to adopt a more ascetic ethic (see especially his rebuke of those who glory in their fasting in *Mand.* 5). Some scholars have suspected the presence of an ascetic tendency in *2 Clement* (cf. in particular chs. 5, 6 and 12), but if it is present, it does not seem very strong.

internal boundaries within the Church (on this see above). When he does so, however, these boundaries relate primarily to questions of doctrinal purity. Other writers, while acknowledging the reality of sin in their communities, assume the efficacy of repentance, without passing comment on the sins that render someone beyond even repentance (see *1 Clem.* 7f; *2 Clem.* 8.1f). The restoration of individuals to the community seems sometimes to be more important than their exclusion (see Polycarp, *ad Phil.* 11 and the bishop's plea for the restoration to the community of the wayward presbyter Valens and his wife); and some writers appear to deal with the problem by adopting a realistic view of the ethical potential of their communities. This seems to be the way to read the Didachist's statement which forms a part of his concluding statement about the Two Ways: 'For if you can bear the whole yoke of the Lord [perhaps the Two Ways], you will be perfect, but if you cannot, do what you can' (6.2).[19]

The presence of perfectionists who see no place in the Church for those who sin after baptism emerges as a considerable problem in *Hermas* (*Mand.* 4.3.1). Here we have a much stronger sense of a Christian writer struggling with the problem of the disjunction between ecclesial vision and reality. When Hermas has a vision of the Church, it is a vision of an old woman, whose age reflects not only the fact that she was created before the world (*Vis.* 1.3.4; 2.4.1), but the fact that her 'incarnation' in the form of the Church in the world has rendered her an altogether more feeble creature than she was in her pre-existent state,[20] a point that is indirectly confirmed by the fact that she becomes more youthful as Hermas' moral state improves (*Vis.* 3.11–13; on this see Brox 1991:524–25). But *Hermas* is written with the purpose of justifying post-baptismal repentance within certain constraints (see especially *Vis.* 3; *Sim.* 8 and 9, and the discussion in Tugwell 1989:84). Furthermore, Hermas himself, who is 'an ordinary sort of bloke', appears to find solace in his visions, mandates and similitudes. These two facts show that the work is not as rigorist as some have argued. The author does accept, within certain limitations, that the Church on earth is a mixed bag, a '*corpus permixtum*', even if there do exist some tensions on this point between his understanding of the Church in his third vision and his ninth similitude.[21]

[19] On this verse and the Didachist's 'realism' in general, see Tugwell 1989:13f. Some might see his interpretation as faulty in the light of 16.2 where Christians are warned that 'the whole time of your faith will not avail you, if you are not made perfect at the last time'. But Tugwell interprets this verse in the light of 16.5 where it is stated that those who remain in their faith will be saved, where 'faith' means faithfulness.

[20] See also *2 Clem.* 14 where the Church is similarly seen as a pre-existent entity that, like Christ, has enfleshed itself amongst humans, and risks becoming corrupted.

[21] In the third vision only those stones which represent sinless people are placed in the tower, but in the ninth similitude stones representing sinners are found in the tower (4.5–8; 6.3–5), and are only removed subsequently. For a discussion of this apparent inconsistency and its resolution, see Brox 1991:528f.

But while the majority of the AF, insofar as we can judge, seem, up to a point (and those points probably varied), to have accepted the morally mixed nature of the Christian Church, they knew that at the end, whatever form that might take, God would judge individuals on the basis of their moral state (*1 Clem.* 26; *2 Clem.* 9; *Did.* 16; *Barn.* 6.18, etc.). Then there would be no chance of a second repentance. Salvation was not brought about solely by entry into the Church (*Barn.* 4.14; 6.17f), and once baptized, the call was to persevere in the face of a final judgement (*1 Clem.* 35.4; *2 Clem.* 7.1; *Barn.* 4.11).

6. Conclusion

To try and write about the vision of the Church in the AF is in some sense an artificial exercise. Not only does each writer promote a different vision with different emphases, but also some writers afford the reader more information on this matter than do others. So, for instance, it is not too much of a problem to describe Ignatius' ecclesiology, whereas it is much more difficult to do such a thing for *Barnabas*.

In what has preceded, an attempt has been made to discuss different writers' approaches to a variety of subjects which it was felt come under the umbrella of the theme 'vision of the Church'. What emerges from this is, to a greater or a lesser extent, a picture of a somewhat introspective Church (none of the texts are addressed to outsiders), made up of tightly-knit communities, intent upon the promotion of unity and the maintenance of an identity which finds much of its inspiration from a particular moral vision of what it is to be a Christian. Such a vision is strongly communal in its orientation even in a writer like Ignatius who spends so much time promoting the authority of the bishop; and it is also strongly practical.

It is impossible to know how representative of early Christianity the AF are. The fact that they are a heterogeneous group of writings, that they were preserved by the Church, and that some of them, most notably *Barnabas* and *Hermas*, nearly achieved canonical status, indicating a certain popularity, could be taken as signs which affirm their representative character. But, given our limited knowledge of Christianity at this time, judgements in this respect can only be of the most provisional kind. However we judge this question, they remain important witnesses to the emerging perception of Christian identity on the part of a variety of Christians from different parts of the Roman Empire.

BIBLIOGRAPHY

Bardy, G. 1945. *La Théologie de l'Église de saint Clément à saint Irénée.* Paris: Les Éditions du Cerf.

Bowe, B. E. 1988. *A Church in Crisis: Ecclesiology and Parenesis in Clement of Rome.* Minneapolis: Fortress Press.

Brox, N. 1991. *Der Hirt des Hermas.* Göttingen: Vandenhoeck & Ruprecht.

Grant, R. M. 1964. *The Apostolic Fathers, vol. 1, An Introduction.* New York: Thomas Nelson & Sons.

Grant, R. M. and H. G. Holt. 1965. *The Apostolic Fathers, vol. 2, First and Second Clement.* New York: Thomas Nelson & Sons.

Kraft, H. 1963. *Clavis Patrum Apostolicorum.* Darmstadt: Wissenschaftliche Buchgesellschaft.

Kraft, R. A. 1965. *The Apostolic Fathers, vol. 3, Barnabas and the Didache.* New York: Thomas Nelson & Sons.

Lightfoot, J. B. 1890. *The Apostolic Fathers.* 5 vols.; 2nd edn. London: Macmillan & Co.

Lightfoot, J. B. and J. R. Hamer. 1891. *The Apostolic Fathers: Revised Greek Texts with Introductions and English Translations.* London. Rev. edn. by M. W. Holmes. Grand Rapids: Eerdmans 1989.

Niederwimmer, K. 1989. *Die Didache.* Göttingen: Vandenhoeck & Ruprecht.

Osiek, C. 1983. *Rich and Poor in the Shepherd of Hermas: An Exegetical-Social Investigation.* Washington, DC: Catholic Biblical Association of America.

Pernveden, L. 1966. *The Concept of the Church in the Shepherd of Hermas.* Lund: Gleerup.

Schoedel, W. R. 1980. 'Theological Norms and Social Perspectives in Ignatius of Antioch'. In E. P. Sanders (ed.), *Jewish and Christian Self-Definition vol. 1.* London: SCM Press. 30–56.

Schoedel, W. R. 1985. *Ignatius of Antioch.* Philadelphia: Fortress Press.

Streeter, B. H. 1929. *The Primitive Church.* London: Macmillan & Co.

Trevett, C. 1992. *A Study of Ignatius of Antioch in Syria and Asia.* Lewiston/Queenston/Lampeter: Edwin Mellon Press.

Tugwell, S. 1989. *The Apostolic Fathers.* London: Darton, Longman & Todd.

Wengst, K. 1984. *Didache; Barnabasbrief; Zweiter Klemensbrief; Schrift an Diognet.* Schriften des Urchristentums II. Darmstadt: Wissenschaftliche Buchgesellschaft.

Williams, R. D. 1991. *The Wound of Knowledge.* 2nd rev. edn. London: Darton, Longman & Todd.

15

Universalism and Particularism: Twin Components of Both Judaism and Early Christianity

JOHN M. G. BARCLAY

Or is God the God of Jews only? Is he not the God of Gentiles also? Yes, of Gentiles also, since God is one; and he will justify the circumcised on the ground of faith and the uncircumcised through that same faith. (Rom 3.29–30, NRSV)

THUS Paul triumphantly declares the achievement of the Christian mission he spearheaded: it bridged the ancient gulf between Jews and Gentiles, creating a transcultural movement which was in principle blind to ethnicity. The sound of this triumph sounds throughout the NT (cf. Eph 2.11–22; Rev 7.9–17; Acts *passim*), though Paul is unique in linking it theologically to the cornerstone of Jewish belief, the oneness of God. His rhetoric might be taken to imply that Jews, despite that belief, considered God to be God only of Jews, not of Gentiles. At the very least, it provokes questions about how confession of the one God of all humanity can be combined with belief in the election of Jews as God's special people. But the sensitive reader will feel the undertow of a similar question facing Pauline theology too: if God is one, is he the God of unbelievers as well as believers? In abandoning Jewish ethnic particularism, has Paul done away with all particularisms, or has he implicitly reimposed one of his own?

In his brilliant essay on this topic (1977), Nils Dahl warned of the potential of Pauline rhetoric to spawn a theological stereotype according to which Christian 'universalism' is contrasted with Jewish 'particularism', 'nationalism' or 'exclusivity'. That stereotype was foundational to F. C. Baur's construction of early church history which stands at the root of much NT scholarship. Baur claimed that the universal spirit of Christianity was the culmination of the political and spiritual universalism effected by the Roman Empire, in which nations 'tended inevitably not only to melt away the stiffness and unsociableness of their previous attitude to one another, but even to obliterate all merely national or individual distinctions, and to produce a broad sense of universality' (1878:3). Christianity, for Baur, embodies that 'universal form of consciousness' to which the human spirit had been moving, and in its freedom from 'everything merely external, sensuous, or material' constitutes the 'absolute religion' (1878:5, 9). In particular, while drawing on Jewish monotheism, it was necessary that Christianity should be freed from Jewish 'particularism', the 'narrow range of vision of the Jewish theocracy', which constituted the Jewish 'national one-sidedness and defectiveness' (1878:18). It was Paul's achievement to uproot Jewish particularism and to 'expose the baselessness of its prejudices and pretensions' through his 'magnificent dialectic' (1878:198).

Baur's scheme of theological history, drawing on a well-developed post-Enlightenment ideology, encouraged the production of numerous caricatures of Judaism, and it was perhaps inevitable that such confidence in Christianity's universal achievement would rebound in resentment towards the Jews as the token of unassimilated difference in the heart of 'Christian' Europe. But the basic stereotype, contrasting Christianity with a 'nationalistic' or 'exclusive' Judaism, is still operative in many contemporary forms of NT scholarship, not least in the 'new perspective on Paul'. J. D. G. Dunn, its foremost proponent, takes our lead text (Rom 3.29–30) to signal Paul's attack on 'Jewish national righteousness', that is, 'Jewish claims to exclusive rights before God', the 'Jewish assumption of God's favour and overconfidence in election' (1988:193). Where Paul speaks elsewhere of the 'curse of the law' (Gal 3.10) he 'has in mind the specific short-fall of his typical Jewish contemporary, the curse which falls on all who restrict the grace and promise of God in nationalistic terms, who treat the law as a boundary to mark the people of God off from the Gentiles, who give a false priority to ritual boundaries' (1985:536). Other scholars in this line of interpretation have spoken of Paul's attack on Israel's 'national pride' and 'racial exclusivism' (Barclay 1988:240, 246) and of the Mosaic law as, in Paul's view, 'given to Jews and Jews only, which relates to Gentiles simply in that it forms a barrier to keep them out of the covenant' (Wright 1991:173).

Although I have just cited myself among those who have employed such language, I am now alarmed by its proneness to stereotype Judaism. Should we not be disturbed by the ease with which Judaism is invested with epithets – 'particularistic', 'exclusive', 'restrictive', 'tribal', 'nationalistic', 'narrow', 'clannish', 'ethnocentric', etc. – which read like a vice-list of post-Enlightenment discourse? In recent years, several scholars have objected to the simplistic contrast between 'particularistic Judaism' and 'universalistic Christianity' (e.g. Boccaccini 1991:251–65, Segal 1994, and Levenson 1996), noting that many variants of first-century Judaism had their own kinds of universalism, and that the early Christian movement was itself 'exclusive' and 'particularistic' in its attitudes to non-believers.

More radically, one might also question whether the modern assumption that 'universal' is better than 'particularist' does not carry its own cultural and political baggage. Recently, for instance, the Jewish post-modernist Daniel Boyarin has read Paul's universalism not, with Baur, as a higher stage of religion, but as an inherently imperialist drive to 'coercive sameness', which threatens to obliterate 'the rights of Jews, women and others to retain their difference' (1994:233). From Boyarin's post-modern perspective, particularism, in the sense of preservation of difference, is a necessary attribute of humanity, not an impediment to its progress. Thus Baur's value-system, with its acclamation of a 'universal' Christianity, is turned entirely on its head.

In what follows I offer some comparisons of Judaism and early Christianity which can give only the outlines of a broad and complex field, while attempting to minimize the apologetic factor which has typically played a large part in the self-presentation of both Jews and Christians. It will be helpful to distinguish between different kinds of 'universalism' (cf. Levenson 1996:144–45), and I shall suggest that both Judaism and early Christianity contained elements of universalism and particularism to varying degrees and in various forms. In particular, by calling attention to the different *kinds* of particularism typical of Judaism and early Christianity – the one an aspect of ethnicity, the other of a voluntarist association – I hope to highlight the essential incommensurability of the two traditions and also to further reflection on the problems and possibilities facing the contemporary Church.

I. JEWISH VARIETIES OF PARTICULARISM AND UNIVERSALISM

The vast and multicoloured entity we call 'Judaism' is obviously far too complex to be analysed in a few pages, but some broad reflections could at least help structure further study. Jon Levenson has surveyed 'the universal horizon of biblical particularism' (1996), insisting that the Jewish concept of election need not entail either indifference to, or contempt of, Gentiles, nor does it rule out an all-embracing hope of salvation in the eschaton. The resulting balance of particularism and universalism could take many shapes, but we may here explore its manifestations in post-biblical Judaism in relation to three topics: (*a*) God, Jewish election and humankind in history; (*b*) eschatological expectations for humanity; and (*c*) social relations with non-Jews.

(*a*) God, Jewish Election and Humankind in History

The biblical tradition juxtaposes God's care for all nations and all creation with his special selection of the Abrahamic family, and it is no surprise to find later Jewish theology working in the tension of these two convictions. Philo explains how Israel is the 'portion' of the universal Lord (Deut 32.7–9) by reference to kings who rule over all their subjects but have a special relationship to their household servants, or own the whole land while having their own personal property (*Plant.* 54–60).[1] God's universal attributes, as Father and Saviour of all humanity, are central to Philo's theology, but he finds these compatible with the notion of a special people who are distinguished by their piety and virtue, and whose role in the world is that of a priest, making up for the deficiencies of other nations (*Spec. Leg.* 2.163–67). Similarly, The Wisdom of Solomon presents God as giver of wisdom to all who seek her, offering universal benefits without any ethnic limitation (6.12–9.18); but it also presents the Saviour of all as, in particular, the Saviour of his beleaguered people, who are chastened where other nations are destroyed, and who can claim an ultimate superiority over others because 'we are yours, since we know your power' (12.20–22; 15.1–4; see Barclay 1996: 170–76, 181–91).

Of course, the presentation of this balance of universalism and particularism, and the relative weight given to each, varies in sources of different characters and milieux. It would be wrong to present Palestinian Judaism as necessarily more 'particularistic' than a 'universalistic' diaspora, since in both regions social and theological reactions to the Gentile world varied greatly (Hengel 1974; Barclay 1996). Jews in either location could draw on the potential universalism of the Jewish wisdom tradition or make appeal to the common ground they shared with Hellenistic culture, positing perhaps a 'moral minority' among Gentiles who attained to the level of virtue practised by Jews (e.g. Philo's *Quod Omnis Probus Liber Sit*), or depicting philosophical, moral and even theological agreement between Jews and educated Gentiles (e.g. *The Letter of Aristeas, The Sentences of Phocylides*). The later construct of the 'Noachide laws', which detailed the basic morality required of Gentiles (Novak 1983; Bockmuehl 1994–95), is the specifically rabbinic form of a long tradition of respect for 'righteous Gentiles', whose ability to discern God's will might also be explained by reference to 'natural' law or revelation. In apocalyptic circles there was perhaps a greater degree of pessimism concerning the capacity of Gentiles, and even of Jews, to understand or obey God (e.g. at Qumran), but that could lead to a different form of universalism, the universalism of the human plight

---

[1] Compare the later rabbinic saying, *b. Sanh.* 39b: 'R. Eleazar opposed [two verses]: It is written, "The Lord is good to all" (Ps 145.9), but it is also written "The Lord is good unto them that wait for him" (Lam 3.25). This may be compared to a man who has an orchard. When he irrigates it, he irrigates the whole; but when he prunes, he prunes only the best [trees].' On rabbinic discussions concerning God as God of the nations, and as God of Israel, see Dahl 1977.

(4 Ezra; cf. the message of John the Baptist). In general we may say that some sense of Jewish 'distinction' – in the sense of Jewish difference and/or Jewish superiority – was integral to the efforts of Jews to maintain their cultural integrity, but it would be inaccurate to present this as if it necessarily excluded a vision of God's interest in the whole world or of the capacity of non-Jews to relate to God's will. It would be misleading also to depict either element as awkward, ill-fitting or merely traditional. Much Jewish theology thrived precisely in the tensions inherent in being God's people in God's wider world.

(b) Eschatological Expectations

One way in which those creative tensions could be theologically resolved was in hopes for the ultimate salvation of the world. Here it is important to note the distinction between what is expected of Gentiles in history and what is expected of, or for, them in the eschaton: a largely pessimistic view of the 'ungodly nations' in the present might well be complemented by hopes of the ultimate salvation of all humanity, and on terms which did not necessarily match those applied to conversion into the present-day Jewish community (see Fredriksen 1991). Like all eschatological hopes, speculation on the fate of Gentiles was extremely varied and often imprecise. The biblical tradition gave ample scope for expectations ranging from the total obliteration of the godless Gentiles to hopes of the gathering of the nations when Israel's destiny is realized (e.g. Isa 2.1–4; 56.3–8; 60.10–14). Even in passages depicting destruction, God's judgement is sometimes specific to 'the rulers' or 'the oppressors' and does not imply the annihilation of all Gentiles (e.g. Ps. Sol. 17); sometimes, also, 'destruction' turns out to mean only subjugation to Israel's authority, or a purging from sexual and religious 'perversions' which precedes eschatological restoration (Sibylline Oracles 3).

In a tradition which may go back to the early second century, we find two rabbis debating the implications of Ps 9.17, 'The wicked shall go into Sheol, and all the nations which forget God' (Tosefta Sanh. 13.2): does that mean that all nations forget God, so none will have a share in the world to come (R. Eliezer), or could it mean that only those nations which forget God will be banished to Sheol, allowing 'righteous people among the nations' to share in the world to come (R. Joshua)?[2] The notion of 'the righteous among the nations' mirrors Philo's concept of a Gentile 'moral minority', those Greeks and barbarians who, like an ember in a fireplace, keep the flame of virtue from extinction (Spec. Leg. 2.44–48). But Philo also hopes for a 'redemption' of Gentiles on a much larger scale that this. He believes that when Israel's fortunes are restored 'others will

---

[2] See Sanders 1977:206–12 on this passage and variant rabbinic views on the salvation of Gentiles.

abandon their own traditions, and bid farewell to their ancestral customs, and turn to honour ours alone' (*Mos.* 2.44).

In general, expectations of Gentile salvation leave unspecified how many Gentiles will be saved and what will change in the lives of the Gentiles concerned. The reorientation of the nations towards Israel, the temple in Jerusalem and the one God are common themes, but there was no need to spell out exactly how Gentiles would participate in the eschatological salvation (see Sanders 1992:264–70, 289–98). Such vagueness might signal lack of interest but it could also suggest open-ended hope. Although some strands of Judaism (e.g. the members of the Qumran community) might look forward to the destruction of all Gentiles, in other cases even an antagonistic attitude to 'immoral' and 'idolatrous' Gentiles could co-exist with a generous imagination concerning their future. Thus Jewish particularism in this context does not necessarily preclude a universal vision for the redemption of all creation. Indeed, one might say that Jewish particularism is in some senses here the *necessary prerequisite* for universal salvation, since it is only through the faithfulness of God's 'sacred race' (*Sib. Or.* 3.573) that all humanity will renew its proper worship of the one God. As Levenson comments in relation to late biblical eschatology, 'Israelite particularism, in this vision of things, is not destined to disappear. It is destined to reach its universal horizon' (1996:164).

(c) Social Relations with non-Jews

Even if all the above is conceded as integral to Jewish theology, Christian complaints about Jewish 'exclusivity' remain insistent in relation to the limits of Jewish social intercourse with Gentiles. It is thus especially important here to clarify both where and why those limits were set and to identify the type of 'particularism' which they entailed.

In the first place, it is important to insist that Gentiles were *not* in principle excluded from membership in the chosen people, since Jews had long allowed the practice of proselytism, by which it was possible for Gentiles to join themselves to the Jewish nation. We do not know how many proselytes there were, nor how eagerly they were sought (Feldman 1993 gives a maximal and Goodman 1994 a minimal answer to the latter question, while Carleton Paget 1996 helpfully suggests a mediating solution); but there is abundant evidence for the existence of proselytes and for reflection by Jews about Gentile conversion (e.g. the depiction of conversion in *Joseph and Aseneth*). Although there was discussion, at least among the rabbis, about the precise status of proselytes, and although their distinct designation in some inscriptions as 'proselytes' might suggest that first-generation 'incomers' were an ambiguous category, that is only what one would expect of 'naturalized' citizens or of those who become members of a family through adoption or marriage; in the long term what matters is their grafting into the people of God, which ensures that their lineage is henceforth truly Jewish. Thus, Judaism was not an 'exclusive' entity in the sense that Gentiles were automatically or permanently debarred from entry.

However, what the Jewish practice of proselytism demonstrates, somewhat paradoxically, is that Judaism was primarily an *ethnic tradition*, that is, one based on allegiance to 'ancestral customs' (Greek, τὰ πατρία or τὰ πατρία ἔθη, Philo, *Mos.* 1.31; Josephus, *Ant.* 20.100 and *passim*). Here heredity is fundamental and Jewish families constitute the principal bearers of the tradition. Many of our sources indicate that to become a proselyte was to undergo a radical resocialization, in which not only one's cultural but also one's ethnic identity was somehow redefined.[3] Modern notions of 'race' are potentially misleading here, since the Jewish awareness of belonging to a 'nation' (ἔθνος or γένος) had nothing to do with genetic or physiological characteristics. The most appropriate model is rather that of a family: a group which outsiders may join (through marriage or adoption) but whose consciousness is based on ancestral inheritance, and where relatedness to others is defined principally through heredity. It is ethnicity (thus defined) which characterizes Jewish particularism, creating the possibility of accretion through proselytism but also making stringent demands on the convert who so radically alters his or her social and ethnic identity.

Proselytism appears to have been necessary for the fullest intimacy with the Jewish community. Josephus, deflecting criticisms of Jewish unfriendliness, insists on the welcome given to 'those who wish to come and live under our laws' (i.e. proselytes), but admits that 'to secure our customs from corruption' it is necessary that 'casual visitors are not allowed to associate with us on an intimate level' (*Contra Apionem* 2.209–10). But it would be absurd to suggest that Jews thereby stood aloof from all non-proselyte Gentiles. In the same work, Josephus proudly mentions the many instances of Gentile imitation of Jewish practice – for instance, abstention from work and lighting of lamps on the Sabbath – which could only come about through social contact with Jews. In fact, both Josephus's works and other Jewish sources (literary and epigraphic) are replete with reference to Gentiles who respected Judaism in various aspects and who supported Jewish communities in the social, political and economic sphere to various degrees. Such Gentile 'sympathizers' are

---

[3] See Bamberger 1968. I find puzzling Neusner's claim (1995) that rabbinic Judaism was not ethnic on the grounds that (*a*) for the rabbis Israel was a 'supernatural entity' and (*b*) joining it had 'nothing in common with joining an ethnic group' (285). The argument appears to confuse theological claims with sociological realities. Both insiders and outsiders understood the social and cultural redefinition involved in becoming a proselyte; see e.g. Philo, *Spec. Leg.* 1.52 and Juvenal, *Sat.* 14.100–01. I have argued this case in relation to the diaspora in Barclay 1996:408–10.

of multiple types (see Cohen 1989), but they form an important feature of Jewish experience, especially in the diaspora. Although some diaspora communities at some times were at loggerheads with their Gentile neighbours, most cultivated the patronage or support of Gentiles: old images of 'ghetto' conditions have now been proved grossly inaccurate by archaeological and inscriptional evidence (see e.g. Trebilco 1991 and Rutgers 1995). The famous Aphrodisias inscription (early third century CE) is a fine case in point, and illustrates perfectly the importance to Jews of both proselytes and 'God-fearers', as well as the social distinction between them (on the *stele* the proselytes are listed with Jews, while most of the 'God-fearers' constitute a separate category of donors [Reynolds and Tannenbaum 1987]).

Judaism thus allowed, indeed fostered, a range of social contact with Gentiles, and can hardly be characterized in this respect as 'narrow' or 'exclusive' without gross distortion. Of course, it had boundaries and was concerned to preserve them for the sake of its own survival. Those which had greatest effect on the social interaction of Jews and Gentiles were Jewish abstention from iconic, polytheistic and other 'alien' cults, dietary laws, observance of the Sabbath and the practice of circumcision (see Barclay 1996:428–42). (Other cultural differences, like Jewish distinction in sexual morality, created a platform for criticism of Gentile culture, but had less impact on day-to-day life.) These boundaries, which came to embody Jewish ethnic distinctiveness, certainly limited Jewish involvement in many of the customs of Graeco-Roman society; they sometimes also caused resentment among non-Jews, leading to charges of 'misanthropy'. Nonetheless, the preservation of Jewish ethnic particularity did not necessarily curtail the interest or counteract the attraction of Gentiles towards the Jewish community. Indeed, it was perhaps precisely the clarity of the ethnic boundary, limiting full 'intimacy' to Jews and proselytes, which made it possible to identify a broad social terrain in which Jews and Gentile 'sympathizers' could encounter one another without anxiety about the terms of their association. Knowing where they stood, Gentiles were able to play well-defined roles in relation to the Jewish community, without uncertain or unrealistic expectations creating confusion or provocation on either side.

2. SOME CHRISTIAN VARIETIES OF PARTICULARIST UNIVERSALISM

It is as hazardous to generalize about early Christianity as about its contemporaneous Judaism. We may here take Paul as the central figure in our study, since his claim to 'universalism', epitomized in our opening quotation, has been the most powerful influence in the debate about particularism and universalism. We may explore Pauline theology and practice in the same three dimensions as were examined above.

(a) God, Election and Humankind in History

Given Paul's grounding in the Jewish tradition, we are not surprised to find in his theology the same juxtaposition of convictions concerning God's universal role as Creator and his particular interest in his 'chosen' people. The notion of universal revelation in Rom 1 is closely parallel to that depicted in *Wisd. Sol.* 13, though in Paul an apocalyptic pessimism has thrown a particularly dark shadow over all Adamic humanity. The distinctive Pauline twist is to redefine the category of 'the chosen' in such a way as to undermine Jewish ethnic particularism. Paul will allow (almost) no room for the characteristic Jewish claim of a permanent special relationship to God (Rom 11 is here the partial exception), and thus applies the notion of universal divine sovereignty in a new way to dissolve the distinction between the circumcised and the uncircumcised (Rom 3.30; cf. Gal 5.6; 6.15). This move is made all the more provocative by the retention of many Jewish election labels – 'the children of Abraham', 'the elect', 'the saints', 'the Israel of God' – which are now applied to a group without any necessary association with the Jewish people. Thus Paul invests his converts with a pseudo-ethnicity, and carries over into his churches a quasi-Jewish particularism which retains the sense of difference from 'the Gentiles who do not know God' (1 Thess 4.5; cf. 1 Cor 5.1), although that difference has no longer anything to do with ethnicity.

But Paul's prescription for the Church's identity by no means abolishes particularism: it simply erects, in place of an ethnic particularism, an ecclesial particularism defined by faith in Christ. If there is 'in Christ no Jew or Gentile' (Gal 3.28), there is now a new divide between those who are, and those who are not, 'in Christ'. And for Paul, even if not for all his converts, the distinction between 'the church' and 'the world', the 'new creation' and 'the present evil age', is quite as significant as that he formerly maintained between Jews and Gentiles. He battles throughout 1 Corinthians to maintain that distinction (see Barclay 1992), and draws quite as sharp an ideological boundary between 'brothers' and 'outsiders' as we ever find in Jewish forms of particularism (1 Cor 5–6). Mirroring The Wisdom of Solomon, Paul also suggests a preferential judgement of Christians: God chastens them in judgement, so they will not be condemned along with the world (1 Cor 11.31). Thus, while God justifies both circumcised and uncircumcised on the ground of faith (Rom 3.30), his justice maintains as clear a distinction between faith/obedience on the one hand, and unbelief/disobedience on the other, as was ever created by the old ethnic divide.

Paul, like his Jewish contemporaries, might soften this dualism on occasion. The rulers who support what is 'good' in Rom 13 (contrast 1 Cor 2 and 6) are not wholly dissimilar to that 'moral minority' which we found in Philo, and, in the course of levelling the position of Jew and Gentile, Paul hints at a 'natural' observance of the law by both Jews and Gentiles (Rom 2.6–16). But it is instructive that such potential is mentioned only in a context where the gospel of Christ is presented as the sole path of salvation (Rom 1–3). For the predominant note of universalism in Paul is that of universal sin and death. Analysing the human condition as a universal plight, Paul can present the gospel of divine grace as blind to ethnicity: even Jewish salvation can take place only through grace and by the justification of the ungodly (Rom 4, 11).

Thus, the dark shading of Paul's apocalyptic theology does not wholly obliterate a sense of God's present interest in the whole world (cf. 1 Cor 8.4–6), but it tends to shift the realization of that universalism away from the present and into the future, while investing the present with the urgency of communicating a gospel of salvation. Other early Christian voices present similarly pessimistic views of the relation between unbelieving humanity and God, whether they be outsiders who can neither see nor understand (Mark), or representatives of the 'world' whose ways are in darkness (John), or enemies whose fate is sealed (Revelation). In all such cases the foreground of ecclesial particularism practically obliterates a universal horizon.

(b) Eschatological Expectations

We saw in relation to Judaism that the creative tensions of particularism and universalism might be brought into some sort of theological resolution through eschatology; and much the same could be said of Pauline and other early Christian eschatology. Eschatology was of immense significance in the formation of early Christianity, and the vivid metaphors of Christian expectations often mirrored their particularist concerns. Paul works with a clear distinction between those 'on the way to salvation' and those 'on the way to destruction' (1 Cor 1.18), and can draw up a list of those who will be excluded from the kingdom of God (1 Cor 6.9–10; cf. Rev 21.8). If there are vessels of grace, there are also vessels of wrath prepared for destruction (Rom 9.22–23). Matthew's 'wailing and gnashing of teeth' and the Apocalypse's reapers, horsemen and burning pits merely give further symbolic shape to such grim future prospects.

Thus, as in Jewish eschatology, the Christian eschaton can be presented as a cataclysm of destruction for all outside the people of God, their present sin finally reaping its just reward. But also, as in Jewish eschatology, a brighter hope can flicker around the edges of those dark expectations, often vaguely expressed or seemingly in contradiction to the predictions of utter destruction. It is arguable that there is a glint of this universalist hope in Paul's presentation of Christ as the representative of a new humanity: 'as in Adam all die, so also in Christ shall all be made alive' (1 Cor 15.22; cf. Rom 5.18–19). Certainly the eventual victory of Christ is anticipated as a moment when 'every knee will bow and every tongue confess that Jesus Christ is Lord' (Phil 2.10–11). There may be some ambivalence as to whether this final realization of divine sovereignty will be effected through the destruction or the reconciliation of hostile forces (cf. Col 1.20; 2.14–15), but it is striking that in all these cases the christological particularism of the Church is not erased but made integral to the univeralist expectations for the world. When Paul declares that 'God has assigned all to disobedience in order that he may have mercy on all' (Rom 11.32), one feels the same open-endedness as in some Jewish literature, though perhaps made more insistent by the sense that the power of grace, so vividly experienced in the Christian present, is ultimately unstoppable.

(c) Social Relations with non-Christians

Thus far we have found many similarities between the possible combinations of particularism and universalism in Judaism and early Christianity. It is in relation to our third dimension, that of social relations, that greater differences begin to emerge, not in the degree of particularism but in its character.

   In the first place, we would have to recognize that early Christianity was more consciously and deliberately a 'missionary' movement than its contemporaneous Judaism, in the sense that the winning of 'converts' was not supplementary to its natural continuation through the generations, but was essential for its establishment and maintenance. In his *Mission and Conversion* (1994), Martin Goodman has drawn a sharp contrast between Judaism and early Christianity in this respect, insisting that only the latter could be said to have sponsored a 'universal proselytizing mission'. To some extent this contrast is exaggerated: Goodman minimizes Jewish interest in the attraction of converts (and Jewish hostility towards Gentile 'idolatry'), and exaggerates the difference between 'a willingness to accept' and 'a positive desire to acquire' converts (e.g. p. 137). Judaism did attract converts, and at least some Jews went to some effort to aid that attraction (through conversation or literature). Yet the early Christian movement was clearly much more intense and self-conscious in its missionary efforts. That is at least partly explained by the difference between, on the one hand, an ethnic tradition whose continuation is guaranteed by family loyalties to 'ancestral customs', and, on the other, a voluntary association which cuts across hereditary ties and wins members on the basis of their own convictions rather than their familial connections. Of course, some Christians entered the movement in 'households', and it spawned many a familial or ethnic metaphor. But the impression conveyed by all early Christian literature is that the new Christian associations were not primarily founded on some 'natural' or 'given' connection, such as birth, family or race; rather, they created artificial 'kinships' formed by a declaration of faith in Christ which often mortally offended the converts' families and fellow-nationals. The creation and maintenance of such voluntary associations required the acquisition of converts and encouraged minimal consideration of ethnic or status differentials. Armed with a radical theology of universal sin, and having crossed into the terrain of 'the nations', the early Christian mission set itself, in principle, the widest possible horizon.[4]

But does this make the early Christian churches in general less 'exclusive' and more 'universal'? It is certainly the case that, in the course of their mission, many early Christians ignored significant Jewish barriers. They did not, in general, dismantle the barrier created by Jewish abhorrence of 'idolatry' (see further below), but some other Jewish distinctives, of great significance in daily social intercourse, were largely abandoned in the increasingly Gentile movement, notably the practice of male circumcision, the Jewish dietary restrictions and the observance of the Sabbath. This made the Christian movement to some extent less culturally specific, and thus transplantable to a variety of cultural contexts. But some Jewish social barriers remained and – what is important to note here – new barriers were also erected which made the Christian churches just as 'particularistic' as the Jewish community, only 'particularistic' in a different way. The following five points illustrate some of the ways in which ecclesial particularism was defined.

(1) *Rejection of 'Idols'* This barrier, inherited from Judaism, had far-reaching social effects in family and community life. Since Gentile Christians (soon the majority in the Church) had themselves turned 'from idols to the true and living God' (1 Thess 1.9), they were inclined to condemn 'idolatry' with special enthusiasm. They were also vulnerable to criticism of 'impiety', having broken with their familial and cultural traditions. Having paid so dearly for their conversion, Christians were bound to view 'idolatry' with special emotion.

(2) *Sexual Differentiation* Criticism of Gentile sexual morality was a standard feature of Judaism, and it played an important, even an enlarged,

---

[4] This sociological factor does not preclude other ideological or practical motivations for the early Christian mission, but it is oddly ignored by Goodman 1994. Simon, however, noted that 'Judaism, being an established body, national and religious at the same time, indissolubly bound up with Israel and founded on the concept of the chosen people, was less spontaneously and less unanimously inclined than most post-Pauline Christianity ever was to gather in the nations to hear its gospel. For early Christianity was not an existing body but one that was still growing and coming into being' (1986:392).

role in the boundary-definition of early Christianity. The fact that so many Christians had themselves once 'transgressed' in this area gave particular bite to their criticism of 'the lusts' of unbelievers. Indeed, since they could not demarcate themselves from 'the world' by ethnicity or by the practice of publicly visible customs (cf. the 'ancestral customs' of the Jews), early Christians were inclined to invest most in their *moral* differentiation from non-believers. In this regard, it is notable how often sexual morality features in Christian self-definition (e.g. in lists of vices). It is possible that the radical stance of total sexual abstinence, which became surprisingly common in early Christianity (Brown 1988), was an attempt to inscribe such moral differentiation into the script of everyday life. (Repudiation of abortion or the exposure of children concerned, by contrast, only occasional events.) Refusal to succumb to fleshly 'lusts' to any degree could then be displayed repeatedly as the flag marking the Christian front-line in the battle with 'the world'.

(3) *Experience and Expectation of Hostility*   Both the features just mentioned were liable to create within the Church a sense of antagonism to 'outsiders'. We know that in some situations that did not occur (e.g. in Corinth), but it is notable how often early Christian literature is suffused with the expectation of hostility from outsiders. Since the Christian message focused on a suffering Christ, and since the experience of many early leaders and churches was of conflict with non-Christians (Jews or Gentiles), it is not surprising that the Christian tradition should adopt a 'conflict mentality', even in situations where no actual conflict existed. Imbued with the ethos of a beleaguered minority, Christians were bound to erect strong ideological boundaries around themselves.

(4) *The Intensity of Participation*   The early Christians had a strange constitution, since 'they are distinguished from the rest of humanity neither in land, nor in language nor in customs' (*Ep. Diog.* 5.1–4). When we ask what Christians did in everyday life that was clearly and dis-tinctively *Christian*, we are hard pressed to find an answer, except in terms of their communal activities. Thus, everything hinged on joining and participating in a specific community, whose intimacy required careful protection of its boundaries. The sacred zone formed by the circle of the Church was reinforced regularly in communal meals (which feature very prominently in early Christianity), and especially at the Lord's Supper (Meeks 1983). Paul reacts with swift judgement to anything that pollutes or disrupts the table-fellowship of the community (Gal 2.11–14; 1 Cor 5, 11; Rom 14) precisely because it defines Christian belonging more clearly than anything else. Eating with an unbeliever is invested with comparatively little significance (unless it involves idolatry), because it is not an event which constitutes Christian identity; but eating with a fellow

believer is of such significance that any internal pollutant has to be immediately expunged (1 Cor 5.9–11). Thus, the gathering of the community, its worship and its meals are invested with huge significance, and the identification of who properly belongs there as a 'brother' or 'sister' is crucial. 'Outsiders' or 'unbelievers' are not thereby banned, but it is made clear on what basis they attend. It was almost certainly in some liturgical context that Christians said, 'If anyone does not love the Lord, let him be anathema' (1 Cor 16.22).

(5) *Faith and Confession*   As the opening quotation of Rom 3.29–30 showed, the new particularism forged by early Christianity was defined by 'faith', which was given in this new context a distinctive christological content. Hence the focus of communal identity resided in convictions, and although these were believed to have practical effects, it is the convictions themselves which constitute the most novel feature of the Christian communities and their most essential bond. The rapid production of creeds and confessional statements in early Christianity illustrates this point clearly enough, while subsequent Christian history was to show the potential for dispute about the proper expressions of belief and the proper meaning of those expressions. Moreover, unbelievers could be considered morally responsible for their 'disobedience' to the message (Rom 10); their failure to join the Christian movement could not be considered dispassionately as a 'natural' loyalty to their ethnic traditions.

Thus, early Christian communities necessarily drew their own boundaries, often with a special intensity, creating their own form of particularism. By contrast to the ethnic particularity of Judaism, Christian particularism was not a 'natural' or 'given' phenomenon. As voluntarist associations, Christian communities had to be created and maintained, and their boundaries continually declared and reinforced against prevailing, and far more 'self-evident', social and political realities. By contrast to Jews, Christians were, as Meeks has it, 'pseudo-aliens' (1993:47), and their sense of alienation needed to be continuously maintained. Such a social dynamic helps to explain why early Christian rhetoric is so often provocatively 'exclusive' and 'particularist'.

We may illustrate the effect of this dynamic in one further respect. In contrast to Judaism, there is a marked absence in early Christianity of the category of the non-member who can nonetheless be regarded as a 'sympathizer' or 'God-fearer'. We noted above the significance of this Gentile penumbra to the Jewish community, involving a range of political, economic, social and religious support for Jews and Judaism. In early Christianity, however, at least as far as its 'official' representatives are concerned, no such 'mid-way' level of support for the Church is to be encouraged. Of course, Christian communities were not public institutions which could naturally appeal for political or economic support: they were too small, too novel, too secret and too politically dubious to attract the patronage of interested non-members. Nor is it easy to see what Christian 'practices' could be imitated by non-members, in the way that Jewish customs could be copied by Gentile sympathizers; the only common example of such a phenomenon is the use of the name of Jesus by non-Christian exorcists (e.g. Mark 9.38–40; Acts 19.13–17). But these social factors were compounded by the prevalent early Christian ideology that there are only two sorts of people, 'insiders' and 'outsiders': interested and supportive 'outsiders' are to be encouraged only so that they might be brought 'inside'. Paul can imagine non-Christians attending Christian worship, but it is his hope that the style of worship will induce a conversion experience (1 Cor 14.20–25; see Sweet 1966–67). He can also tolerate Christians remaining in marriages to unbelievers, but his ambition, and that of 1 Peter, is that such spouses will be 'saved' (1 Cor 7.12–16; 1 Pet 3.1–6). Christians are encouraged to remain in good standing with outsiders as far as possible (1 Thess 4.10–12; 1 Pet 2.13–17), but the world is still neatly divided between 'the righteous' who are saved and 'the wicked' who 'disobey the gospel' (1 Cor 6.1–8; 1 Pet 4.17–18). Luke is the NT author with the fullest capacity to conceptualize a category of righteous non-Christians who support or protect the Christian movement: Jewish and Roman officials, for instance, protect the early Christians (Gamaliel, Acts 5.33–39; Gallio, Acts 18.12–17) and occasionally even 'believe', without baptism or church membership (Sergius Paulus, Acts 13.7–12). But even in Luke's narrative world, the inward pull of the Christian movement is strong, and Agrippa feels himself pressurized to move from sympathy to Paul to becoming a Christian (Acts 26.25–29). In general it seems that the dynamic of early Christianity pressed those it contacted into unequivocal commitments (cf. Taylor 1995). Since the boundary of the Christian movement was artificially created and not formed by 'natural' (e.g. genealogical) factors, it was not so easy as in the case of Judaism to negotiate a terrain in which non-Christians could be associated with the Christian community without finding themselves drawn unambiguously into the circle of faith.

Thus, Christianity forged its own peculiar combination of universalism and particularism, disregarding ethnic differentiation and proclaiming itself open to all, while forming communities whose artificiality and intensity created new and well-defined social distinctions. While embracing a mission of universal outreach, Christians in fact gained a reputation for clannishness and even 'hatred of the human race' (Tacitus, *Annals* 15.44; Benko 1986). The 'triumph' of Christian universalism was proclaimed in conjunction with a social particularism often sectarian in nature. Loving all humanity yet being persecuted by all was a paradox Christians learnt to endure and even embrace (*Ep. Diog.* 5.11–17).

3. CONCLUDING REFLECTIONS

It would be foolish to attempt to measure which of early Christianity or its contemporary Judaism was 'more' universalistic or particularistic. For a start, one would have to distinguish between different streams in both traditions, whose diverse realities were far more complex than this over-simplified map; one would also have to break down the categories of 'universalism' and 'particularism' still further, with regard to their different dimensions and aspects. But, more to the point, we are dealing here with different *kinds* of particularism, which are hardly commensurate in a quantifiable way. Both Judaism and early Christianity were particularistic in important respects, but their two particularisms were different phenomenologically, corresponding to their different social formations as, respectively, an ethnic community and a voluntary association. 'Particularism' in itself is not a negative or regressive phenomenon: any community needs to define itself with boundaries, and difference may be validly preserved against the imperialist claims of 'universalism'. However, as Boyarin has argued (1994:228–60), both Jewish and Christian forms of universalist-particularism bear the potential for dangerous consequences. Jewish tolerance of non-Jews, but simultaneous focus on ethnic difference, can lead to a haughty *indifference* to all but fellow Jews. On the other hand, Christian universalism linked to christological exclusivism, when given the power to enforce its will, can result (and sometimes has resulted) in coercion or repression of all that refuses Christianization. Both communities face severe challenges in the present pluralist environment in which differences and convictions have to be re-expressed or re-negotiated in forms which meet the requirements of civility and tolerance.

During the long era of Christendom, Christianity acquired many natural boundaries which it did not possess in its primitive form: family, social class, country, even continent and empire became solidly 'Christian'. But its new status in the post-Christian West requires it to reassemble artificial boundaries like those it employed in its first centuries. Thus, there now re-emerges the danger of a self-enclosed sectarian spirit which lurks in the New Testament vision of the Church. Perhaps what is required of Christians now is an honest recognition of Christian particularity (*pace* Baur and his modernist successors), a renunciation of past imperialist ambitions, a commitment to exploit the world-affirming aspects of the Christian tradition, and a liberality which recognizes the complementary contributions to human welfare which are made by those outside the Christian community. As well as the sectarian saying, 'He who is not for us is against us' (Matt 12.30 // Luke 11.23), the Synoptics record Jesus' statement that 'He who is not against us is for us' (Mark 9.40 // Luke 9.50). That 'us' signals the ongoing particularism of a community which preserves its loyalty to Jesus; but the recognition accorded to those who are 'for us' also encourages a Christian universalism which applauds and supports the work of divine grace wherever it is manifested.

BIBLIOGRAPHY

Bamberger, B. J. 1968. *Proselytism in the Talmudic Period.* New York: KTAV.

Barclay, J. M. G. 1988. *Obeying the Truth: A Study of Paul's Ethics in Galatians.* Edinburgh: T. & T. Clark.

Barclay, J. M. G. 1992. 'Thessalonica and Corinth: Social Contrasts in Pauline Christianity'. *JSNT* 47:49–72.

Barclay, J. M. G. 1996. *Jews in the Mediterranean Diaspora from Alexander to Trajan (323 BCE–117 CE).* Edinburgh: T. & T. Clark.

Baur, F. C. 1878. *The Church History of the First Three Centuries.* 3rd edn. London: Williams & Norgate.

Benko, S. 1986. *Pagan Rome and the Early Christians.* Bloomington: Indiana University Press.

Boccaccini, G. 1991. *Middle Judaism: Jewish Thought 300 B.C.E. to 200 C.E.* Minneapolis: Fortress Press.

Bockmuehl, M. 1994–95. 'The Noachide Commandments and New Testament Ethics'. *Revue Biblique* 102:72–101.

Boyarin, D. 1994. *A Radical Jew: Paul and the Politics of Identity.* Berkeley: University of California Press.

Brown, P. 1988. *The Body and Society: Men, Women and Sexual Renunciation in Early Christianity.* New York: University of Columbia Press.

Carleton Paget, J. 1996. 'Jewish Proselytism at the Time of Christian Origins: Chimera or Reality?' *JSNT* 62:65–103.

Cohen, S. J. D. 1989. 'Crossing the Boundary and Becoming a Jew'. *HTR* 82:13–33.

Dahl, N. A. 1977. 'The One God of Jews and Gentiles (Romans 3:29–30)'. In *Studies in Paul.* Minneapolis: Augsburg Publishing House. 178–91.

Dunn, J. D. G. 1985. 'Works of the Law and the Curse of the Law (Galatians 3.10–14)'. *NTS* 31:523–42.

Dunn, J. D. G. 1988. *Romans 1–8.* Word Biblical Commentary 38a. Dallas: Word Books.

Feldman, L. H. 1993. *Jew and Gentile in the Ancient World.* Princeton: Princeton University Press.

Fredriksen, P. 1991. 'Judaism, the Circumcision of Gentiles, and Apocalyptic Hope: Another Look at Galatians 1 and 2'. *JTS* n.s. 42:532–64.

Goodman, M. 1994. *Mission and Conversion: Proselytizing in the Religious History of the Roman Empire.* Oxford: Clarendon Press.

Hengel, M. 1974. *Judaism and Hellenism.* London: SCM Press.

Levenson, J. D. 1996. 'The Universal Horizon of Biblical Particularism'. In M. Brett (ed.), *Ethnicity and the Bible.* Leiden: Brill. 143–69.

Meeks, W. 1983. *The First Urban Christians: The Social World of the Apostle Paul.* New Haven: Yale University Press.

Meeks, W. 1993. *The Origins of Christian Morality: The First Two Centuries.* New Haven: Yale University Press.

Neusner, J. 1995. 'Was Rabbinic Judaism Really "Ethnic"?' *CBQ* 57:281–305.

Novak, D. 1983. *The Image of the Non-Jew in Judaism.* Lampeter: Edwin Mullen Press.

Reynolds, J. and R. Tannenbaum. 1987. *Jews and Godfearers at Aphrodisias.* Cambridge: Cambridge Philological Society.

Rutgers, L. V. 1995. *The Jews in Late Ancient Rome.* Leiden: Brill.

Sanders, E. P. 1977. *Paul and Palestinian Judaism.* London: SCM Press.

Sanders, E. P. 1992. *Judaism: Practice and Belief, 63 BCE – 66 CE.* London: SCM Press.

Segal, A. F. 1994. 'Universalism in Judaism and Christianity'. In T. Engberg-Pedersen (ed.), *Paul in his Hellenistic Context.* Edinburgh: T. & T. Clark. 1–29.

Simon, M. 1986. *Verus Israel: A Study of the Relations between Christians and Jews in the Roman Empire (AD 135–425).* Tr. by H. McKeating. Oxford: Oxford University Press.

Sweet, J. 1966–67. 'A Sign for Unbelievers: Paul's Attitude to Glossolalia'. *NTS* 13:240–57.

Taylor, N. H. 1995. 'The Social Nature of Conversion in the Early Christian World'. In P. F. Esler (ed.), *Modelling Early Christianity.* London: Routledge. 128–36.

Trebilco, P. 1991. *Jewish Communities in Asia Minor.* Cambridge: Cambridge University Press.

Wright, N.T. 1991. *The Climax of the Covenant: Christ and the Law in Pauline Theology.* Edinburgh: T. & T. Clark.

Select Bibliography
of the Writings of J. P. M. Sweet

Early Christian Thought in its Jewish Context, co-edited with J. Barclay. Cambridge: Cambridge University Press, 1996.

'Revelation'. In *Early Christian Thought in its Jewish Context*, edited by J. Barclay and J. P. M. Sweet. Cambridge: Cambridge University Press, 1996. 160–73.

'Identity and Tradition: A Theological Reflection'. In *The Renewal of Common Prayer. Uniformity and Diversity in Church of England Worship: Essays by Members of the Liturgical Commission of the Church of England*, edited by M. Perham. London: SPCK, 1993. 68–77.

'Antichrist' and 'Revelation, The Book of'. In *The Oxford Companion to the Bible*, edited by B. M. Metzger and M. D. Coogan. New York/Oxford: Oxford University Press, 1993. 31–2 and 651–55, respectively.

'A House Not Made with Hands'. In *Templum Amicitiae: Essays on the Second Temple presented to Ernst Bammel*, edited by W. Horbury. JSNTSup 48. Sheffield: JSOT Press, 1991. 368–90.

'Old Wine in Old Bottles'. In *The Weight of Glory: A Vision and Practice for Christian Faith. The Future of Liberal Theology: Essays for Peter Baelz*, edited by D. Hardy and P. Sedgwick. Edinburgh: T. & T. Clark, 1991. 231–39.

Revelation. London: SCM, 1979. Revised edition London/Philadelphia: SCM Press/TPI, 1990.

'Miraculous, Interpretation of the'. In *A Dictionary of Biblical Interpretation*, edited by R. J. Coggins and J. L. Houlden. London: SCM Press, 1990. 465–67.

'"Taking Satan Seriously": A Reply'. *ExpT* 101 (1989–90) 266–67.

'The Zealots and Jesus'. In *Jesus and the Politics of His Day*, edited by E. Bammel and C. F. D. Moule. Cambridge: Cambridge University Press, 1984. 1–9.

'The 3d Sunday after Epiphany'. *Theology* 86 (1983) 3–7.

'Maintaining the Testimony of Jesus: The Suffering of Christians in the Revelation of John (and Use of Zech 12–14 in the NT)'. In *Suffering and Martyrdom in the New Testament*, edited by W. Horbury and B. McNeil. Cambridge: Cambridge University Press, 1981. 101–17.

'Miracles and Faith (II): The Miracles of Jesus'. *Epworth Review* 3.2 (May 1976) 81–91.

'A Saying, a Parable, a Miracle'. *Theology* 76 (1973) 125–33.

'A Sign for Unbelievers: Paul's Attitude to Glossolalia'. *NTS* 13 (1966–67) 240–57. Reprinted in *Speaking in Tongues*, edited by W. Mills. Grand Rapids: Eerdmans, 1980. 141–64.

'The Theory of Miracles in the Wisdom of Solomon'. In *Miracles: Cambridge Studies in their Philosophy and History*, edited by C. F. D. Moule. London: Mowbray, 1965. 113–26.

'The Kerygma [Second Thoughts VIII]'. *ExpT* 76 (1964–65) 143–47.

'Commentaries on Romans'. *Theology* 67 (1964) 382–87.

List of Contributors

JOHN M. G. BARCLAY is Lecturer in Biblical Studies, University of Glasgow

RICHARD BAUCKHAM is Professor of New Testament Studies, St Mary's College, University of St Andrews, Scotland

G. K. BEALE is Professor of New Testament and Director of the Th.M. in Biblical Theology, Gordon Conwell Seminary, South Hamilton, Massachusetts

MARKUS BOCKMUEHL is Lecturer in Divinity and a Fellow and Tutor of Fitzwilliam College, University of Cambridge

JAMES CARLETON PAGET is Assistant Lecturer in Divinity and a Fellow of Peterhouse, University of Cambridge

ANDREW CHESTER is Lecturer in Divinity and a Fellow of Selwyn College, University of Cambridge

MICHAEL GOULDER is Emeritus Professor of Biblical Studies, University of Birmingham

MORNA D. HOOKER is Lady Margaret's Professor of Divinity, University of Cambridge

WILLIAM HORBURY is Reader in Jewish and Early Christian Studies, and a Fellow of Peterhouse, University of Cambridge

C. F. D. MOULE is Lady Margaret's Professor of Divinity Emeritus, University of Cambridge

J. C. O'NEILL is Professor Emeritus of New Testament Language Literature and Theology, University of Edinburgh

CHRISTOPHER ROWLAND is Dean Ireland's Professor of the Exegesis of Holy Scripture, University of Oxford

DAVID SECCOMBE is the Principal of George Whitefield College in Cape Town, South Africa

STEPHEN S. SMALLEY is Dean of Chester Cathedral

MICHAEL B. THOMPSON is Director of Studies and Lecturer in New Testament at Ridley Hall, Cambridge

CHRISTOPHER M. TUCKETT is Lecturer in New Testament Studies and a Fellow of Wolfson College, University of Oxford

Index of Ancient Sources

9. Other Ancient Authors

Index of Modern Authors

243

Index of Subjects

Kingdom of God 22, 24f, 28, 30, 36, 38f, 42,
45–49, 51, 53, 59f, 118f, 143, 155, 157–59, 175,
196, 201–203, 216

Last Supper: in John 82f, 90; *see also*
Eucharist
Law: in Matthew 25–27; in Q 68f, 74; in Paul
116; in James 155f; *see also* Judaism
Leadership 8, 115, 147, 196–98
Logos 79f
Love 27, 29, 72, 101, 103f, 108, 112f, 130, 146f,
165, 199

Martyrdom 40, 136, 184f, 201; *see also*
Persecution; Exile
Matthew and Paul 27–31
Miracles x, 10, 15, 51f; *see also* Signs
Moses and Messiah 8

New Creation 106
New People 5, 11, 39, 106, 135, 139f, 160

Order 15
Outsiders 41f, 189; *see also* Church and
World

Pagan Deities 8
Parrhésia 15
Paul and Jesus 117, 127
People of God 9–11, 14, 139–41, 160f; *see also*
New People
Persecution 136, 219; *see also* Martyrdom;
Exile
Peter, James and John 20
Peter and Paul 19
Posture in worship 130
Poverty 29–31, 158f, 199; *see also* Wealth
Praise 6f, 129; *see also* Worship
Prayer 92, 129
Priesthood 138f, 144, 162, 197, 210; *see also*
Sacrifice

Prophecy 6f, 70
Proselytism 212–14; *see also* Gentiles
Psalms 129; *see also* Hymns; Scripture
Purity 10, 109f, 124, 142f, 146, 157

Radicals, wandering 29f
Readership: of LXX 1–3; of Hebrews 136; of
James 154; of 1 Peter 159f; of Apostolic
Fathers 194
Repentance 6of, 143, 204
Reproof and Correction 73, 142f, 204f; *see
also* Church Discipline; Heresy

Sacrifice 121–23, 130, 136, 140, 147, 162f; *see
also* Priesthood
Saints 13–14, 146f; *see also* Holiness
Scribal interpolations 81–89
Scripture 1–17 *passim*; 129f, 145f, 172–76,
200
Sexual ethics 110, 218f
Signs and Wonders 51f; *see also* Miracles
Son of Man 35, 167f
Son, Church/Israel as 12
State, the 115f, 203; *see also* Church and
World
Synagogue in LXX 13; in Acts 55; in John's
Letters 100; in Rev 100; in Paul 112,
128f; in Hebrews 137; in Apostolic
Fathers 196

Teaching 50f, 130
Temple 4, 11, 123, 128, 134n, 139, 162f
Theory vs. Practice 105–20, 203–05
Thirty-Nine Articles 5n
Unity 52f, 110–14, 141f, 195f

Wealth 52, 158f, 186f, 199; *see also* Poverty
Wholeness 155–57
Women and Men 4, 42, 113f, 130, 139
Worship 121–32 and *passim*; *see also* Praise